A selection from
the 2012 Reading List

W9-BZC-309

FOR *Mark.*

....

Enjoy, Goul

J.P.Morgan

BY
INVITATION
ONLY

BY INVITATION ONLY

HOW WE BUILT

GILT

AND CHANGED THE WAY
MILLIONS SHOP

ALEXIS MAYBANK *and*
ALEXANDRA WILKIS WILSON

COFOUNDERS OF GILT GROUPE

PORTFOLIO / PENGUIN

PORTFOLIO / PENGUIN
Published by the Penguin Group
Penguin Group (USA) Inc., 375 Hudson Street,
New York, New York 10014, U.S.A.
Penguin Group (Canada), 90 Eglinton Avenue East, Suite 700,
Toronto, Ontario, Canada M4P 2Y3
(a division of Pearson Penguin Canada Inc.)
Penguin Books Ltd, 80 Strand, London WC2R 0RL, England
Penguin Ireland, 25 St. Stephen's Green, Dublin 2, Ireland
(a division of Penguin Books Ltd)
Penguin Books Australia Ltd, 250 Camberwell Road, Camberwell,
Victoria 3124, Australia
(a division of Pearson Australia Group Pty Ltd)
Penguin Books India Pvt Ltd, 11 Community Centre, Panchsheel Park,
New Delhi – 110 017, India
Penguin Group (NZ), 67 Apollo Drive, Rosedale, Auckland 0632,
New Zealand (a division of Pearson New Zealand Ltd)
Penguin Books (South Africa) (Pty) Ltd, 24 Sturdee Avenue,
Rosebank, Johannesburg 2196, South Africa

Penguin Books Ltd, Registered Offices:
80 Strand, London WC2R 0RL, England

First published in 2012 by Portfolio / Penguin
a member of Penguin Group (USA) Inc.

3   5   7   9   10   8   6   4   2

LIBRARY OF CONGRESS CATALOGING IN PUBLICATION DATA
Maybank, Alexis.
By invitation only : how we built Gilt and changed the way millions shop / Alexis Maybank and
Alexandra Wilkis Wilson.
p.   cm.
Includes index.
ISBN 978-1-59184-463-1
1. Maybank, Alexis.   2. Wilson, Alexandra Wilkis.   3. Gilt Groupe.   4. Luxury goods industry—
United States.   5. Discount houses (Retail trade)—United States.   6. Electronic commerce.
7. Entrepreneurship.   I. Wilson, Alexandra Wilkis.   II. Title.
381'. 14206573—dc23
2011043725

Printed in the United States of America
Set in WarnockPro
Designed by Jaime Putorti

To our loving
and supportive families

CONTENTS

RELATIONSHIPS. EXECUTION.

In 2007 we—Alexis Maybank and Alexandra Wilkis Wilson, avid New York City sample sale shoppers and the best of friends since graduate school—launched, with our cofounders Mike Bryzek, Phong Nguyen, and Kevin Ryan, a business located squarely at the charged intersection of fashion and technology, where things tend to come and go quickly.

We were barely thirty.

We'd never worked together—or with Mike, Phong, or Kevin—professionally.

We had no proof the concept would work. And actually, it struck a lot of people as outlandish. *Online sample sales?*

The idea that you'd have to become a member in order to shop on an exclusive luxury e-commerce site? Or that tens of thousands of women would wage a war of the mouses by attempting to buy the exact same designer shoe at the exact same time? *Unheard* of.

While e-commerce and fashion were separately booming, high-end brands still preferred to sell their wares exclusively in stores. Luxury executives believed customers would throw down their credit cards only if they could touch and feel their purchases.

Yet we had guts, perseverance, a lot of trust in each other, and just enough naïveté, not to mention the valuable experience we'd accumulated working for companies like eBay and Louis Vuitton. We also had our own instincts as shoppers. We knew we were creating a site *we* wanted to shop on—and, more than that, a site we'd be willing to drop everything to visit at noon each day.

We named the business Gilt Groupe.

And together with Mike and Phong (Gilt's two brilliant founding engineers) and Kevin (our founding chairman, whose idea it was to bring online flash sales to the United States), we raised millions of dollars, created a totally unique online customer experience, established a strong corporate culture, overcame the Web site and warehousing challenges of rapid growth, and hired an amazing staff to execute our vision. We launched an ambitious business that, in three and a half short years, investors would value at one billion dollars. Gilt Groupe changed fashion and e-commerce and fundamentally altered the way millions of people shop for everything from shoes to luxury vacations.

Nowadays, we're asked often about our story. As we travel the country, speaking on panels and meeting customers at events or over coffees and meals, the same questions come from men and women of all backgrounds, of all ages, in all professions. At first it surprised us that they didn't want to know when Gilt would next sell Vera Wang or Brooks Brothers Black Fleece or why we had run out of their sizes during our last Christian Louboutin sale or what Mr. Valentino is like in person. They didn't press us for the date when the Parker Palm Springs would next appear on Jetsetter, Gilt's luxury travel site. Instead, they asked—and still do—"How did you meet? How did you convince such amazing brands to sell on Gilt? How did you make sure the business didn't destroy your friendship? What are you each responsible for? How do you find good engineers? Can you read my business plan and tell me what you think?"

Coming from marketers or bankers, students or entrepreneurs, fashionistas or stay-at-home moms, these questions reveal the same interests and aspirations: to start a company, to galvanize a family business, to innovate in the context of a larger corporation. They speak to a powerful human desire: to create something and to watch it grow into something larger than oneself. We definitely relate to these feelings. And we are proof that amazing things can happen when you team up with the right people to take risks and act on them.

In recounting our backgrounds, key decisions, and hard-won wisdom in this book, we hope to inform, inspire, and help pave the way for others who want to start something new, advance in a career, or—especially—build a business that grows to employ dozens or even hundreds, modernize industries, and change people's lives. Whether you have already started your own company, are tackling a new opportunity inside a big organization, or just have a great idea, some entrepreneurial spirit, and no idea what to do next, we are putting forth our story with the goal of offering concrete suggestions on how to handle some of the challenges that lie ahead. We've provided a mix of smaller anecdotes and larger takeaways, of personal perspectives on well-worn themes and interrogations of widely accepted truths.

Keep in mind as you read this book that it is just *our* point of view, a forthright and at times self-effacing account of our early days at the center of a fast-growing, wildly influential New York start-up. We've helped lead Gilt Groupe from a tiny upstart based out of a dingy Manhattan office, where we sat shoulder to shoulder with Mike and Phong, to the much larger operation it is today, with more than nine hundred team members handling everything from merchandising to engineering to photography to marketing. The site once hosted two or three sales per week; it now hosts more than twenty-two per day in order to cater to more than five million members. Gilt has expanded far beyond women's fashion to offer everything from Volkswagen Jettas for $5,995 to a two hundred thousand dollar villa rental in the Bahamas (on Jetsetter; it sold).

While there were many factors that helped make Gilt what it is today, we believe they are best distilled down to just two: *relation-ships* and *execution.* These are what we hope to focus on in this book.

Ours is a story about friendship. Though people mistake us for each other constantly—we have similar names, and we're told we look alike, too—we're not the type of best friends who finish each other's sentences or share all the same interests. Most of the time neither of us knows what's going on in the other's head.

Far from making things difficult, we believe our different person-alities and points of view have been our secret sauce, the potent rec-ipe behind our success as cofounders. One of us (Alexis) marvels at her friend's ability to form and sustain relationships with thousands of people simultaneously; the other (Alexandra) shakes her head at her friend's capacity for risk and preternatural calm in any situation. We complement each other's strengths and weaknesses. Each of us genuinely believes the other is the best out there at what she does. We have always turned to each other for advice, coaching, honest feed-back, and emotional support. And we know that no disagreement involving the company we've helped build over the last five years is worth jeopardizing the friendship we've built over the last fifteen.

You may have noticed that we also happen to be women. While this isn't the most important thing about our partnership, it does make us unusual in the tech world. When we started Gilt Groupe, we weren't aware of any other close female friends who'd launched ambi-tious, disruptive businesses, at least not in the Internet space. Since we tend to be a bit competitive (though not with each other—and this is key), this only increased our resolve. From Bill and Paul to Larry and Sergey to Steve and Steve, it was hard to ignore how many game-changing companies had been borne of friendship.

In addition to our friendship, Gilt benefited from the deep rapport between our cofounders Mike and Phong, who had worked together in Silicon Valley for many years pre-Gilt and shared an unshakeable trust and respect. When we all joined forces, these long-standing bonds of trust (Alexandra/Alexis and Mike/Phong) allowed us to move incredibly fast, often independently in different directions, to boldly take on upstart competitors and even some of the largest incumbent businesses in our industry. This trust formed the rock-solid foundation of our start-up business.

We believe that Gilt Groupe is powerful proof that strong pre-existing relationships between cofounders—coupled with a focus on relationships with customers, vendors, and employees—is a potent formula for both success and personal fulfillment. In other words, starting a business with a best friend—*especially* if you bring complementary skills and personalities to the table and both happen to value each other more than any enterprise you could start together—makes you more effective, and makes the adventure more meaningful. We are two people who've always worked hard in our careers, spending long days at the office through our twenties. We'd never considered until we cofounded Gilt Groupe that work could feel so much more significant when shared with someone we love and value personally. As much as our friendship has always defined and strengthened our approach to this business, this business has deepened and fortified our friendship, and has made the last five years the most rewarding of our lives.

Which brings us to *execution*. Quite simply, we believe that our relationship helped us *execute* better than our competitors. Ideas are cheap and easily replicated these days; it's the execution that really counts. For us, that meant starting with high-end luxury products (before later expanding to include more affordable offerings), employing innovative word-of-mouth marketing techniques, embracing cutting-edge technology like mobile commerce, and prioritizing ethical, long-term relationships with our brands, shoppers, and employees. All these things helped Gilt execute a popular idea better than any other site out there. We've focused in these pages on how our relationship helped us take critical early steps that fueled a rush of customer, vendor, and employee confidence and catapulted Gilt forward at breakneck speed, with wide-ranging effect on shoppers and brands.

Since cofounding Gilt Groupe, we've each taken on many roles. We've been merchants, marketers, saleswomen, ambassadors, and general managers. We've become mothers. We've learned rudimentary Japanese. We've met Madonna. But detail-oriented Alexandra still sends Alexis the same text three times before getting an answer, while spontaneous Alexis, who cuts it dangerously close when heading to the airport, still rolls her eyes at Alexandra's insistence on departing hours before a flight. And now that Alexis is pregnant with her second child, Alexandra will surely stand in at key meetings and conferences for her, and we'll tag-team New York sample sales so Alexandra can try on investment pieces for both of us, just as Alexis did for Alexandra in 2010, when she was pregnant.

In the last few years, the tech scene in New York has exploded. We're active mentors to many start-ups, and we're constantly impressed by the pluck and ingenuity of the newest wave of entrepreneurs we meet here and in other places around the country. We've even seen dozens of female friends starting fashion and technology businesses. We're proud that many of these start-ups even come out of Harvard Business School (HBS), our alma mater, which began teaching a case study on Gilt Groupe in 2009. It is our hope that future entrepreneurs will see us and today's other young female entrepreneurs as proof that women can attract millions in venture capital investments and start ambitious businesses, too. And that for reasons both personal and professional, they *should*.

We've written in a communal "we" voice to make the book easier to read and to emphasize that when it comes to the origins of Gilt, the stories of Alexis and Alexandra are fortuitously intertwined. We couldn't have done it without each other. Nor would we have wanted to.

But because we're so different, we also wanted to highlight our individual backgrounds and personalities and the roles we played in certain situations. In these instances, we've written in the third person, which we acknowledge can sometimes be an awkward solution to a vexing narrative conundrum. We hope our fluid take on tenses will give you a better idea of who we are as people and of the texture of our friendship and partnership.

In this book (as in real life), we haven't attempted to write the last word on Gilt Groupe. Instead, Gilt's story, and ours, too, is ongoing.

There are *many* chapters still to write.

BY
INVITATION
ONLY

ZAC POSEN IN DANIEL ISLAND, SOUTH CAROLINA?

New York City, November 13, 2007.

By 7:00 A.M. our cramped, makeshift office on West Nineteenth Street was buzzing. Two hours later we were due to start our very first sale at Gilt.com, a selection of pants, shirts, and handbags by the American fashion designer Zac Posen, a prodigy who had been championed by Anna Wintour, the editor of *Vogue* and the most influential person in fashion.

We—along with a handful of employees and team members, all packed at a long desk pushed up against the wall—were giddy, excited, and admittedly a little bit nervous. We'd been unreachable to the outside world for months as we worked around the clock readying the site. We probably hadn't gotten a full night's sleep for ten days. But we had outlined a detailed plan for our first live sale.

Out at the Brooklyn Navy Yard, a small team led by Mike Bryzek— our cofounder, Gilt's multitasking chief technology officer (CTO), and the engineering genius who had built much of our Web site—was to man our tiny warehouse space, which was stuffed into the corner of a cavernous building that also housed acres of religious textbooks and Pokémon trinkets. There we had four rolling racks of clothes, a small safe for fine jewelry, a shipping label printer, and some boxes. Mike, assisted by a buyer and an intern, was to print out bar code labels, slap them on boxes, and send our first customers' purchases off to locations around the country (we hoped).

Back in Manhattan, Phong Nguyen, another cofounder and our lead engineer—not to mention our fastest typist—would oversee the Meebo chat we planned to use for customer support. Alexandra, meanwhile, not unlike a drive-through operator at a fast-food restaurant ("Would you like fries with your order?" echoed in her mind), was to man the phones on a headset, fielding calls from customers who wanted more information about fit, fabric, or color. She'd already decided—after discussion with the rest of the team—how the Gilt team should address customers properly over the phone, because etiquette was important in luxury retail. She knew that part of the drill well, from her time working on the sales floors of Louis Vuitton and Bulgari.

Alexis was to concentrate on the glamorous—and Herculean, we were sure—task of e-mail customer support. She had created dozens of ready responses to the multitude of questions she anticipated. Despite the fact that we hadn't yet staged a real sale, we'd invited potential members to join our site with a massive e-mail blast just days earlier, on October 31, and had successfully signed up more than thirteen thousand people. We figured they'd have hundreds of finicky questions . . . right? After all, there were no other e-commerce sites like Gilt in the U.S. market. We were asking people to shop in a completely unfamiliar way.

In the days leading up to our first sale, we'd supplemented our thousands of e-mail invites with targeted personal entreaties, calling up friends we knew loved Zac's clothes to invite—er, *beg*—them to become members and sign on and buy something. Anything! Now we steeled ourselves for an onslaught of communications that morning as the thousands of siblings, friends, former colleagues, former colleagues' girlfriends, cousins, cousins' best friends' aunts, Facebook friends, and Facebook friends' friends we'd invited to join our site made their way (virtually) to our Zac Posen sale.

We knew we'd done everything we could do.

But deep down most of us were worried about what would happen when the clock struck nine eastern that morning. Would customers buy in droves? Would anyone even log on to the site at all? Would we have to take our heels off and put on flats so we could move faster to fill customers' orders and answer their questions? Would we—

The truth is, we were deeply afraid that we'd sell nothing.

In Manhattan we sat frozen in anticipation. And for the first seven minutes of our sale, our worst fears seemed to come true: we sold nothing.

But then, at precisely 9:07 A.M., as we stared, transfixed, at our screens, an order trickled in from a buyer in New York for two pairs of pants, one a navy classic cuff, the other a fitted chocolate trouser, for a total of $503.48. Two minutes later we sold a taupe Antonia handbag for $535, down from $1,200, to a woman in San Francisco. But oops, we felt bad that she'd gotten up so early to shop our sale! How could we possibly have shown so little consideration for our West Coast members? (Right then we decided to move our next sale back a couple of hours to 11:00 A.M.) Our third purchase was from Daniel Island, South Carolina. We remember thinking, Really? Do we know someone in Daniel Island, South Carolina? "Alexis?" "Alexandra?" "Mike?" But we didn't recognize any of the purchasers popping up on our computers until Alexis's friend Sumana later placed an order for a pink ruffled blouse.

On our computer screens, we watched the orders appear. It was strangely addictive, and something we continued to do for about a dozen more sales, until the pace of purchases became too fast and furious to follow. We saw where they were coming from, what sizes and colors women were buying. We became obsessed with clicking "refresh" (we couldn't stop!) in order to follow the orders in real time and see where they'd be shipped. It was so gratifying to see purchases popping up on the screen, out of nowhere, one after another, made by women we'd never met or heard of, from towns we'd never visited. They'd all somehow gotten wind of our site and decided to sign on and check it out.

In the beginning, we could almost always track an order back to a specific friend or a family member's network, or at least to the Gilt employee who had sent the original invitation. But it was doubly encouraging when, after attempting to trace an order back ten steps to the person who initially invited the customer to join our site, we still couldn't identify its source. "We don't know anyone in Arkansas!" someone would announce triumphantly. Our eyes would meet across the room, and we'd exchange a silent cheer. It was proof that our word-of-mouth marketing techniques were working—and that news of Gilt was spreading virally, exponentially, taking on a life of its own.

That first day, while the orders began coming in at a respectable clip, the silence in our office was deafening. Not a single shopper contacted us via Meebo chat or phone, and we got a whopping one e-mail. *One!* Unlike at Bulgari and Louis Vuitton, Alexandra's former employers, where customers were demanding, exacting, and prone to grilling employees about a product's provenance, the Gilt customer immediately revealed herself to be savvy, self-directed, and efficient, with no need (or perhaps time) for hand-holding. We got the immediate sense that she didn't want us or anyone else to get in the way of her purchase. *"Let me be,"* roared this customer with her silence. OK! we thought.[1]

Of course the day wasn't without hiccups. Out in Brooklyn, Mike was forced to handle not only order fulfillment but also quality con-

---

1. Relative to other e-commerce businesses, we still get far fewer customer inquiries to this day.

trol. Keep in mind he's a tech guy, not a fashion expert, who initially questioned the need to develop a "hoyce-ery" (hosiery) category in the database (what *was* that anyway?). Several hours into the sale, he deftly observed that one of the handbags we were about to send out to a customer was missing a chain. Thinking quickly, he swapped the chainless bag for an intact one that was heading off as a surprise gift from his father to his mother. "To this day my mom has a chainless Zac Posen bag," Mike recalls. "And our customer got a high-quality, perfect bag." We were quickly learning that in a start-up business, everyone has to think on his toes, be flexible and creative, and wear many hats.

Our Zac Posen sale was a huge success. Roughly half the orders went to New York, 17 percent to California, 10 percent to Massachusetts, 6 percent to New Jersey, and the rest to Maine, Alabama, Missouri, South Carolina, and Illinois. At least five of the orders went to Alexandra's personal friends, and each time she saw one trickle in over the screen, she thought, Thank you. But despite the fact that we were located in the fashion capital of the country, we'd already gone viral and national, thanks to the power of the Internet, reaching customers we didn't know personally. We would have been thrilled to make three hundred dollars, so we were beyond elated.

Kevin Ryan visited our office around noon with champagne, and our nervous energy in the office dissolved into celebratory glee. As the afternoon wore on, the celebration gave way to focus: Alexandra, our lead merchandiser, had just four more brands confirmed to sell on Gilt: Alvin Valley, Judith Ripka, Rachel Roy, and Notte by Marchesa. Now that the Zac Posen sale had been a success, she felt equipped to bring on many more. We also had to expand our word-of-mouth marketing efforts. And we needed to build a robust and reliable site that was capable of growing exponentially larger for an hour or so each day, as customers rushed through our virtual doors at the same time and tried to buy many of the same things simultaneously. We had to build out our operations, hire a lot more people. And we had to raise money for all of this.

We had a *lot* of work to do.

We still couldn't have imagined that just a couple of weeks later, after three more successful sales for Alvin Valley, Judith Ripka, and Rachel Roy, we'd get a call from Greg Kwiat, of the diamond brand Kwiat, and promptly sell seventy-five thousand dollars' worth of his fine jewelry on our site on one day in December, just in time for the holidays. Or that we'd get another call, this time from Stuart Weitzman: "Hello, Alexandra? This is Stuart Weitzman. Do you know who I am?" Needless to say, we nearly died.

But on that first day we sensed something revolutionary was happening: people were genuinely excited about Gilt. We had created a Web site that could potentially change the rules of retail, for both shoppers and brands. If shopping was traditionally a slow, leisurely activity that might consume an entire weekend (the exception being sample sales), it would now be competitive, addictive, urgent, thrilling— a rush delivered at the same time each day via the Internet. It would be the appointment you couldn't miss, at a time *we'd* specified. We'd bring the thrill of the hunt for designer fashion to people all over the country, and allow them to experience that feeling of triumph that comes with beating other invisible shoppers to a choice purchase, a rush similar to gambling. There might even be virtual cart snatching.

Shopping would become not just easier but so much more *fun*.

By our third sale we'd settled on noon EST as our daily start time, and lunchtime on the East Coast—breakfast on the West—would never be the same.

CHAPTER 1

THE PERFECT COMPLEMENTS:

Our Journey from Cambridge to New York

(Featuring eBay, Louis Vuitton, Plenty of Sample Sales,

and One Fabulous Wedding in Miami)

The A's, as they call themselves, met in Portuguese class
while undergrads at Harvard.
—*TIME STYLE & DESIGN*, APRIL 2009

The line was long, stretching from the door of John Harvard's up
a few concrete stairs and around a bend, up some more stairs, and finally out onto Dunster Street, a quaint side street off Harvard Square. The crowd buzzed in anticipation, each person giving his name at the door before entering the dark subterranean pub, a Cambridge institution. It was a warm September night in 2002, and we'd both returned to Harvard to pursue MBAs. Tonight, the first of the semester, we were attending a mixer with our new classmates. OK, it was a little bit dorky, but we were excited. We'd been working demanding jobs for years (for Alexis, a challenging and exhilarating four-year run at eBay; for Alexandra, three years of long nights as an investment banker at Merrill Lynch), and we were relieved to be students again.

Alexis was three or four people away from finally making her way out of the winding stairwell and through the door of the pub when she heard her name. "Alexis!" She spun around. At the top of the stairs, waving with excitement, was Alexandra Wilkis. Alexis remembers

Alexandra looking chic in white jeans and a pink kaftan top, her tan suggesting she'd just flown in from somewhere exotic.

Six years prior, in the spring of 1996, we'd met as Harvard undergraduates. Our shared love for Brazil—Alexis had backpacked through South America while studying in Argentina, and Alexandra's best friends in high school had been Brazilian, so she'd traveled with them all over their country, from Rio to the Pantanal to Petropolis—had landed us in the same Portuguese class. It was taught by an affable but quirky professor from Cape Verde who organized dinners at quaint Brazilian churrascarias and restaurants in Cambridge. We were two of the more outgoing and engaged students in the class, and we shared a deep fascination for Brazilian history, culture, music, food, and politics. So we'd go out of our way to sit next to each other at these little dinners in Cambridge and had always enjoyed trying new foods and attempting to mimic our professor's funny Cape Verdean accent.

We'd never become more than casual acquaintances in college, but Alexis was thrilled to see that Alexandra was in her business school class. She thought, Phew, someone to hang out with! Alexis has always been guided by her very strong intuition. In that moment, entering John Harvard's, she had a feeling that she and Alexandra would be very close, lifelong friends.

We entered the bar, a place we knew well from our undergraduate days, when we'd spent plenty of evenings gabbing away with our respective groups of girlfriends over subpar nachos and above-average beers. It was as dark, smoky, and New England preppy as we remembered it, with stained glass windows and endless local beers on tap. But the crowd was older now and much better dressed. Instead of starry-eyed idealists, the room was packed with—well, capitalists. We started recognizing people we knew from our high school days, our undergraduate years, or our recent work experiences.

Throughout the night we'd break off to greet friends or acquaintances, then loop back to introduce these people to one another, our conversations alternating among English, Spanish, and Portuguese (and, for Alexandra, an occasional phrase in French or Italian). We were never more than a few feet apart, despite the fact that we each talked to dozens of people. Little did we know we'd end up working a room in this manner for years to come, at both social and business functions.

We left John Harvard's together, Alexis behind the wheel; this too became standard in our friendship (Alexis likes to joke that Alexandra won't get behind the steering wheel unless she absolutely has to, yet will happily hop into an itty-bitty plane to visit some remote Latin American city, navigating cheerfully in the local language). While the end of the night is a bit hazy, we do know that by the time Alexis dropped Alexandra off at her apartment in Cambridge, we'd managed to catch up on everything that had happened in both our lives since that undergrad Portuguese class. It was almost as if we'd spent the last five years not working totally different jobs, for the most part in different countries, but becoming the best of friends. Alexandra had been reminded that Alexis had a mischievous twinkle in her eye and was always game for anything fun, and Alexis had got to experience anew Alexandra's uncanny ability to connect with and quickly befriend people of all backgrounds and personality types.

From that day forward, we were inseparable wingwomen. We hopped on a plane every time we had a school break, or even a day off, to visit New York or discover another part of the world. In two years we visited fourteen cities in seven countries, from Punta del Este to Verbier, as well as some remote destinations like the rain forests of Costa Rica.[1] Alexandra would corral the group and research and plan the itinerary, and Alexis would chauffeur, since she was almost always

---

1. Now we are up to thirty-six cities in fourteen countries; we've been far more places together than either of us has been with her husband.

the only one who could drive a manual transmission. We'd both excitedly soak up as much local culture, shopping, food, music, and nightlife as we could, making friends along the way.

The more time we spent together, the more we confused our classmates, who, apparently thrown off by our similar hair and height, started calling us by each other's names. Instead of being annoyed, we simply learned to answer to both. By the end of our time at HBS, we'd turn around in unison when someone cried, "Alexis, Alexandra, Alex—"

Luckily, we both thought it was kind of flattering to be mistaken for each other, because this continues today in the halls of Gilt Groupe's 2 Park Avenue offices, where many new employees and even the veterans confuse one of us for the other and then turn bright red upon realizing their mistake.

ALEXANDRA: THE GO-GETTER

While our business school experiences quickly fused into one big joint adventure, we weren't nearly as alike as people always seemed to assume. And we'd returned to Harvard for very different reasons. Goal-oriented Alexandra was on a mission that bordered on obsession: to get out of her grueling job in investment banking and into high fashion, an industry she'd been drawn to for as long as she could remember. She had actually stated on her business school application essay that she intended to work for a global fashion conglomerate like LVMH upon graduation (of course, planner that she is, she *would* end up working for LVMH). As soon as the semester started, she subscribed to the fashion industry trade newspaper *Women's Wear Daily* at the student rate of ninety-nine dollars—she was probably the only subscriber on campus—and began systematically contacting, befriending, and picking the brains of the top executives at brands like

Donna Karan, Chopard, and Lilly Pulitzer in an effort to figure out how to become one of them as quickly as possible.

Alexandra had grown up on Manhattan's Upper West Side, the daughter of loving, supportive parents who always believed in her and encouraged her in everything she did. Her mother, Elsa Fleites Wilkis, was a teacher at a private Manhattan boys' school and an early refugee from Castro's Cuba who had grown up in a family of progressive, professional women. She prized education above all else. Alexandra's time was always heavily scheduled; when she wasn't in school, she took intensive piano lessons, practiced an hour every evening, and performed in monthly Saturday concert recitals.

At an early age, Alexandra decided that her dream was to attend Harvard. As a result, she was always a driven student who put in long hours in return for solid grades. During her high school years at Exeter in New Hampshire, she also wrote for the school newspaper, played squash, and ascended to captain of the varsity tennis team—a dizzying schedule that left little time for sleep. At the age of eighteen, her hard work paid off with a big fat acceptance letter to Harvard. She'd never felt so excited, and relieved, in her entire life.

As an undergraduate Alexandra allowed herself to relax and have some fun for the first time since—well, ever. Though her parents encouraged her to study economics, she decided to create her own major: romance studies, which allowed her to indulge her love of Spanish, Portuguese, and French literature (she'd grown up a native Spanish speaker, and languages came easy). Before graduation, Alexandra wrote a thesis entitled " 'Un Soleil Couchant': Dandyism and Decadence from France to Latin America and Portugal," and, thrilled by her topic, which incorporated fashion, the arts, *and* languages, turned it in three days before the deadline.

Part of what drove Alexandra to succeed was a nagging feeling that she had to work twice as hard as her friends and classmates to achieve the same results. She'd felt different since the end of third

grade, when her family fell on very hard times financially and emotionally and could no longer afford her school or their lifestyle. Though
Alexandra was young, she'd understood that from then on, nothing
would be easy anymore. Her father, Robert Wilkis, an entrepreneurial
businessman, had stressed to her the importance of resilience. And
rather than pull her out of Brearley, the private school she loved,
Alexandra's parents arranged for her to stay with the help of a schol-
arship, which most of her friends don't know about to this day. Alexandra remembers her mother saying, "No matter what happens, no
one can take away your education."

But she lacked access to the luxuries enjoyed by her classmates
and friends. Alexandra never felt resentful about this—her childhood
was full of more love and opportunities than most people's. Still, this
was Manhattan, a competitive, over-the-top place. She couldn't help
feeling the need to be extraresourceful in order to keep up. Her family's means had been seriously cut back, but Alexandra figured out
how to start seeing the world through creativity and various side jobs
during her high school years: she completed an exchange program in
London and a summer internship in Paris, and she visited her Brazilian high school friends in their homeland. Partly to afford all this
travel, she tutored in the summers, both in New York and on family
trips to Key Biscayne, Florida.

Alexandra always thrived on setting clear goals for herself and
working hard to achieve them; this gave her peace of mind. She never
went to sleep hoping a problem would be resolved or bemoaning a
fate that had befallen her; instead, she drew up realistic, step-by-step
plans and took deep satisfaction in checking items off her list. She
took this approach not just with academics but later with her career
and motherhood. To this day she feels a little lost when she isn't working diligently toward her next concrete goal.

It was Alexandra's mother who first introduced her to fashion.
Elsa Wilkis had an eye for aesthetics that extended easily from art to

clothing. She loved well-made pieces, understood fine construction and fit, and could spot real couture a mile away. But because designer clothes were for the most part out of the family's price range, she taught Alexandra to appreciate the value of a bargain, a *ganga,* as she jokingly called it. Alexandra has many happy memories of browsing through stores with her mother and her mother's mother (Alexandra's beloved *abuela*) in New York, Boston, and Miami, where they always did more bonding than buying.

Alexandra felt an almost magnetic pull toward fashion. It was always more about the mystery and craftsmanship of fine clothing and accessories than about any burning need to have the right handbag du jour. By the fifth grade she had turned an entire wall of her bedroom into a collage of her favorite magazine ad campaigns, from Claudia Schiffer posing for Guess to Paulina Porizkova vamping it up for Estée Lauder. Surrounding the ads, she taped cutouts of her favorite accessories, culled from magazines like *Vogue, Elle, Harper's Bazaar,* and *W.*

By the time she went away to high school, she'd become an expert comber of designer sale and discount racks. On the weekends she often went to Boston (where her *abuela* lived) to blow off steam with fashion-inclined friends at the oldest off-price retailer in the United States, the original Filene's Basement at Downtown Crossing.[2] This was the mid-nineties, and the girls at school were dressed head to toe in J.Crew and L.L. Bean. But while Alexandra could rock the preppy look, she was captivated by the exquisite vintage Givenchy and Nina Ricci dresses she stopped to admire at secondhand boutiques on Newbury Street.

Inevitably Alexandra approached her budding love of fashion with the same work ethic and resourcefulness she applied to her schoolwork. It was not enough just to get something on sale; she had to get

---

2. The store shut its doors just two months before the launch of Gilt Groupe.

a better price than anyone else did. She became a connoisseur of quality fabric and fit and honed the practical quantitative fixations of a professional merchandiser. She'd mastered the low-tech markdown system at the Filene's Basement Boston flagship by the age of fifteen: about two weeks after goods hit the sales floor, they dropped to 25 percent off the already discounted price; a few days later, 50 percent; and finally the price plunged to 75 percent off. At eight weeks items were donated to charity or, in rare instances, left on the floor, where you could continue to buy them for 75 percent off the already discounted price. Alexandra relished running the math on these discounts in her head and always compared prices all over town before buying even the smallest item. In high school she bought her first designer piece, a long navy blue Prada skirt with two slits up each side, for fifty dollars. She knew buying one at full price, had it even been possible, wouldn't have felt nearly so good.

Later, during her years as an investment banking analyst in London, Alexandra traveled throughout Europe on business and learned to navigate the shops on Via Montenapoleone and Via della Spiga in Milan at lightning speed, zipping through the side streets on foot in her black Fay motorcycle jacket. She had some disposable income to spend for the first time in her life but was never able to shake her love of a bargain. She perfected an agile mental currency converter that helped her stay on top of fluctuations among the dollar, the euro, and the British pound and always refused to pay retail without satisfying herself that an item couldn't be had cheaper anywhere else in the world. She practiced her romance languages on flabbergasted shopgirls across Europe, always paying several visits to a store to view an item before pulling out her wallet.

The natural gravitation she felt toward fashion, and the delight she took in scoring a deal, were always in sharp contrast to the lack of enthusiasm she felt for investment banking. One early morning in 2001 Alexandra found herself on a flight from London to Bilbao exhausted from a week's worth of all-nighters in the office. Eager for a mental break but not wanting to appear unprofessional to her boss, a managing director named Pacho, she wrapped a copy of the *Financial Times* around what she really wanted to read, American *Vogue*. She thought she was being clever, but Pacho wasn't fooled. "Alexandra," he said gently, "please promise me that after you get your MBA, you'll go into fashion and not back to banking. It's so obvious where your heart is."

She never forgot that.

When she got to Harvard Business School, Alexandra was determined to graduate from it with a job in fashion. During her second year she became copresident of the Luxury Goods Club, an inactive association of mostly French students, and got to work brainstorming ways to generate buzz and grow its membership. The answer, it turned out, was to call an HBS alumna at the Swiss luxury goods conglomerate Richemont (which owns brands like Cartier and Van Cleef and Arpels) to ask if any of the Richemont brands might donate product to help "increase brand awareness" among students at HBS. Alexandra happened to be working on a field study project for Cartier at the time, so the loot soon flowed in: voluminous rust-colored Longchamp totes inscribed with Baume & Mercier logos; Panerai baseball caps; Jaeger-LeCoultre Dopp kits. She packaged all these exciting freebies inside huge bright red Cartier shopping bags for new members, and joining the Luxury Goods Club suddenly became a very enticing proposition! At an annual event at the start of the school year showcasing the school's various extracurriculars, she signed up 180 new members, 10 percent of the student body. Huge red Cartier bags proliferated all over campus (obviously, Alexis joined so she could get one), and the club has maintained a strong presence since.

Clearly, Alexandra was destined for a future in fashion—and had a knack for building excitement around an idea.

ALEXIS: THE RISK TAKER

If Alexandra had come to business school with a clear agenda, Alexis most certainly had not. In fact her entire life's journey had involved far less detailed planning and much more spontaneous decision making. More than anything, she'd enrolled in business school for a break. For four years she'd held demanding positions at eBay, then the world's fastest-growing company, and she was feeling a little burned out. She'd endured hundred-hour workweeks for nearly her entire tenure, with few vacations, and had burned through three cars while commuting two hours daily. It didn't help that the tech bubble had burst in 2001 and a general air of defeatism had started to settle over Silicon Valley, with businesses shutting down and young techies leaving town in droves. Although eBay continued to grow, it was increasingly alone. Alexis, a perpetual optimist, had loved her time at eBay—it had been exhilarating and life-changing—but at twenty-seven, she found her life had started to feel a little predictable. She had a strong gut intuition that it was time for a change of scenery. Business school was a chance to move east, immerse herself once more in university life, be inspired by new ideas, and decompress for a couple of years.

Alexis's approach to life, like Alexandra's, can be traced to her childhood. One of six siblings, she grew up peripatetic and independent, splitting the year between her mom's place in New Jersey and her dad's in South Carolina. Her parents divorced when she was five, so she spent half her time as a Yankee, visiting New York City, Maine, and the Adirondacks; the other half she spent in Dixieland, having adventures in Charleston, up in the Smokey Mountains, and on her dad's cattle farm in the middle-of-nowhere Abbeville County. Since her father worked full-time, she and her closest-in-age sister, Lilly Maybank, ran wild and almost entirely unsupervised on the farm, galloping on their horses for hours every morning through neighboring fields and woods. Alexis learned some early lessons in responsibility while shuttling her sister between New Jersey and South Carolina from a young age.

Frank Maybank, Alexis's father, was an entrepreneur. He'd grown up in a house of two boys and attended all-boys schools through college. So when he had a large brood of mostly daughters, he raised them, well, pretty much like sons. He insisted they learn to drive a tractor, take their driving tests on a stick shift, and shoot a shotgun for self-protection. Before he and Alexis's mother divorced, he'd started his own financial firm in New York City; he eventually moved it to the Carolinas, where he had grown up, and grew it over several decades before selling it to a large southeastern bank. The only businessman in a family of mostly artists and architects for a generation in either direction, he was self-directed and self-made, and Alexis learned from his focus, determination, and ability to triumph over any personal or professional hardship. When Alexis later became an entrepreneur, she often turned to him for business advice and insight.

Up in New Jersey with her mother, Alexis's life was very different. Her mother, Deborah Macy Osmun, and Alexis's grandmother Maisie Macy were active outdoorswomen, world travelers, and multilingual sophisticates who made their way through the world on their terms, with intelligence, tenacity, and wit. Because Alexis's grandfather had worked for Pan Am, the family traveled far and wide as a benefit of his employment. Deborah had attended school in Switzerland from the age of fifteen before matriculating at nursing school in Germany, while Maisie, an avid painter, had explored, primarily alone (after her husband's untimely death), Europe, the South Pacific, Colombia, and other parts of the Americas, highly unusual for a woman at the time. She passed her love of travel and art on to Alexis's mother, who introduced Alexis to the thrill of visiting far-flung countries and cultures. Deborah was fearless, having lived abroad and alone from an early age. She embraced the world head-on.

Alexis was generally a good student, conscientious about homework, though she never felt pressure from either parent to perform a certain way in school, nor can she remember even once being asked for a report card. She just decided what interested her and pursued it with everything she had. When she was growing up, that meant sports. She went away to school in Connecticut at the age of fourteen and became captain of the cross-country team and an all-American lacrosse player. She always figured she'd play college lacrosse at a big state school like the University of Virginia, which was appealingly located betwixt the North and the South. She applied to Harvard only because the lacrosse coach recruited her heavily. And when she got in—and not into UVA—she was surprised but also thrilled. Unlike Alexandra, she'd never set her sights on the Ivy League or any other schools; she'd just always assumed things would work out. And they usually did.

As an undergrad, Alexis found environmental science interesting and harbored vague dreams of becoming a female Jacques Cousteau. But she treated lacrosse as her major. She got playing time immediately but also clashed with the coach. In hindsight, Alexis recognizes she had a minor problem with authority, arguably an asset as an entrepreneur, but not as a freshman lacrosse player. While she helped the team make it to the Final Four as a freshman, she was unceremoniously cut as a sophomore, a blow she had not anticipated. At the time it seemed like a tremendous setback, a failure of almost unimaginable proportions and a loss of her entire sense of self. Athletics had been the place she felt most at home and the arena in which she'd learned the thrill of being in the trenches with a team, the responsibilities of leadership, and, as a captain, the importance of leading by example. Now she'd lost her berth on the lacrosse team for reasons that had nothing to do with her skills as a player. It was confusing and disorienting, and it stung.

She now thinks it was one of the best things that could have happened to her.

Her natural response wasn't to lick her wounds, dwell on her foibles, place blame, or feel sorry for herself. It was to put her head down and push forward with increased motivation. Screw it, I'm just going to do something different, she thought. And better! Being independent from a young age and having responsibility for younger siblings made Alexis comfortable setting off in her own direction and confident in facing unexpected challenges. She was always oriented toward the future and the next thing, rather than let negative thoughts churn in her head and slow her down. Within a week of her humiliating setback, Alexis had regrouped, picked herself up off the floor, and, with a hint of competitive smugness, decided to spend a year abroad having more fun than she would've running sprints on the lacrosse field. She settled on Argentina, probably because it had looming mountains and an extremely exciting capital city, Buenos Aires. Most alluringly, Argentina was the farthest point away in the Americas. With pictures of the Andes swirling in her head, she applied for a program that would allow her to study political science and economics—interesting, she now thinks, since Argentina excels at neither.

Alexis's time in Argentina turned her into a traveler. During her remaining years of college she ventured to some of the most remote places on the globe, including Antarctica and indigenous regions of the Amazon, rearranging her studies to suit her passion for South America. While traveling, she carried what you might expect—hiking boots, rain gear—but she also couldn't help packing a couple of fantastic outfits and a pair of high heels . . . just in case.

Alexis's travels in South America, as well as being one of the most exciting times in her life, increased her appetite for risk and taught her to be resourceful in any environment or situation and to be ready for anything. To this day there is not much that makes her nervous, from a board meeting to a live interview on national television. We often joke that if Alexandra needs to spend time calming her nerves before a media interview, Alexis needs to chug a couple cappuccinos in order to appear sufficiently energized.

When she graduated from college, Alexis took a job in investment banking. She figured that becoming an ace in business would help catapult her to the top of a worthwhile global nonprofit, where she'd be able to make a difference for the environment or in international development. She chose Alex.Brown, a firm that would also take her to California, a place, like Argentina, that appealed to her sense of adventure. She was assigned to be an analyst in the New Media Group, which sounded cool, though she didn't know fully what it meant yet.

Within weeks, she found herself smack in the middle of the very first initial public offerings (IPOs) in the Internet space. At the time, 1997 and early 1998, there were only five or so public Internet companies: Amazon, AOL, and a few more that no longer exist. Promising start-ups were just beginning to raise money, be acquired, and go public. Alexis's small team saw its workload explode as the sector took off. The group was so understaffed that Alexis was soon attending management meetings, running due diligence sessions, and organizing documents and finances for companies preparing to go public—all at the age of twenty-two. All-nighters were a weekly occurrence. Her bosses also sent her to conduct meetings in far-off cities like Lahore, Kuala Lumpur, and Jakarta, places they had no interest in visiting themselves but which did—unbeknownst to them—appeal to her.

It was while she worked at Alex.Brown that Alexis got to know Jeff Skoll, one of the founders of eBay. A few months after their meeting, he wooed her over to his scrappy start-up, or, as her father warned her, his "online flea market." It was a far less stable job than finance, to be sure (Internet companies were viewed even more so as risky ventures in 1997, just flashes in the pan). But Alexis liked Jeff, and her gut told her to go work for eBay, so she did.

She joined a small team of no more than fifty people based in a single suite in an industrial office park in San Jose, California. The eBay headquarters had a ragtag feel: think cubicles decorated with snow globe collections, some even covered by homemade tents. But what the company had going for it was an incredibly creative, driven team of people. Alexis remembers being swept up by all the optimism coursing through the office. Instead of cynical bankers, she was now surrounded by idealistic young tech entrepreneurs who shared a common goal of building something big—ideally, something that would help people or answer a need. She felt imbued with a sense of purpose: eBay was aiming to inspire socially positive change by creating a platform whereby a mom in Idaho could sell her used laptop right alongside established companies like IBM. The site could be used to start businesses, make livings, get off welfare. It became a backbone for millions of entrepreneurs around the country, and then around the globe. It was the first time Alexis had considered that a profit-driven company could also alter behavior and change lives.

Jeff Skoll had stepped down as president that year to pave the way for Meg Whitman, the shrewd and seasoned executive whom Jeff and his cofounder, Pierre Omidyar, had recruited from Hasbro. As it organized to go public, eBay was in a period of exciting transition. Alexis joined Jeff's newly formed strategic planning team as an analyst alongside Reed Maltzman and later Simon Rothman, who, with Jeff, are some of the most innovative and strategic talents she's worked with to this day. Her job was to help predict the future of e-commerce. Where would eBay be in two years? In five? With her team, she helped identify and remove obstacles to the company's growth. Back then there weren't even credit card payment mechanisms that allowed Larry in Des Moines to pay Sue in Charlotte or insurance policies that would cover either one of them. Alexis found that working on the bleeding edge of an industry—clearing the messy roadblocks to its existence and growth—was thrilling.

It didn't hurt that the business as a whole was experiencing the single greatest growth spurt in corporate history. Spreading mostly through word of mouth and spurred on by eBay's grassroots marketing techniques, customer demand spiked, the number of sellers surged monthly, and the company struggled to hire enough people to keep pace. By the time Alexis left in 2002, the company had exploded from forty employees to a staggering five thousand.

This enabled Alexis to volunteer for assignments far beyond her level of experience. At twenty-four, she launched and ran eBay Canada. With the U.K. and Australia, Canada was one of eBay's initial forays outside the United States, and Alexis was by far the youngest person tasked with launching and running one of these international businesses. She moved part-time to cold, snowy Toronto, where she hired a Canadian product manager and found office space on a shoestring budget. She drafted a business plan, identified prospective partners to approach, and learned to navigate an extremely confusing tax system. Toiling practically around the clock, she schooled herself in product marketing, business development, engineering, and financial planning. When she couldn't figure something out, she would improvise rather than slow down. As eBay Canada's de facto media consultant, she even convinced native Canuck Jeff Skoll (a person who has never sought the limelight) to fly North for a grueling round of newspaper and TV interviews tied to the launch. She was thrilled when eBay Canada hit the market with a splash, earning ten million dollars in revenue in its first year and quickly becoming the largest e-commerce business in the Great White North.

Because she didn't want to live in Canada permanently, Alexis hired a Canadian country manager, returned to California and took on a completely different challenge: helping Simon Rothman, still her most important mentor, launch eBay Motors, eBay's largest category to this day. The company had acquired a crazy car auction company in Indiana, and Simon was charged with figuring out the automotive category and turning it into a thriving business. Alexis joined him for the ride. Much as in Canada, Alexis knew nothing about cars, but that soon changed. She found herself in boardrooms in Detroit, seated beside Simon across from twelve intentionally intimidating GM executives whose business cards said things like "Negotiator." She was usually the youngest in the room by at least twenty years, and a woman to boot, even stranger in the car business.

Alexis's focus at eBay Motors was business development, so she threw herself into understanding everything from the motorcycle industry to the used parts industry and developing a plan to sell the business to its target audience. She and her team wanted to promote eBay Motors through word-of-mouth (or viral) marketing. They aimed to find bike enthusiasts and car collectors, the kind of passionate hobbyists who would tell all of their friends about the new way to buy and sell cars, motorcycles, and parts that eBay was pioneering. Hopefully, word would spread among friends until raves for eBay grew into an exponential chain reaction with a life of its own. Word-of-mouth marketing would be cheap, but it would also be the most efficient way for eBay Motors to reach the consumers who would naturally be most interested in the site. This is because word-of-mouth marketing is fueled by two intuitive truths: First, people who are passionate about something talk about it a lot, whether it's cars or fashion. And second, a personal recommendation from a friend or trusted source will always be more powerful than any other mode of advertising.

So Alexis traveled regularly to places like South Dakota, where she attended the weeklong Sturgis Motorcycle Rally, which attracts half a million bikers. There she tried to turn bikers into eBay converts— and encouraged them to tell their friends. She also took some incredible pictures.

Her team's tactics worked. Soon the business was responsible for selling a billion dollars' worth of vehicles annually. And Alexis had learned a priceless lesson in the power of grassroots and word-of-mouth marketing that she'd later apply to Gilt Groupe.

BECOMING A&A

Arriving from such different places and experiences, we admired each other from the start. Alexandra got a kick out of the way Alexis marched to the beat of her own drum, never getting caught up in things that stressed out other MBAs, like micromanaging her job search. (Alexis just assumed she'd find something, and besides, she had tons of contacts in the Bay Area. Who needed HBS career services?) Alexis meanwhile loved Alexandra's chameleon gene, her uncanny ability to blend into any culture or environment. There was scarcely a place we visited in our two years at business school that Alexandra didn't have a close friend or friend of a friend.

As students we couldn't have been more different. If Alexandra was the type to front-load stress, finishing papers a week in advance so she could review them with the professor and get a good night's sleep the night before they were due, Alexis was the opposite: she hardly gave any assignment a passing thought until the night before the deadline. From the beginning of our friendship, our different personalities made us a great pair, because we approached the same challenges with different skills and perspectives.

Right before graduation we got our first taste of what it would be like to actually work together. The previous summer Alexandra had completed an internship at Financo, working under Marvin Traub, a retail guru who is the former chairman and CEO of Bloomingdale's. Through Marvin, she'd met the Posen family: the twenty-two-year-old fashion designer Zac Posen and his mother, Susan Posen, a lawyer who was then CEO of her son's business. During our final semester at HBS, Alexandra arranged a field study project with the Posens to gain more retail experience and to help her in her job search, which had become incredibly frustrating. (Why was she being offered jobs only in finance?) Because she was offering to work for free, it wasn't hard to sell Susan on the idea. Now Alexandra just needed a partner. Her dear friend Alexis did not harbor dreams of working in retail, but she, too, loved and followed fashion, and had certainly been the best-dressed person in her corner of Silicon Valley, preferring skirts over pants and reading fashion magazines like *Bazaar* in her spare time. Alexandra knew Alexis also had a thing for high heels. She asked her if she wanted to join her on the Zac Posen project. Alexis readily agreed.

Working with Susan, we created a project that would analyze successful examples of businesses that had launched secondary, or "contemporary," lines of clothing; think Marc by Marc Jacobs or D&G by Dolce & Gabbana. The ultimate goal was to create a business plan for a hypothetical Zac Posen diffusion line. We learned about the less glamorous but important side of fashion, from licensing and branding to distribution. Our independent study project was definitely not the best work we've ever done because it was the spring of our second year. But we were pleasantly surprised by how much we really enjoyed working together in a professional context.

It was Susan Posen—she could *not* tell us apart—who began referring to us as A&A or just the As. We thought it was funny. Little did we know she wouldn't be the last person in the fashion industry to address us this way, and that designers, fashion executives, and some of our own future employees would call us A&A, too.

In a professional context, as in real life, we'd started to become two distinct parts of a greater whole.

PARTNERING UP (IN MORE WAYS THAN ONE)

We both graduated with MBAs in 2004.

After a year of frustration and a couple of retail job offers so low as to be borderline insulting, Alexandra had managed to land a job in fashion, not a moment too soon, at Louis Vuitton, her dream brand. She moved back to New York to join the company's MIT (Management in Training) program. But this was the highly glamorous fashion job she'd envisioned in name only. In reality she was selling accessories in the Louis Vuitton boutique at Saks Fifth Avenue, learning to use a cash register, merchandising the display areas, and interacting constantly with customers. On the upside, she got to use her language skills, as there were plenty of foreign tourists in Saks. But she'd occasionally wonder why she'd worked so hard to get an MBA only to find herself sweeping the floors at a department store.

Alexis also took a job in New York City, as general manager of AOL's real estate, automotive, and dating sites. For the first time ever, we both were living in Manhattan. This was exciting!

We quickly zeroed in on a hobby both of us loved: sample sale shopping. At least a couple of times a month, we'd duck out of our respective offices to hike to the remote empty storefronts, hotels, or rented spaces where luxury brands liquidated excess merchandise. Among our favorites were Louis Vuitton, Fendi, Givenchy, Pucci, Valentino, and Carolina Herrera. When any of these designers had a sample sale, we'd e-mail each other to coordinate our plan of attack, regardless of what else we had going on at work that day. Luckily, Alexandra's job at Louis Vuitton ensured that we were on all the right e-mail lists in the first place and got invites to the best sales.

We shopped as a team to increase our chances of beating other designer bargain hunters to the best stuff. Surely many of our future Gilt customers would have been shocked to see us hastily trying on 75 percent off gowns and cocktail dresses right in the middle of chaotically cluttered showrooms and event spaces in the garment district—most sample sales don't have dressing rooms—but we did this all the time. Pandemonium was part of the deal, and it only added to the thrill of the chase when we could snag an amazing find in one of our sizes. Sample sales stoked Alexis's competitive juices, and for

Alexandra, an expert shopper who'd been marooned in Cambridge, they were almost too good to be true.

_____

In May 2007, three years after we moved to New York, Alexandra married Kevin Wilson in Miami. In hindsight, the wedding was not just a blowout party; it represented a turning point for both of us professionally and a major step toward our future partnership.

Alexandra had first spotted Kevin on the dance floor at Fizz, a now-defunct restaurant and nightclub at Fifty-fifth and Lexington. Kevin, who knew one of Alexandra's college friends, had an MBA from Kellogg and worked in finance at Citigroup. He'd been born and raised in the Midwest but had attended high school in Switzerland, and was fluent in French. Alexandra fell in love with him immediately. A year later, in July 2006, he got down on his knee on the beach in Key Biscayne, Florida, where Alexandra had spent time with her family since childhood. They began planning their wedding bash at the Biltmore Hotel in Coral Gables, Florida.

Alexandra wanted the wedding to embody the old-world glamour of Cuba in the 1950s. Because she was unable to choose any fewer, Alexandra appointed sixteen bridesmaids and five greeters, her best friends from every stage of her life. Alexis and her fellow maids wore floor-length mango-colored gowns, and the groomsmen (a smaller contingent by roughly half) wore white dinner jackets and escorted the bridesmaids down the aisle, one on each arm.

There was just one problem—well, two. Alexis's longtime boyfriend Jerome McCluskey, whom she had met in freshman year of college when they were assigned to the same dorm, dated for the better part of her adult life, and would later marry, was a corporate lawyer who worked punishing hours. That weekend, he ended up getting stuck in the office and was forced to cancel his trip to Miami on Friday night. This would have been disappointing under any circumstances, but Alexis was weathering an epically bad week.

She had finally tired of the bureaucracy of slow-moving AOL and, after two years, had left it six months before to cofound her own Internet business, Spinback. The idea, which was slightly before its time, was to reward bloggers for sales they generated for e-commerce sites through apps bloggers could embed on their pages.

But things at Spinback weren't going so well. The week of Alexandra's wedding Alexis had finally been forced to admit that she and her partner had conflicting goals and that the company was dead in the water. She flew to Miami for the wedding knowing that on Monday, when she returned to New York, she'd have to break the news to her four employees, who had left more stable jobs to join her start-up based on what had seemed like a promising idea. Failing was bad enough, but letting down employees who had taken leaps of faith to join her would be excruciating.

Alexis was determined to keep her stress from Alexandra on her wedding day. The last thing she wanted was for Alexandra to feel the need to have a long conversation with her or to focus on anything but her own joy. Like she'd done with her lacrosse setback, Alexis forced her disappointment out of her mind. And she hit the dance floor.

While Alexandra honeymooned, Alexis attempted to regroup from her disappointment, which felt different from, and larger than, any setback she'd previously experienced. Spinback was the failure of a partnership more than an idea, which somehow made it worse. Her cofounder was an entrepreneur she'd met through a venture capital (VC) firm she'd worked with in the past. In hindsight, it's clear that they were not the right people to execute the idea, at least not together.

In fact, from the beginning, red flags had abounded. Did he really plan to dedicate himself fully to this start-up? Was he more focused on control of the business than its ultimate success? All these doubts and signs that they had completely different objectives for the business she'd ignored, downplayed, or missed altogether in her eagerness to escape the big, tedious corporate battleship of AOL and get back to a more challenging and fast-paced entrepreneurial environment. Alexis had started Spinback trying to recapture the excitement and sense of purpose she'd felt at eBay. But she'd never paused to think about the fact that at eBay, she had trusted partners and mentors at every stage. At Spinback this was not the case.

Alexis had believed deeply in a concept and had underestimated the human side, the importance of a good partner who could support and complement her. In her optimism, she had overlooked the nagging sense that something wasn't right, and over the six-month period she worked on Spinback she began to question her cofounder's motives. Did he want to spend time in the office at all? When they began fund-raising, all the issues they'd buried in their haste to get the business up and running suddenly rose to the surface; it became glaringly obvious that their partnership could not survive. Their goals and principles just did not align. Alexis had thrown everything she had into getting the business off the ground, including plenty of her savings, so it was incredibly deflating when this didn't turn out to be enough. When Alexis sold her portion of the company to her partner, she felt as if she'd been punched in the gut.

She emerged from the experience wary and very scarred. She knew she'd never again enter into a partnership that had any obvious (or even not-so-obvious) red flags. Instead, she'd go into business only with someone she knew well and respected, who augmented her strengths and compensated for her weaknesses, someone she could trust completely.

But make no mistake, Alexis was more determined than ever to make her next start-up successful.

As it happens, the failure of Spinback had come just as a new opportunity emerged.

Alexandra had left Louis Vuitton a little more than a year earlier to take a job managing North American retail operations for Bulgari, the Italian luxury watch and jewelry behemoth. At first she'd liked the job, which sent her to places like Hawaii, Los Angeles, and Palm Beach, where she visited Bulgari retail stores and familiarized herself with the most relevant corners of luxury retail real estate in the United States. It had also left her plenty of time to plan her wedding because her role wasn't all that stressful. But by the time her big day rolled around, she'd started thinking about her next move and had already put out feelers to contacts in the industry indicating she'd be open to something new.

Alexis didn't know that Alexandra was thinking about starting a job search when she got back from Bali. For the first time in our professional lives, we'd be looking for a new challenge at the same time. Not unimportantly, Alexandra, who usually has less of an appetite for risk than Alexis, would also be married, with a partner whose job might allow her to consider stepping off her secure career path.

It was possible she'd be willing to try something a little more risky—and potentially *much* more rewarding.

CHAPTER 2

THE HISTORY OF AN IDEA:

Dreaming Up Gilt Groupe

Most online shopping mirrors brick-and-mortar stores. They're not taking advantage of what's uniquely possible online, the heightened sense of entertainment and competition. A big part of the Gilt brand promise is discovery: You come every day and it's new every day.

—GILT GROUPE CHAIRMAN SUSAN LYNE,
QUOTED IN *FAST COMPANY*, FEBRUARY 17, 2010

Spinback hadn't been dead for more than a few weeks when Alexis met a New York investor and entrepreneur named Kevin Ryan. Confident and whip smart, Kevin was founder, along with his partner Dwight Merriman, of AlleyCorp, a network of technology and media start-ups; his portfolio included ShopWiki, Music Nation, Panther Express, Business Insider, and later 10gen (at the time multitasking Kevin was also acting as CEO of both ShopWiki and Panther Express). The introduction came through Karen Rosenbach, a recruiter who had first called Alexandra to ask if she was interested in speaking to Kevin about a new business idea. Though Alexandra was looking for something new, the word *Internet* gave her pause, and she suggested to Karen that Kevin speak instead with her good friend Alexis. Alexis had worked at eBay and AOL; the online world was much more her thing.

In hindsight, it's a little uncanny that Alexis and Kevin might never have connected had it not been for Alexandra.

Alexis was immediately intrigued when she heard Kevin's name.

She'd met him once before, while she was working at Alex.Brown. Kevin had come to meet with her boss, Bob Packard, the managing director of New Media, about a small prepublic online advertising business called DoubleClick. Alexis had sat in on the meeting. She'd later watched with interest as DoubleClick had grown from a start-up to a $1.1 billion business,[1] with Kevin as its chief financial officer, then president, and finally CEO. DoubleClick was sold to the private equity firm Hellman & Friedman in 2005 (the firm then sold it to Google in 2008 for $3.1 billion).

In June 2007, Kevin invited Alexis to his AlleyCorp offices on lower Fifth Avenue. They quickly hit it off, despite the fact that he was punctual (if not early) and she was running her usual fifteen minutes late.

Though Kevin's portfolio was heavy with male-dominated tech start-ups, he wanted to talk about a French Web site called vente-privee (private sale) that was changing the face of e-commerce in France. With temporary online flash sales lasting four to five days, vente-privee liquidated large volumes of merchandise for mostly mass-market retailers like Adidas and Bisou Bisou at highly discounted prices. Kevin, whose wife is French, had heard of the site while traveling in France on both business and vacation, and a little digging had convinced him there was nothing remotely like it this side of the Atlantic. Since May, Mike and Phong had been working on building out the back end of a site inspired by vente-privee. For the time being, the project's name was FirstLook.

Alexis had never had any burning desire to work in retail; much like AOL, big luxury brands seemed too bureaucratic and slow-moving for her taste. But she'd always been fascinated by fashion. She thought immediately of the sample sales she and Alexandra knew

---

1. Web site of Hellman & Friedman LLC, www.hf.com/investments/Investments .aspx?tag=doubleclick.

oh-so-well. What if she could apply the French e-commerce model to the New York sample sale?

Energized by her conversation with Kevin, Alexis went home and did some furious brainstorming.

Everyone likes to hear about aha! moments, but the truth is, it can require ten aha! moments to produce one great idea. The Gilt model was no exception: it was ultimately shaped by a series of good ideas that we enhanced, tweaked, and rejiggered along the way. Kevin's vente-privee idea got Alexis thinking about sample sales and how they'd been a beloved local institution for years, offering fleeting bargains on coveted designer brands to select groups of insiders. They weren't just shopping; they were *events*. To savvy, fashion-conscious New Yorkers, a Louis Vuitton or Hermès sample sale was a drop-everything-and-run proposition. Once there, you basked not only in the bargains but in being part of (and often trampled by) an elite, stylish, in-the-know crowd.

Why not bring this singular phenomenon online, Alexis wondered, instead of liquidating mass-market sneaker brands? If women (and even men) in New York got so excited about designer sample sales, wouldn't similar shoppers across the United States? *Sex and the City* and other popular media had already introduced the concept to the rest of the country, and Alexandra and Alexis regularly fielded requests from friends and family members in other states to grab something, *anything,* in their sizes when their favorite brands hosted sample sales.

As Alexis saw it, sample sales had a huge untapped customer base online. Factors like reality TV, celebrity weeklies, the proliferation of secondary designer lines, and years of a flush economy had turned more men and women on to designer fashion than ever before. Yet in many states you couldn't even find brands like Oscar de la Renta and Carolina Herrera at full price, let alone 70 percent off.

Alexis met Kevin again a week later, this time with a ten-page

Word document in hand, to present her ideas and plan of attack. She was late again, but Kevin seemed increasingly willing to overlook this once she started laying out the specifics of her plan. She proposed that FirstLook focus on the more rarefied luxury end of the market—basically, that it be an online sample sale site. She emphasized that this made sense from a practical economic standpoint because working with higher price points would help achieve higher margins during the cash-strapped early months of the start-up phase.

But she also saw luxury brands as a long-term branding strategy. They would help the site amass a much bigger, more passionate audience, and quickly, by tapping into the singular excitement of consumers for the brands they coveted. FirstLook could re-create that urgent thrill of being invited to an exclusive, fleeting event; of being fast enough to score a highly sought-after handbag or pair of shoes for a great price. Designer brands would naturally attract their preexisting groups of devotees, as well as aspirational purchasers (as a Dolce & Gabbana fan Alexis knew she'd shop *any* Web site that offered access to Dolce at insider prices). She couldn't picture customers of a mass brand like Nike being quite so excited to plan their days around the sale of widely available sneakers. Designer brands would also lend a positive halo effect to the fledgling site. Their association with excitement, glamour, and intrigue would reflect positively on the FirstLook brand.

Alexis had also observed over the years that it was easier to start high end and expand into mass market than vice versa. She could think of a slew of designer brands that had started successful secondary lines, either on their own or through collaborations with retailers like Target and H&M, and in the process had attracted hordes of new customers hungry for a piece of those brands' cachet. But she could hardly think of any names from the middle of the spectrum that had succeeded in elevating their brands into the luxury sphere.

Take Lord & Taylor, the mid-range department store that tried to reposition itself as higher end in the early 2000s, remodeling its stores and cutting mainstream brands from its sales floors and replacing them with trendier collections. The department store lost millions of dollars before abandoning the strategy and returning to its roots.

Whereas Facebook, moving in the opposite direction, began as an exclusive online networking site for Harvard students and quickly grew to blanket all universities and later the entire world without ever really losing the cachet of its original market positioning (or the mystique of its founding story, as evidenced by the movie *The Social Network*). By launching at one of the most prestigious universities in the world and then slowly expanding to other elite colleges, only later admitting users unaffiliated with any university, the brand maintained the trust and the sense of privilege it had initially enjoyed as a forum for Harvard students. Even when millions of people were allowed to join, these members somehow felt as if they were being admitted to an exclusive club.

Alexis thought FirstLook should associate itself with the Fendis, the Christian Louboutins, and the Marc Jacobses of the world. In the future she could perhaps see expanding into lower-priced or less widely recognized brands. But first the site had to become a club that everyone wanted to join. The lure of exclusivity and access to sought-after merchandise would enable the business to use word-of-mouth marketing tools like the ones Alexis had learned at eBay to grow quickly, cheaply, and efficiently.

Another one of Alexis's points of reference at the time was ASmallWorld, a buzzy social networking site populated by the international jet set. It had a large global following and aimed to connect people of a certain influence and taste level from around the world. Importantly, the only way to join was via an invite from a friend. (Alexandra, incidentally, had the largest network on ASmallWorld of anyone Alexis knew.) The site made members feel special, as if they were chosen and in the know. That naturally incentivized them to tell their friends; it sped the pace and effectiveness of word-of-mouth marketing.

Alexis knew that making FirstLook not just high-end but members only would help it market itself. It would cultivate an air of mystery and imbue it with the allure of exclusivity. People would want to join for the deals, but also because of the perception that not everyone could.

When Alexis wrapped up her presentation to Kevin, he seemed encouraged, even excited by her ideas. He expressed some hesitation about moving toward a luxury positioning, since it might be easier to find suppliers in the mass market, and vente-privee had already been successful selling mid-level brands. But he heard Alexis out, and he liked her passion and confidence.

In July, Alexis began officially working with Kevin to add another start-up to the AlleyCorp portfolio. She initially came on board as chief operating officer, or COO, to flesh out the concept, run the business, and make the idea a reality. A few months later—though she's never been concerned with titles—she would formally become CEO, a role she was already filling. She would remain CEO throughout the company's critical first fifteen months.

Alexis was elated. With Kevin's support, she now had a chance to start a business she was truly passionate about as a consumer and to move on from Spinback to another chapter altogether.

Alexis began working immediately with Mike and Phong, with whom she hit it off famously. Mike knew absolutely nothing about fashion, but he shared Alexis's love for working on fast-moving, bureaucracy-free online businesses in the start-up phase. Like her, Mike was impulsive, upbeat, extremely extroverted, and driven primarily by intuition. Phong meanwhile was a good counterpoint: he was measured, quiet, and detail-oriented, with a great read on people.

All three were excited by the prospect of building something from scratch. "We all got along so well," recalls Phong. "I was so impressed that we were able to find that caliber of team right at the very beginning."

Mike and Alexis spent most of the summer focused on operations and on building the site's front end or customer experience, while Phong built out key parts of the technology and site infrastructure, including our e-mail system (which would ultimately be tasked with delivering millions of e-mails to our members within a few minutes each day). Both Mike and Alexis felt strongly about building the simplest, fastest shopping experience on the Web, one that minimized the number of mouse clicks standing between a shopper and the pair of Michael Kors gladiator sandals she passionately desired. They wanted to allow members to be able to log into the site and, with just a couple clicks—in *seconds,* not minutes—arrive at the checkout screen. They were obsessed with the proper placement of buttons on the screen, and with excising all needless words, links, and pages from the shopping experience. Mike even advocated for saving customers' credit card information after their first purchase and absolving them from re-entering their card's security code on subsequent purchases. The ease of Gilt's site now causes customers to marvel— and sometimes lament—that it's all so *fast* that they can buy hundreds or even thousands of dollars' worth of items without even realizing what they've done!

Our relentless focus on customer experience did not start and end with Gilt's Web site, however. It also extended to customer support and warehouse operations. Mike was particularly focused on streamlining our logistics so that items purchased could be shipped on the very same day. In order to make this happen, he visited dozens of warehouse spaces in New York and New Jersey and systematically assessed each facility's technological prowess, flexibility, and willingness to work with us as we tested complex new inventory management systems. He even kept an eye out for the warehouses' treatment of employees. He figured that the better a company treated its employees, the better it would treat our inventory and customers; the more a facility valued and understood technology, the more potential longevity it would have as our partner; and that a high degree of flexibility would enable the warehouse to more easily take our growth in stride.

Alexis remembers visiting the top three facilities that summer with Mike and learning skills she never anticipated she'd need, such as how to appraise whether a warehouse was likely to have mafia ties. At one New Jersey facility, she saw doors bound by chains during employee work hours, effectively signaling that employees were not allowed to leave their posts and they'd better not even *think* about stealing. Another potential partner balked at the limited amount of space we were seeking and questioned our business's real potential for growth. Though tech-savvy, this facility obviously did not have the stomach to put up with the unpredictability of a start-up.

By the end of August, Mike and Alexis had chosen a tech-savvy, highly flexible warehouse facility in Brooklyn's Navy Yard, one that treated its staff and hourly employees with respect. This facility would house our inventory during the business's critical early years, and it would ultimately grow with us for four years and counting. We started out with a small safe and four rolling racks. Today, with fulfillment having moved to a large facility in Kentucky, the Brooklyn space houses eight photo studios, props and samples for photo shoots, and our customer support team.

With our warehousing needs settled, we shifted our focus to an important matter for any luxury e-commerce business: packaging. We spent *weeks* discussing in minute detail how to provide our customer with the best possible package-opening experience. Should her purchase be wrapped in black or gold tissue paper? Should it include a personal, handwritten note of thanks? What could we do to re-create the rush she'd hopefully experienced while buying the item in the first place? That summer and even into the fall, Alexis and Mike devised detailed packing instructions for our new warehouse that included information on how to fold various types of apparel; how to use rulers to make the folds *neat*; which items should be inserted first in the box; where the gold sticker should be affixed to the tissue paper; and what the customer should see first upon opening the box. Mike, world-class engineer that he is, even led a folding training session for our packers!

We wanted each box shipped out from our warehouse to feel to the customer like a gift she was delighted to receive. Mike, in particular, was fastidious with the details so that the thrill customers felt shopping on our site extended all the way to the moment they received and opened their box at home.

———————

But while the core team was coming together and the business starting to take shape, there was still something missing. Alexis knew she needed a merchandising expert who could liaise with the fashion industry and lure the right high-end brands to the site, someone who understood fashion intimately and was a go-getter. This person needed a large preexisting network of contacts in the industry, and the gumption to convince them to entrust us with their valuable wares. For all her experience on the Internet, Alexis's career had not exactly put her in touch with any fashion CEOs; although she knew many people in Silicon Valley, she knew no one in New York City's garment district.

But she knew someone who did.

CHAPTER 3

FROM THE BEST OF FRIENDS TO
BUSINESS PARTNERS:

How to Know When You've Met Your Match

> I can never underestimate how important that initial team is. Ideas are cheap and available—it's all about the execution. A team that's well-rounded, complementary and has personalities that gel is critical in building a strong and sustainable business.
>
> —ALEXIS MAYBANK, QUOTED IN *THE WALL STREET JOURNAL*, OCTOBER 19, 2010

Alexis had thought of her dear friend Alexandra during that first meeting with Kevin Ryan.

After all, Spinback had taught her a valuable lesson: in start-ups, the execution is much more important than the idea. No matter how brilliant or timely your business proposition, if you don't have a team capable of effectively executing it, and executing it together, it will never work. Alexis knew she needed a great partner if she was ever going to be successful getting FirstLook off the ground. She knew little about the inner workings of the fashion industry but had a feeling it was chock-full of divas, drama, and politics.

She also knew enough to know that many luxury brands were still terrified of the Internet, which to them still seemed somehow déclassé, and that it would be no small task to convince them to sell at a steep discount online. FirstLook's final cofounder needed not just contacts but heaps of persuasive gifts and charm. Without the right brands, the site wouldn't be able to generate excitement and spread virally among groups of friends. It wouldn't be able distinguish itself from the many other lackluster fashion e-commerce sites already out there, most of which weren't performing well at all. There was a reason fashion e-commerce as a whole had been left for dead (like local discounts, incidentally—another category that would soon be spectacularly resuscitated, via Groupon).

But more important than any contacts, Alexis wanted a partner she could trust and rely on completely. She understood that Spinback had been doomed more by her lack of chemistry with her partner and their different goals for the business than by its lack of potential as a business.

By the summer of 2007 Alexandra's job at Bulgari, overseeing North American retail operations, had become monotonous and unchallenging. Upon returning from her honeymoon she'd been temporarily assigned to manage the Bulgari retail store on Madison Avenue while the company did some internal reshuffling and hired a new manager from the outside. Alexandra had a spacious office and sole responsibility for millions of dollars' worth of exquisite jewels and watches. But it was a little depressing to be working retail on New York's Upper East Side in the summer months, when most residents clear out for extended stays in places like the Hamptons. Days regularly passed without a single sale. Forget challenging—she found the job downright boring. Every morning Alexandra put on gloves and painstakingly removed the many trays of watches and jewelry from the basement safe, then carried them up to the sales floor, where she laid them out in pristine cases and storefront windows. On a good day this tedious process took at least twenty-five minutes. Then she and the sales associates spent the day waiting in vain for a customer to walk through the door.

It was a quiet weekday morning when Alexis, in yoga pants, showed up unannounced at the Bulgari boutique. She was in good spirits. She'd wandered up from her nearby apartment to ask Alexandra out for coffee. It was a typically sluggish day on Madison Avenue, so Alexandra had all the time in the world. We left the store in the hands of one of Alexandra's coworkers and ducked out around the corner to a diner on Madison Avenue. We sat there drinking coffee and nibbling on a fruit plate for more than two hours while Alexis made her honest, direct pitch.

Although Alexis isn't really a planner, she'd thought long and hard about how to present the idea to Alexandra. While she and Kevin were also interviewing a couple other candidates as backups, she knew there would be absolutely no one better than Alexandra with whom to launch a sample sale Web site. For one thing, she had the luxury retail experience to complement Alexis's tech and start-up backgrounds. She knew how the design and production process worked, she knew about sales and discounting, and from the inside of two of fashion's most storied companies, she'd versed herself in luxury brand marketing and merchandising. She was well connected in New York's fashion industry, with a large Rolodex of friends and contacts. And she had the chutzpah to work those connections, with no fear of cold calling. Alexandra knew exactly whom to contact at most brands and, even if she didn't know them personally, could find a way to get in front of just about anyone for a meeting. Surely she could charm the most hardened, skeptical fashion CEOs and decision makers.

But Alexandra didn't just have a complementary skill set; she had a complementary personality. If Alexis was fearless and spontaneous, a big-picture thinker, Alexandra had meticulous follow-through and an amazing ability to fit more work into the average twenty-four-hour day than most people. She was persistent and relentless and brought all ideas she pursued to closure.

More important still was trust. Alexis knew her friend was a truly good person, that she shared Alexis's values. This idea was too good to risk pursuing with a cofounder about whom she had *any* doubts, and with Alexandra, there were none. Alexis trusted her completely and knew that ethics and integrity would form the core of the working relationship. Of all the things we shared, this was the most valuable. We'd waste no time testing each other or being suspicious of decisions one or the other of us made. There would be no jockeying for power. We'd root for each other from the bottom of our beings and seek success and recognition for the other person as much as, if not more than, for ourselves.

As friends we'd never been even the least bit competitive. It's probably because we're so different, from our academic interests to our personalities to the separate careers we were building in luxury fashion and the tech space. We can understand how friends with the same skills who are working in the same industry would be tempted to compare themselves or even to begrudge each other's promotions or recognition. But even in graduate school, this was never an issue for us. We have each always been self-aware enough to know that the other had skills we couldn't touch—and vice versa!

This would work to our advantage as cofounders. We'd be responsible for completely different areas of the business (for Alexis, team-building, operations, product marketing, and fund-raising, and for Alexandra, merchandising and liaising with designers). We'd combine forces to tap our networks and grow our membership from scratch, and we'd certainly strategize together, support each other, and constantly compare notes, but we both were self-starters and would be free to do our own thing, trusting each other implicitly.

Alexis knew that whatever happened, we'd be in it together, supporting each other, lending perspective to disappointments, amplifying all joys, and, she believed, having as much fun together as we always had.

She really wanted Alexandra to say yes.

But she had a tricky line to walk. She didn't want to undersell how amazing an experience it was to launch a business. Alexandra had never worked at a young, fast-growing company, and we'd talked casually for years—ever since our field study project for Zac Posen—about how fun it would be to start something together. FirstLook was an uncannily perfect blend of our respective expertise. We both were also barely thirty, enjoying that rare moment in life when we still had plenty of energy but did not face unwieldy personal responsibilities at home.

At the same time, Alexis didn't want to sell the idea *too* hard and risk Alexandra's being unhappy in a start-up environment or regretting her decision to leave Bulgari. Bulgari was an internationally known company with an esteemed heritage and prestige. How would Alexandra adapt to a four-person team and a dingy little rented office space?

Finally, Alexis couldn't imagine ever having to tell her friend Alexandra, as she'd just recently had to tell her four loyal employees at Spinback, that things weren't going to work out and the business was shutting down. This fear loomed larger than any other. What if they didn't succeed? It would be Alexis who had convinced Alexandra to give up her hard-won position at Bulgari. Alexis worried more about straining a close friendship than she did about personal failure.

But while she fretted about how it would impact the friendship should things not work out, Alexis also knew that if Alexandra joined the team, it would vastly increase FirstLook's chances of success.

It was ultimately a risk she was willing to take.

————

Alexandra listened as Alexis laid out the concept, explaining Kevin's idea to bring a model like vente-privee's to the United States and her own interest in replicating the New York sample sale. Before Alexis even finished, Alexandra's head started filling with names of people she could call for help: executives she'd met while still a graduate student, powerful people she'd worked with in the fashion industry, and many of her friends. Surely there were hundreds, if not thousands, of people she could enlist to help get this idea off the ground. She also thought of her hundreds of girlfriends who would be perfect customers for this site.

We did some initial brainstorming on what kinds of brands First-Look would target (Alexis's dream brand was Dolce & Gabbana; Alexandra's, Valentino or Alexander McQueen), where we'd position the site in the market, how we'd make inroads in an industry that was still quite scared of the Internet.

For Alexandra, the conversation was a revelation. Tossing around creative ideas—ideas she might actually be able to directly implement—was exactly what was missing in her job at Bulgari. She couldn't remember the last time she'd been asked to brainstorm about anything truly creative or come up with a new way of doing things! At the end of the day all important decisions at Bulgari were dictated by "Rome," where the company's corporate headquarters was located.

Alexandra knew it would take a lot of discussion and careful planning before she'd be able to work up the confidence to take her chances on a start-up. But when she returned to the boutique later that afternoon, her mind was racing. Suddenly the stately confines of Bulgari felt more like a dungeon.

That summer we became more and more excited and increasingly convinced that together, we could turn FirstLook into an amazing business. But while we knew shoppers would love it, luxury brands' enthusiasm for the site was far from assured. The idea was risky, exciting, overwhelming, and a little bit scary.

Though Alexandra took her time committing to the opportunity, she quietly started compiling Excel documents of executives in the fashion world with whom she had solid relationships, fashion industry contacts she'd approach for access to luxury brands where she didn't have contacts, and friends and acquaintances she'd invite to join the site as members. She knew she'd want to hit the ground running if she were able to work up the nerve to dive into a start-up. In her basement office at Bulgari, Alexandra worked on her lists through the summer.

Many of her contacts dated to business school, where, after reading an interesting article about a brand in *WWD*, she'd fire off an e-mail directly to the designer or the brand's CEO explaining that she was a student and would love to meet for coffee. Often she'd initially be ignored or told that the company wasn't hiring MBAs, but she'd politely persist, explaining she just wanted to *meet* because the person or company inspired her. The truth is, flattery will get you everywhere, or at least somewhere! More often than not, even the very powerful and well-known executives acquiesced. In this way Alexandra had coffee or phone calls with over one hundred top executives in the fashion industry during her second year of business school alone, from Philippe Bonay, then president of Panerai North America, to Jeffry Aronson, then CEO of Donna Karan, to Tim Schifter, then CEO of LeSportsac.

Alexis attests that there were at least two thousand names on Alexandra's lists, all people who worked, or formerly worked, or knew someone who worked at key brands in the fashion industry. And these weren't just people Alexandra had met or e-mailed with once or twice. Many were people she'd kept in thoughtful, close touch with for years, it seemed, sending handwritten notes after meetings or coffees, remembering birthdays, and, when appropriate, facilitating helpful introductions. In her thirty years, Alexandra had made many friends and business acquaintances and lost very few (if any). Alexis had never been nearly as good at, or interested in, keeping in touch with as many people and was impressed by her friend's ability to remain genuinely close to so many people.

Alexandra knew that the position at FirstLook would be harder than any job she'd ever had. In a way, as FirstLook's connection to designer brands she'd be tasked with single-handedly convincing an entire industry to sell in a new, untested way. But she felt increasingly confident that she could break down this task and systematically attack it.

Before making her final decision, she sought advice from two key people in her life, her husband and her father. When she proposed the idea to her husband, his reaction was what she expected. "If you believe in the concept and want to do it, you should go for it," he said. So she took the idea to her dad. Alexandra's father had always been her closest adviser and confidant. She often felt he knew her better than she knew herself. Alexandra wasn't yet sure she was ready to abandon her cushy luxury gig for an Internet start-up but was hoping she was and knew her father would be a rational sounding board to help her through this important decision.

As he'd done so many times in the past, before nearly all the big academic and professional crossroads Alexandra had faced, he helped her lay out the pros and cons of the opportunity. Alexandra believes his questions are the ones everyone should think about before joining a start-up venture.

---

checklist:
IS THIS RISK A GOOD RISK?

1. DO YOU BELIEVE IN THE CONCEPT? (Yes, I do. I understand the psychology of how women shop, and know that if we execute well, this idea could fundamentally change the retail industry.)

2. DO YOU BELIEVE IN THE FOUNDING TEAM? What is the track record of everyone involved? (Yes. Alexis is a hard worker who is never afraid to get her hands dirty. She's genuine and authentic. She thrives at the helm of small, growing businesses, like the two—eBay Canada and eBay Motors—she started and helped start, respectively, at eBay. Kevin has shown a knack for identifying market opportunities at AlleyCorp and is a businessman with proven successes behind him at DoubleClick. Mike and Phong are top-notch engineers with remarkable work ethics.)

3. DO YOU BRING UNIQUE CAPABILITIES TO THE TABLE? (Relationships with the brands we'd want to sell on the site. Thousands of potential customers to invite to join. Drive. Resilience. I won't give up.)

4. WHAT KIND OF FREEDOM WILL YOU HAVE (IN THIS CASE, TO HIRE, BUY INVENTORY, AND TRAVEL TO MEET WITH DESIGNERS)? (This was a good question. I needed clarification from Alexis on my budget and our plans for raising capital.)

5. WILL YOU LEARN AND GROW? (Definitely.)

6. ARE YOU PREPARED TO FAIL? (I think I can handle failure, but I'd obviously rather avoid it.)

7. IS YOUR PARTNER (SPOUSE) SUPPORTIVE OF YOU TAKING THIS STEP? (Absolutely.)

8. WHAT DO YOU HAVE TO LOSE? (Not much. A job that doesn't challenge me anymore.)

9. WHAT DO YOU HAVE TO GAIN? (A lot. The chance to finally make my mark on an industry I'm passionate about.)

After her conversation with her father, Alexandra knew that she'd take the job.

While Alexandra finalized the details of her decision, Alexis arranged a dinner at DB Bistro Moderne in midtown Manhattan so that Kevin Ryan could spend time with us both outside a conference room (Alexandra had already met with Kevin at his office, and they had gotten along well). Over sirloin burgers, pommes frites, and plenty of red wine, we got our first taste of how much we'd all like working together as a team. We talked excitedly for hours. By the end of the night it was clear that Alexandra had Kevin's blessing and that we all were very likely going into business together. That was when Kevin gave us a piece of advice we'll never forget.

"If you are really good friends," he said, "make sure your professional relationship doesn't busnify your friendship."

He explained that in his years involved in start-ups, he'd seen plenty of business partnerships fail because of personality clashes between partners who were ill matched from the start. And he'd seen many more friendships become all business, as friends became business partners and eventually found that all they talked about was work; business had essentially replaced their personal rapport and made it hard for them to connect on a deeper level. Kevin didn't want this to happen to us, and we appreciated that. It spoke well of his integrity. He advised us to go into our partnership with eyes wide open and to actively manage the balance we wanted to strike between our professional relationship and our long-standing friendship, which both of us valued above all else.

Kevin's advice gave us an opportunity to talk about what exactly our business relationship would look like. The biggest potential issue, of course—at least from the outside—was that one of us would have to be in charge (in any business, even in an equal partnership, someone ultimately needs to be responsible and answerable). We already knew this person would be Alexis. As chief merchandising officer, Alexandra would manage an area of the business Alexis knew nothing about but would report to her friend. For some pairs this might be awkward. But to be honest, it never even occurred to us to feel bothered by it. Partnering up just felt right, and we had no time to lose. Besides, compared with working for her previous bosses, Alexandra thought reporting to Alexis sounded liberating and fun! Still, we made sure to spend some time talking about how we'd divide responsibilities, make decisions, handle disagreements, and whether we'd tone down our close relationship to keep our coworkers from feeling that Alexandra was getting special treatment. We decided to keep our conversations in the office strictly professional, to voice any differences openly and honestly as colleagues, and to retreat to a conference room if we needed to have a more heated debate, though we really couldn't imagine what we'd disagree about. We also talked about Kevin's warning and agreed to talk about things other than work. The truth was, with so many friends in common, it would be hard to avoid talking about our personal lives. But these conversations we'd save for coffee dates, travel, and the taxi rides that we shared frequently enough.

We also discussed how much fun it would be to walk to work together from the Upper East Side, where we both lived. Unfortunately, *that* never happened; we were soon moving around town exclusively at a sprint or in a speeding cab or subway car, rushing from our warehouse in Brooklyn to meetings with brands to coffees with potential hires.

We both recognized that we were in theory putting a lot on the line by launching a business together. If conventional wisdom says you shouldn't rent an apartment with your best friend, then cofounding a company is surely an even faster way to combust a friendship. But these conversations about our partnership always felt kind of perfunctory; we had them because we felt we should and because other people told us to have them. We were never all that concerned about working together. We were concerned about convincing luxury brands to sell to us, about beating competitors to market, but not about our partnership. We were friends from business school, and that was different from being, say, neighbors. We'd seen each other's work ethic and drive in action; we were familiar with each other's basic business acumen. Most important, we each had seen the other at her best and worst and knew we would not encounter any surprises as we hit the inevitable highs and lows any start-up faces as it grows. While we may have harbored individual fears of failure and embarrassment, after a decade of close friendship our confidence in each other was absolute.

We knew that between us, we had many of the core traits of successful entrepreneurs: drive, creativity, passion, ability to persevere even in the face of failure, healthy ego and confidence, and enough irreverence to think we could actually pull it off. It's not that we'd have started a business with just any friend. Quite the opposite. We were excited about working with each other specifically and knew that if FirstLook were to be successful, the fact that we were friends would have a lot to do with it.

In a way, entering a business partnership is like entering a marriage. Perhaps you have a friend whom you've advised not to tie the knot with someone because she or he was having trouble with the decision. *The fact that you have doubts is your answer.* For us, the fact that we had *no* doubts was our answer.

Our discussions turned from our partnership to frenetic planning. After working for large and established companies like AOL, Merrill Lynch, Bulgari, and Louis Vuitton, we were excited to be able to mold our company's culture and surround ourselves with people with whom we really wanted to work, rather than inherit the legacy of someone else's hiring decisions. We knew we'd be spending a lot of hours at the office and that working together would bring a sense of meaning and permanence to our jobs.

What went unsaid—because we didn't need to say it—was that our friendship would always be our number-one priority. No business issue, no matter how large, was ever going to warrant jeopardizing our deeper bond. We each knew this—and knew the other knew it too.

On September 13, 2007, Alexis received the e-mail she had been awaiting. "Yes!" read the subject line. Eager to hear about Alexandra's meeting with her boss, François Kress, then the managing director of Bulgari, Alexis had been checking her BlackBerry constantly for two days. Alexandra had already promised to resign, but Alexis was terrified that she'd change her mind at the last minute or that François would make it impossible for her to leave.

But Alexandra had made her decision.

"I am REALLY looking forward to getting started," she had written. When Alexis read the e-mail, she immediately broke the exciting news to Mike and Phong. In that moment what had for years been a vague pipe dream, something we'd discussed on vacations, on long drives, or at our weekly chatty grad school dinners at places like John Harvard's, became very real.

We're starting a business together.

We're starting a business together!

---

checklist:
THE BUSINESS PARTNER DECISION

We firmly believe that our friendship was a big reason we succeeded as cofounders. But we're also convinced that not all friends should start businesses together, no matter how close they are or how great an idea they think they have. Take it from us.

Descending into the trenches of a start-up with someone can be incredibly rewarding—or pretty devastating, if it doesn't work out (as Alexis saw at Spinback). Your friendship will be tested. But if you're the right match, any success will just make it stronger. Before you commit to partner with a close friend or acquaintance, no matter how well you think you know him or her, we recommend you ask yourself these questions:

1. HAVE YOU SEEN YOUR PARTNER HANDLE DIFFICULT SITUATIONS? Have you witnessed his highest highs and lowest lows? Because these moments reveal who a person is and what he is truly made of. Without a doubt, this individual will act the same way during the highs and lows your company encounters. We'd seen each other handle everything from the crushing failure of a company (Spinback) to personal family misfortunes; we each *knew* how the other handled major setbacks and, more important, how she regrouped from them.

2. DO YOU WANT THE SAME THINGS FOR YOUR COMPANY? Do you most want control and to be in charge, or do you want to create something big and get a return on that creation, even if you don't remain at the helm? Do you want to focus on work/life balance? Are you chasing fame? As crazy as it seems to talk about these issues when your business consists of four people sitting shoulder to shoulder in a dingy rented office space, you should. People start businesses for different reasons, all of them valid. But when partners have conflicting goals or measurements of success, this causes tremendous strife and can derail companies if not identified and mediated at the start. If your goals are not in sync, then one of you will likely have to compromise your goals or leave the company.

3. DO YOU HAVE SIMILAR ENERGY AND WORK ETHIC? Are you equally ambitious? We knew what it was like to work hard, having pulled plenty of all-nighters at previous jobs. At eBay, Alexis often worked late with the engineers and slept on couches in San Jose to avoid having to drive sixty miles to her house in San Francisco when she'd have to be back at her desk at 8:00 A.M. Alexandra, meanwhile, in her investment banking days, had often curled up with her pashmina in the bathroom's handicap stall—yes, she slept in the office *bathroom*—while she waited for desktop publishing to make her edits so she could have her pitch books printed (this was the dark ages before BlackBerrys). We both hoped we wouldn't have to repeat these experiences at FirstLook, but if we could work this hard for others' businesses, imagine what we could do for our own!

4. HOW DO YOU FIGHT? Can you be honest with each other and give and accept criticism? Do you let things fester, or do you discuss them openly? We've found that open and direct conversation is key to success, even when you disagree. We both have healthy egos, but neither of us is hotheaded. We listen. When there is an elephant in the room or something that needs discussing, one of us simply brings it up—usually out of earshot of other employees—and we discuss it. We voice our opinions, no matter how ardent they might be, always with respect for each other, and then we resolve the issue, agree to a direction, and move on, rather than open and reopen the debate.

5. IS THERE ANY DOUBT OR RED FLAG . . . *ANY?* On this point it's best to just trust your gut. Is there any distrust or uncertainty around integrity? Are you ignoring any burning negative feeling deep down—something you mentally stumbled upon, no matter how fleeting—in your enthusiasm for your idea? If you're not longtime friends, have you painstakingly checked references and followed your instincts? Have you observed how your partner treats people, from colleagues to subordinates to servers at restaurants? Our preexisting trust and complete faith in each other's integrity and intentions were important. It made our business relationship much more efficient because we never had to waste time testing each other's capabilities or doubting each other's motives.

6. DO YOU HAVE COMPLEMENTARY PERSONALITIES? Complementary skill sets are important, surely, and what most people focus on. More essential, and often overlooked, is the need for complementary personalities. The many ways that we are complementary include sensitivity (Alexis is never afraid to be direct, while Alexandra's higher degree of sensitivity allows her to sense emotional currents in the company and highlight them to Alexis) and appetite for risk (Alexis's is higher, making her a creative and intuitive entrepreneur; Alexandra meanwhile is a measured decision maker and has always been more carefully focused on the details). Because we view and experience the world differently, we are more likely to avoid our own blind spots and to avoid taking on needless levels of risks. We are a balanced unit.

7. IS YOUR PARTNER AN UPPER OR A DOWNER? Does he or she see the glass as half full or half empty? Life is too short to spend time with downers, let alone start businesses with them. You need someone who is grounded in reality, but not someone who will make you doubt yourself or debate why every idea and solution will not work. Instead, you need a partner who can see the possibilities, what *will* work.

In August, while awaiting Alexandra's final decision, Alexis turned her attention to another important matter: the company's name. First-Look sounded bland and flat, like a working title for a project, which it was, and not a distinctive, innovative business in the fashion world.

Alexis knew that as a Web-based business we'd need our name to be, and do, a lot of things. Her years in tech had taught her that, first and foremost, it had to be easy: easy to spell, easy to recall, easy to tell our friends about, and easy to type into a browser, search engine, or e-mail, because it would also be our URL. In fact, Alexis knew that a compact four letters were nirvana as far as Web site names went. We were planning to spread the word about the site primarily through word-of-mouth marketing, so our name had to travel easily from person to person, from dinner table to laptop, from news article to excited e-mail to friends.

With all this in mind, Alexis took to the Internet, using sites like Wikipedia to spur creative ideas. Believe it or not, free-associative Web surfing is a great way to brainstorm names for a business. After hours of typing in terms like *luxury* and *exotic*, Alexis thought to research the thousands of Greek isles and soon stumbled upon Skorpios Island, off the western coast of Greece, where Jacqueline Kennedy Onassis had spent her summers. That seemed to have an exotic flare and conjured up associations with Jackie's timeless elegance. She also found *tipetta*, the Italian slang word for a really cute girl, which of course reminded her of muses and ingénues. *La gamine*, a French siren in the mold of Twiggy or Charlotte Gainsbourg, was similarly appealing. Alexis let these words and a few others bounce around in her head for a few weeks, informally surveying her friends at every opportunity, before narrowing them down to five potential monikers, each fun and exotic in its own way: Skorpios, Tipetta, La Gamine, Gilt, and Modenius (a word Alexis invented that fused moda with genius). Many friends she asked liked La Gamine the best, but Alexis was worried about its strongly feminine meaning and sound. It was impossible to imagine a man telling his friend, "I love shopping on La Gamine!" Still, Mike, a fluent French speaker, liked the name and immediately understood its glamorous connotations.

Because she knew the company would eventually sell to men, the site's name needed to resonate equally with men and women. In fact Alexis believed that in branding and Web site design, a business that wanted to capture men needed to design and name itself specifically with them in mind. By doing so, it could capture women too—but *not* vice versa. This is common sense, but there are plenty of examples out there. Brands like Volvo, Gucci, L.L. Bean, Ralph Lauren, and J.Crew have distinctly masculine logos, aesthetics, and even symbols (Volvo has the symbol for masculinity, ♂, embedded in its logo). But all these brands, despite their solid lines, brass tones, or steely design aspects, appeal to women equally. Women naturally embrace fundamentally masculine design. But brands designed with distinct feminine sensibility, like Oxygen network, Lilly Pulitzer, or *Vogue,* are almost never successful in their attempts to cross over and appeal to men. Inevitably, most male consumers find feminine aesthetics alienating.

At this point, most domain names are already owned, so the trick is to choose one that isn't actually being used or, if it is, one that seems as though you might be able to purchase it. Alexis checked GoDaddy.com, a service that allows you to look up who owns a given URL and contact that owner. She began to reach out to these domains' owners to find out if they'd be interested in selling. Before making a decision, she needed to figure out if it was even possible to secure each name.

Alexis had particular affection for the name Gilt, which was the one option that hadn't come from her Web research. Instead, it had been inspired by her grandmother, who always told her that wearing makeup was like gilding the lily. The phrase was slightly old-fashioned, but Alexis had heard it her entire life. In her mind, *gilding the lily* referred to something that wasn't necessary but that certainly sounded exciting, glamorous, and fun.

To come up with Gilt, she'd taken the word *gilding* and played around with it: *Gilded Age, gold leaf, guild, gilt.* Each sounded romantic and idealistic. She was drawn to *gilt* in particular because of its succinct four letters, but it also seemed to be imbued with the most potential meanings. For her, it conjured the Gilded Age, an era of unfettered luxury, and the phrase *guilty pleasures*. Both applied uncannily well to the site we hoped to build. It would *not* sell basic necessities; instead, it was about emotional purchases that made the customer feel inspired. Luxury fashion is not something anyone needs, but it is something many *have to have*. When Alexis thought about it, our whole business model could be summed up as gilding the lily!

Alexis decided to investigate what our potential customers outside her family and closest friends thought of her proposed site names. She put together a survey on SurveyMonkey, a free online questionnaire tool. The survey listed five potential names: Skorpios, Tipetta, La Gamine, Gilt, and Modenius. Then it asked questions like "Which name do you like the best?" and "What does each word make you think of?" She also asked respondents to spell each name after reading it on a previous page (to assess how well they recalled the name later and whether they were able to spell it correctly) and then to rank their favorite to least favorite via unaided name recall. That meant they had to write in the names in blank fields, using only their memories. She fired off the questionnaire to a couple of hundred of our friends, acquaintances, and contacts.

When the survey came back, Gilt and La Gamine were the clear winners. Alexis wasn't surprised that respondents claimed they preferred La Gamine to the other choices. But when asked to recall the names a few steps later, they had a far easier time remembering and spelling *Gilt*. Perhaps this was why, when they were asked again at the end of the survey to rank their name preferences, they had changed their minds and now said they preferred Gilt to La Gamine.

The words they associated with each name were equally revealing. Everyone agreed that *Gilt* sounded luxurious, but some said it brought to mind gold leaf, others Marie Antoinette or France, and still others, Britain. For men, specifically, Gilt summoned images of King Arthur's Knights of the Round Table, crests and guilds (the takeaway: it must have royal connotations). Meanwhile, anyone Jewish mentioned *gelt*, the Yiddish word for "money" that Alexis had never heard. A few respondents said the name caused them to think of their Jewish mothers or mothers-in-law and to feel anxious.

Nonetheless, it seemed to strike a chord with almost everyone, and bring to mind all sorts of (mostly) relevant and exciting images.

Alexis's mind was now made up. Clocking in at a sleek four letters, Gilt was proved to be associated with luxury, even royalty, and to be highly memorable. In other words, it was a slam dunk.

She took the name to Alexandra.

But Alexandra, who had never even heard the expression *gilding the lily*, had her doubts. She loved the double entendre, the name's association with both *gold* and *guilt*. But she thought it was too short.

"It's curt," she said. "In a fashion context, it doesn't sound very luxurious." She pointed out that there were few, if any, international luxury brands with one-syllable names. Christian Dior, Giorgio Armani, Versace, Emilio Pucci, Yves Saint Laurent, Tiffany, and Louis Vuitton all had multiple syllables. Tod's and Coach were the only remotely high-end global brands we could think of without a multi-syllabic name. Somehow, longer names just felt more luxurious and established, and as we prepared for pitch meetings with these multinational retailers, we definitely wanted to sound more established than we were.

Alexandra suggested to Alexis that we add another word to *Gilt*. This way, even if the name were to be shortened colloquially—as Coca-Cola has been, to Coke—it would retain the distinguished vibe of its more formal name.

Alexis suggested *Group*, which would add some pleasing alliteration to the name and also hopefully make our five-person team seem larger and more established than it actually was; this would help us as we pitched larger fashion brands.

Alexandra liked this but came up with the idea to use the French spelling, *Groupe,* to add an air of exoticism and a certain je ne sais quoi.

Gilt Groupe.

"Done," said Alexis. The whole conversation took about five minutes.

Alexis had a strong feeling that our new name would be just perfect. She took to the Internet again, this time to close the sale of the Gilt.com and GiltGroupe.com domains (we planned to use just Gilt .com for ease, but for obvious reasons didn't want anyone else owning or using GiltGroupe.com. We even bought many misspellings of the name).

Gilt.com was owned by a fiftysomething man in Minnesota who'd purchased it about ten years prior. He said he'd had several offers in the past but was now finally ready to consider selling. Buying a domain name can be tricky because it's a zero-sum game: you're never going to work with the person again, and he knows you want what he has, so he's incentivized to try to get as much money out of you as possible. Alexis was careful to use an ".edu" e-mail address in her exchange with Gilt.com's owner to subconsciously signal that she did not have too much cash to spare, which she didn't. She had less of a personal presence on the Internet back then; she hadn't yet been quoted in newspapers. She offered the man five thousand dollars and, after some discussion, eventually upped it to eight thousand, which he agreed would be a fair price.

We now owned the domain; Gilt Groupe was officially in business. Creating the site's name had been our first highly successful collaboration as partners.

CHAPTER 4

AN IDEA BECOMES REALITY:

Starting Your Business at the Right Time

As we work more and more hours, and as more and more of our social interactions take place online, it only makes sense that we would do the bulk of our shopping on our computer too.

—*FORBES*, NOVEMBER 9, 2010

In 2000 Alexis bought a car on eBay Motors, the site she had helped launch that same year. It was a bright blue Audi S4, the exact vehicle she'd wanted. The car was being offered for sale by a dealership in Oregon. It had logged only three thousand miles and had a four-year warranty. Basically, it was good as new. She put down a deposit and hopped on a plane from San Francisco to Bend, Oregon, where the dealer picked her up at the airport. She then drove the eight hours back to San Francisco. The whole thing couldn't have been easier.

Most people, Alexandra included, would have balked at the idea of buying a car online in 2000. But Alexis worked in e-commerce years before grandmothers, teenagers, and everyone in between began shopping on e-commerce sites; she was already purchasing plane tickets, hotel rooms, shoes, clothes, and all her holiday gifts on the Internet by the late nineties. She regularly visited sites from Amazon to Expedia and, of course, eBay. By 1998 there were approximately three places on earth she could still be persuaded to shop in person: Italy during sale time in January and July, Woodbury

Common (the amazing outlet mall an hour outside New York City), and Manhattan sample sales, which offered discounted designer merchandise she couldn't find online. Otherwise she refused to spend her limited free time tracking down a necessary outfit or the perfect purse or shoes at actual stores when it was possible to do so in ten minutes with a few clicks from her desk.

She and her colleagues at eBay had a feeling that everyone else would soon agree.

Sure enough, by late 2007, as we prepared to launch Gilt Groupe, e-commerce was exploding. The net revenues at eBay for that year totaled $7.7 billion; Amazon had grown from another scrappy start-up into the Walmart of the Web, selling everything from books to deck furniture to the tune of $14.8 billion per year.[1]

Yet despite these crazy numbers, the fashion industry was for the most part holding out. It was almost as if it had spent the first years of the new millennium trying to resist the Internet. Many of the industry's iconic brands believed—rightly so—that e-commerce lacked personalized service and prevented customers from inspecting items up close and trying them on for fit. They saw online shopping itself as mass market and worried that by selling online, they'd lose control over their brands' presentation and cachet (and to their point, there were few Web sites at the time that presented luxury brands in an appealing way). As recently as several years ago few high-end fashion brands had Web sites that one could actually buy anything on, and most didn't sell on anyone else's Web sites either.

Alexandra was in many ways a typical 2007 online customer: She shopped every so often on Amazon; bought groceries on FreshDirect, the popular New York City–area grocery delivery service; received a constant supply of movies courtesy of Netflix; and bought most of her

1. "Amazon Optimistic for Growth," *Forbes*, April 4, 2008; www.forbes.com/2008/04/08/amazon-jobs-closer-markets-equity-cx_mlm_0408markets33.html.

friends' wedding gifts via online bridal registries. But she rarely, if ever, bought designer clothes or jewelry online. So many of the brands Alexandra liked weren't available online anyway. Bulgari, for example, which recognized the importance of e-commerce but remained skeptical of it, began selling its most basic products on its Web site only in 2008. And even this irked the brand's store managers, who still thought the Internet would cannibalize their stores' sales and leave them stuck with returns that would affect their bottom lines. So Alexandra shopped at specialty stores like Intermix, Scoop, and Jeffrey; she hit Bergdorf's, Barneys, and Saks (especially during sales) to stay on top of brands and trends; she also loved visiting outlet malls like Woodbury Common where she went at least a few times every year. And of course, her biggest destination of all, sample sales.

The online options that did exist, like Bluefly.com and department stores' Web sites, seemed at best overwhelming, at worst unexciting. They featured sterile photography—usually on headless mannequins— and pages and pages of hard-to-navigate selections that all seemed to blend together. It was often hard to tell what one was really looking at or to determine the quality. After clicking through twelve pages of dresses, who wouldn't be overwhelmed and tempted to give up? These offerings didn't feel luxurious. Instead, they felt like an online shopping mall; you needed to set aside an afternoon to spend time combing the racks and wares. It was as if these sites were trying to be everything to everyone.

But the strange thing was, in 2007, luxury fashion as a whole was killing it. The U.S. luxury market was raking in twenty billion dollars a year, and shows like *Project Runway* had introduced high-end designers like Michael Kors and Diane von Furstenberg to the masses, propelling desire for designer clothing to all strata of society. Designers had started producing "capsule" collections for mass retailers like H&M and Target and putting out more affordable secondary lines like Marc by Marc Jacobs, A/X Armani Exchange, and Vera Wang Lavender Label.

But though e-commerce and luxury fashion were separately booming, they had yet to combine in a truly exciting way. There were plenty of fashion insiders who thought they never would.

Not long after deciding to join the team at Gilt, Alexandra had a meeting in the lobby of the trendy Royalton Hotel with Robert Souza, an old acquaintance and retail whiz who had worked for years helming sales for Valentino and Hugo Boss. Alexandra had been hoping to pick his brain on how to approach those two luxury brands to sell on Gilt Groupe, since he clearly understood their inner workings. She was even hoping she could score an introduction. But the meeting didn't go as smoothly as she had hoped. Robert was skeptical that any luxury brand would ever sell to us. "This will never work," he declared emphatically. "You will *never* get brands like Valentino and Hugo Boss to agree to work with you." He was adamant that they'd never want to sell through a third party, *especially* at discounted prices and *especially* online, when they already had their own successful, profitable outlet stores for liquidation purposes. He made it clear that big, important high-end brands would never need us, so we should be prepared for lots of rejection. He even said that what we were aiming to do—convince designer brands to sell their excess goods through online sample sales—was pretty much impossible. (Funnily enough, Robert and his wife, Liz Radler, the U.S. president of Alexander McQueen, are now big supporters of Gilt Groupe, and we all look back on this meeting and laugh.)

Coming from someone who knew the fashion industry, Robert's feedback illustrated to us the obstacles we would face not just in launching our business but in convincing an industry to stop fearing the Internet as a backwater sales channel. Alexandra had a moment of panic. She felt confident in our concept, but was it possible it would just be too difficult to execute?

THE VALUE OF NAYSAYERS

We believe that one of the reasons Gilt grew so fast was that it was a big, bold risk. Nothing like it existed in the U.S. market. This helped attract a lot of excitement and attention to the idea.

But it wasn't just a risk for risk's sake. It was a *smart* risk. One of the factors that helped us make it even smarter? The many naysayers we met in the early stages.

When you're starting a business, it's inevitable that you'll face naysayers who will offer up compelling reasons why it won't work. In fact we can pretty much guarantee you'll encounter more naysayers than bullish advocates. In talking informally with friends about our idea, one refrain we heard again and again was "You'll never get men to shop online." It was almost as if online shopping itself had a feminine/masculine branding problem; the popular belief was that men only shopped for music, electronics, and books on the Internet, while women shopped for clothes for themselves *and* their partners. Though it was disconcerting for us to hear these things—and still is, when Gilt is starting a new business or branching into a new category—we never let negative feedback destroy our confidence. Instead, we listened to it and discussed it. We put it into context. Was Jeff Bezos telling us our idea would never work, or was it a friend who rarely shopped online *or* in stores? We cross-checked negative feedback with the reasons we thought the idea would be a smashing success at this moment in time. And usually, the feedback just helped us refine our pitch. In getting to the best decision, plan, or proposition, the friction and doubt cast by contrarians are usually critical to vetting all potential angles and counterpoints before moving forward. Hard feedback inevitably helps you arrive at the best possible plan. In our case, negative reactions to the Gilt idea prepared us for meetings with some of our future brand partners and investors. They made us much better saleswomen.

They also forced us to examine our idea again and again, which made us more confident than ever that the time was right for this business. We'd zeroed in on several key reasons that despite a pessimistic outlook for fashion e-commerce, shoppers and, more important, *brands* in the U.S. market would be receptive to our idea.

One clear indication was the Manhattan sample sale itself. Allow us to paint a picture of the scene circa 2007. The best New York sample sales were accessible to only a limited few: magazine editors, socialites, the brand's employees and friends, and occasionally top customers (even when the invites went out to a larger list, these people often got first dibs on an invitation-only opening day). The sales were located as inconveniently as possible, in no-frills showrooms or warehouses in the garment district, a dingy section of Manhattan's West Side best known for factories, fabric stores, and tchotchkes, not far from the no-man's-land that is Penn Station and Madison Square Garden.

They were also held at inconvenient times, like 10:00 A.M. on a Tuesday. Upon arrival, customers were unceremoniously ordered to check their handbags and other personal effects (signaling the management's fear they might steal something—*really*, how offensive), then forced to endure the indignity of sweaty, coed, communal dressing rooms (à la Loehmann's), provided insufficient access to mirrors, bossed around by surly, overwhelmed employees, and left to fight for the best merchandise with otherwise well-mannered women driven to greed and insanity by the whole experience.

Rather than be turned off by this, we—along with so many other fashion-loving women we knew—kept coming back for more. We even found it kind of fun. The sense of accomplishment we felt after emerging with a great designer piece made the abuse worth it. Finding that same bargain on a sale rack in a dignified department store, where no one else was reaching for it? We had to admit, that wouldn't have been nearly as exciting. Sample sales gave us a rush; they were a game we were addicted to winning. They were as much about the deals on clothes and accessories as they were about the triumph of snagging them before anyone else.

We knew we could re-create this rush in an online format. The key was to secure great designer deals and make each sale an "event" that lasted only thirty-six hours because the fleeting nature of the offer would motivate customers to action. We'd bring excitement to e-commerce, which we found to be sorely lacking in emotion, competition, or any other compelling reason to buy. Vente-privee had introduced some urgency—its sales usually lasted four or five days—but Gilt would ratchet that up by selling more exclusive brands for shorter periods. Shoppers would have to show up at our appointed time or else lose out on our exclusive, limited bargains. We expected that same exhilarating urgency that defines sample sales to be the engine of our business. We'd make shopping a *game,* and a successful shopper would need to hone her tactics and skills.

But while we wanted to preserve that *oh my God, I gotta have it!* feeling, we also wanted to make the experience much more luxurious and convenient. This would be essential to our growth. Despite sample sales' craziness, there were plenty of women who couldn't actually leave work to hike to the West Side on a Tuesday morning, and men who would never hit the famous Barneys Warehouse Sale because they were committed to an after-school sporting event. We'd bring the sample sales to them. We imagined catering to our members with excellent customer service. Why should they have to suffer for bargains? Why should we punish them by assuming they would steal or cheat, as sample sale setups seemed to imply? We didn't think the inconvenience was necessary to the excitement; the essential ingredient was feeling that you were beating others to the best stuff. As dedicated sample sale shoppers we just knew online audiences would go crazy for sample sales the same way New York women (and even some men) did. We sort of couldn't believe no one had thought of this sooner.

On the supply side, one sign that the time was right for Gilt was the buzz being generated by Net-a-Porter. Started by a British former fashion journalist named Natalie Massenet in 2000, Net-a-Porter sold designer and contemporary clothes and accessories at retail (otherwise known as full-price) and shipped internationally. Practically alone in the apparel e-commerce space, Massenet had managed to lure to the Internet a handful of high-end brands—from Stella McCartney to Miu Miu to Jimmy Choo—by offering classy visuals and access to wealthy consumers who didn't necessarily live close to these brands' stores.

Of course we'd be targeting brands with excess merchandise to liquidate and would be selling at deep discounts, so we knew we'd face a tougher challenge than Massenet. Luxury brands would be hesitant to be associated with sales on the Internet. But we hoped the fact that our site was members only, accessible by password only, would help convince them. We'd sell directly to our members, and nothing sold on Gilt would *ever* turn up on a Google search. And each sale would last only thirty-six hours! It would be there one day, gone without a trace the next.

We did not even anticipate one of our major selling points to luxury brand partners. Ron Berk, the CEO (and husband) of Judith Ripka, the third brand we sold on Gilt Groupe, opened our eyes to the fact that even an established high-end brand with sophisticated distribution, one that could liquidate its own excess merchandise, might want to work with us. We'd initially targeted designers who lacked a liquidation strategy, either their own boutiques where they could put merchandise on sale or their own brick-and-mortar outlets. But Ron ended up agreeing to partner with us for entirely different reasons. When Alexandra met with him before our launch, he immediately saw Gilt as an opportunity to gain access to thousands of young, fashion-conscious, educated, time-starved shoppers with disposable incomes. In other words, he liked the idea that people like us and our friends would become exposed to his brand. Our target demographic, affluent but largely strapped to a desk, was increasingly hard to reach for brands whose in-store customer tended to skew older, perhaps fifty to sixty-five years old in Ron's case.

In working hard to attract members, we were inadvertently making Gilt a marketer's dream.

We hadn't even thought about the fact that as early as 2007 the twenty- and thirtysomething urban demographic just wasn't spending as much time browsing stores, malls, or boutiques anymore. Luxury boutiques were intimidating and often empty, making customers feel targeted by eagle-eyed salespeople and pressured to buy, rather than at leisure to browse. Besides, with free time so scarce, who wanted to spend a weekend browsing in store after store? Our friends much preferred to pop into specialty stores like Scoop and Intermix, which sold multiple brands, and were constantly seeking ways to expedite their shopping. Those with small children preferred nearly any other form of self-inflicted torture to shopping for hours with kids in tow. The shoppers we knew were savvy; they liked good value for quality manufacturing and craftsmanship. They also wanted to shop quickly and efficiently and then get back to their leisure activities or their families. Even department stores, which in New York are mostly frequented by tourists and in most other places suffer the disadvantage of being at the mall, seemed like a big undertaking.

By the time Gilt arrived on the scene, fashion and design products were in higher demand than ever, but traditional luxury retail had started to feel stale. Brands needed a new way to capture their next generation of shoppers: Generation X (that's us), Generation Y (our younger siblings), and soon Generation Z.

After our first ten or so sales, we'd begin fielding phone calls from other top executives at well-known luxury companies, the kinds of brands we never thought would *need* to sell with us. Many of these established brands had no other way to reach Gilt's specific shoppers so cheaply and efficiently (we were certainly more cost effective than buying an advertisement in *Vogue*). And our model naturally created not just awareness but excitement around our brands. We were corralling thousands of the most hard-to-reach, highly desirable young customers onto our site every day at noon eastern time and causing them to jockey virtually for the best stuff—basically, to fight it out with their mouses! Shopping on Gilt was an *event*, versus a numbing exercise in clicking page after page of unedited, endless selections, like traditional e-commerce.

This was an engineering challenge—from the beginning, we did 75 percent of our daily business in the first hour and a half of a sale—but a marketing coup, both for Gilt and for our brand partners. We were flipping consumer psychology, teaching the customer that if she arrived late to a sale to find everything sold out, it was *her* fault! No longer was a terrible Fifth Avenue store experience to blame, or a poor selection. Even smaller lines like Lorelei handbags, which didn't come to Gilt with huge numbers of preexisting fans, were immediately highly coveted by our members and disappeared fast. And when we finally sold Dolce & Gabbana in February 2008, Alexis waited excitedly until 6:00 P.M.—the hour at which Gilt staffers were (and still are) permitted to buy at an employee discount items that had not been sold to our members—and was disappointed to find only a single T-shirt still available.

THE NEED FOR SPEED

In the summer of 2007, while we failed to anticipate Gilt's appeal as a marketing channel, we did seize on one other important bellwether. Vente-privee raised two hundred million dollars from Summit

Partners, a well-known American private equity firm, at a billion-dollar valuation. To investors and others who follow the retail, technology, and e-commerce industries, this was like a loud siren: *the flash sale concept is hot!* We felt emboldened but also seized by a sense of urgency. Although vente-privee was more like Costco than a Manhattan sample sale, the business model had inspired Gilt Groupe's, and we knew its one-billion-dollar valuation would spawn imitators—if not drive vente-privee to open a U.S. business.[1] It also signaled what would inevitably be a rush of investors writing checks for similar business models.

We had a small window if we wanted to be first.

We believe that part of the reason Gilt was successful was that it wasn't just a great idea, and it wasn't just introduced by the right people (i.e., by us and our small but capable founding team) but that it also hit the market at the right time.

Sometimes the market just isn't ready for an idea. Take Spinback. It didn't take off in 2007 (admittedly, it also had to do with Alexis and her partner's chemistry), but similar affiliate marketing businesses started to gain traction in 2011.

Groupon, the popular local group buying site, is another example. An earlier version of Groupon, Mercata, was actually founded, funded, and tested in the late nineties, backed by Microsoft cofounder Paul Allen. Back then it was focused on consumer electronics, and the model was confusing to shoppers, who were less willing to shop online than they are now. Mercata shuttered in 2001,[2] and when basically the same model was reintroduced by another set of entre-

---

1. Vente-privee finally launched its first sale in the United States in November 2011, partnering with American Express. In 2011 Amazon also launched its version of a sample sale, MyHabit, after a year of planning.
2. "Mercata is Latest Online Casualty," *The New York Times*, January 5, 2001; www .nytimes.com/2001/01/05/business/technology-briefing-e-commerce-mercata -is-latest-online-casualty.html?scp=1&sq=mercata&st=cse.

preneurs in 2008, this time focused on services and offering a more entertaining site and app, it immediately exploded.

Shazam, the clever music-identifying service, has a similar story. It debuted in the U.K. a decade ago. But back then, mobile platforms had not yet advanced to where they are today; no one had Androids, iPhones, or apps. It was basically a service wherein users would dial a code and then receive a text identifying the song in question. Needless to say, this was clunky and not nearly as cool as the present-day Shazam app, which magically brings information on the song to your screen in seconds, so it sat around in relative obscurity for years. It wasn't until 2008, when the app debuted on the iPhone, that Shazam became the sensation it is today. It's now one of the iPhone's most popular apps, with more than 150 million users.[3]

In contrast, Webvan, an ambitious home grocery delivery service that was launched during the dot-com bubble by the founder of Borders, went bankrupt within two years, in 2001.[4] It was—and still is!—a great idea, but it was overly ambitious and costly and overestimated people's interest in buying their groceries online at the time. Nowadays urban grocery delivery is hot, with companies like Fresh-Direct and Peapod thriving. Amazon bought Webvan in 2009 and is slowly reintroducing it to the market.

Launching when your target customers are primed to embrace your idea and comfortable enough with the technology they need to use to make a purchase is often the difference between success and failure.

While Kevin, our chairman at the time, wanted to launch the site in January or February 2008, when Gilt Groupe would be fully built and tested, we were convinced that we needed to launch sooner, by

---

3. "Mobile Media Discovery Firm Shazam Raises $32M in New Funds," *The Wall Street Journal*, June 22, 2011; http://online.wsj.com/article/BT-CO-20110622-707769.html.
4. "Why Webvan Drove Off a Cliff," *Wired*, July 10, 2001; www.wired.com/techbiz/media/news/2001/07/45098.

November at the latest. We knew the market was ready for the site, and we wanted to capitalize on the holiday shopping season. If there was anything we knew about shopping, it's that you don't want to start a retail business in the frozen tundra of January, when people tend to snap their wallets shut to compensate for holiday over-spending.

But Alexis had also observed up close and personally the impor-tance of speed to market and the benefit of being first, when launch-ing eBay Canada. In her haste to get the site up and running, she'd had to cut plenty of corners along the way. But she'd managed to get the business off the ground in just thirty days, the fastest launch in the company's history. In Japan, sluggish eBay was beaten to market by Yahoo! Japan, which introduced auctions to the country and pre-emptively poached eBay's potential customers. eBay's Japanese busi-ness eventually folded. On the other hand, eBay Canada managed to get a foothold before any competitors launched and became the country's largest e-commerce business.

As it turned out, Alexis's knack for speed was rather prescient. Over the next decade, rushing to launch a company and refining the idea in the public marketplace, with input from customers, became standard. The once common practice of incubating an idea behind closed doors in so-called stealth mode for a year or two (to prevent it from being stolen or copied) became an antiquated concept. The Internet diminished the value of an idea and lessened the time and money it took to execute it. As technologies improved and new busi-nesses required less initial investment, years turned to months or even weeks as launch cycles reduced dramatically, and timing became the difference between breakout success and toiling in anonymity. As *The New York Times* put it in May 2011, "For many, the long trek from idea to product to company has turned into a sprint."[5]

---

5. "The 'Facebook Class' Built Apps and Fortunes," *New York Times*, May 7, 2011.

We always knew that Gilt Groupe wouldn't be the only site to convince luxury designers to sell fashion off-price online. We also knew that being first to hit the market wouldn't necessarily make us the most successful. (Just like if your product is far superior to everyone else's, it matters less when you launch; see the example of Google, which was certainly not the first search engine.) But speed couldn't hurt. Especially since we hoped Gilt would eventually become so ubiquitous as to be synonymous with its category—like TiVo, which was so revolutionary when it launched that it's still used as a verb, despite the fact that there are other DVRs available. We knew we could make the site good enough that customers would embrace it while we worked with Mike and Phong to perfect its inner and outer workings. And being first would allow us to establish relationships with an initial lineup of luxury designers, and, hopefully, to attract buzz in key media outlets like *Women's Wear Daily* and the *Wall Street Journal*. Media attention was particularly important, since we were entering a field with low barriers to entry—meaning, for example, no stringent laws or regulations and relatively low costs required to launch. Many more sites *could* launch, and surely would. We hoped that Gilt's novelty would help kick-start our word-of-mouth marketing. We'd get a head start on attracting customers to our site, and first crack at impressing them. Hopefully, they'd remain loyal once the competition got up and running.

Besides, before we speculated any more about what our customers wanted, it made sense to ask them: to host a few sales and gauge the response. Would anyone buy anything? *What* would people buy? It's critical not to overinvest before getting a fledgling idea, product, or service out into the public market. After all, many businesses end up having to pivot in completely new directions after launching. Minimizing investment and maximizing consumer feedback in a start-up's early days helps save critical time, cash, and resources. We didn't want to do too much work or allocate too much money to building the site before we had proof that customers really wanted to shop this way.

We believed so much in our strategy of launch first, tweak later, that Mike and Phong didn't even build out the code for our returns process before the launch. We all knew it would be at least four days before anyone wanted to return anything, which by Mike's confident (and accurate) assessment was more than enough time for him and Phong to release new code to the Web site that would enable customers to return unwanted items. In the meantime, we had to *attract* those customers. The market was ready for us; in fact it seemed that the tidal wave of online shopping would knock us over if we didn't get out in front of it.

A primary branding strategy became speed.

---

checklist:
HOW DO I KNOW I HAVE THE
RIGHT IDEA FOR THE RIGHT TIME?

A big part of being entrepreneurial is recognizing when you should and shouldn't go forward with an idea. Not every great idea or opportunity that falls into your lap is worth pursuing, or pursuing now. Before proceeding with a concept, ask yourself these questions.

1. IS IT EASY FOR YOU TO EXPLAIN THE CONCEPT IN ONE SENTENCE TO YOUR BEST FRIENDS? (And can they repeat it back to you?) Online designer sample sales were an easy-to-understand concept. The fewer words it takes to explain your idea, the easier it will be to market it to a customer.

2. DOES THIS CONCEPT EXIST IN ANY SHAPE OR FORM ALREADY? Why or why not? Take an honest look at the marketplace. Who else is out there? Who else might be out there *soon*? Has someone already tried this and failed—and if so, why? Have times changed? No one had tried Gilt's idea in our marketplace, and in Europe a similar concept had been wildly successful. The investment money behind vente-privee only confirmed it was a matter of time before online flash sales were replicated in the United States.

3. IS THE TARGET MARKET READY FOR YOUR IDEA? We'd experienced firsthand the furor generated by New York sample sales. And a site called Net-a-Porter had proved that luxury brands could be lured online under the right circumstances. We knew that combining the two—sample sale excitement, high-quality product online—would be a potent formula. Finally, there were our strong instincts as consumers. *We* were our target customers, and we were dying to shop on Gilt!

4. CAN YOU TEST YOUR IDEA BEFORE OVERINVESTING, JUST TO MAKE SURE? These days the best way to make sure that the time is right for your idea is to get it out there and see what people think. Getting customer feedback from the start will help you build a better product, one that will maximize your investment. Plus customers love being partners in perfecting your model; that in turn makes them more loyal because they know they're being heard. We resolved to start our sales as soon as possible, when we could convince a few designers to sell with us. We wouldn't launch to media fanfare: we'd just quietly get up and running, test the waters, market ourselves through word of mouth, and get a chance to work out any kinks before our competitors arrived.

5. ARE YOU THE BEST PERSON TO EXECUTE THIS IDEA? Who or what is your team missing? Can you hire him or her? We were lucky to have an amazing team in place from the start. We had Internet and e-commerce start-up experience (Alexis and Kevin), deep knowledge of the fashion industry and relevant contacts (Alexandra), and technological prowess (Mike and Phong). Later we'd need other personality types and areas of expertise to take us to the next level. But at the beginning the five of us made a powerful team.

CHAPTER 5

NETWORKING OUR WAY
TO A NOVEMBER LAUNCH

Wilkis Wilson's job is to sweet-talk luxury designers into selling their unsold inventory to Gilt. "I have so many brands banging down our door that I have to say no," she says.

—*FORBES*, FEBRUARY 25, 2008

When Alexandra first started at Gilt in September 2007, she experienced a bit of culture shock. The minifridge in our makeshift offices at 33 West Nineteenth Street was filled with candy, Red Bull, beer, and cans of Starbucks Frappuccino—in other words, standard start-up provisions. This seemed normal to Alexis, who had always worked with engineers. But Alexandra recalls watching with amazement as Mike and Phong gulped Red Bull for breakfast at their desks. While the fashion crowd had sipped cappuccinos at Sant Ambroeus on Madison Avenue, the Gilt team chomped candy and wore noise-canceling headphones in order to drown out the sound of one another. Because we each had approximately three feet of space to ourselves, large headphones were a proxy for shutting our office doors. We joked that we were like a science experiment: we could watch a cold or cough start with one person, infect that person's neighbor, and then the next person in the row, eventually traveling from one side of our single long desk to the other and then back again! Even though she'd technically moved only forty blocks south from the Bulgari store, Alexandra couldn't help feeling as if she'd entered another universe.

During Alexandra's first days at the office the pressure was already on. She needed to sign some amazing brands so we could launch by November. Armed with her Excel spreadsheets full of contacts, she was ready for the challenge. Unfortunately she hadn't worked at Gilt long when disaster struck. Somehow, while trying to sync her Black-Berry, the AlleyCorp tech support team managed to wipe out ninety-five hundred names, most of the people Alexandra had planned to start contacting, either to join the site or to help reach out to certain brands. For several days, tensions ran high as AlleyCorp IT scram-bled to reinstate Alexandra's contacts—i.e., the totality of Gilt's mer-chandising pipeline. Without these contacts, Alexandra feared we'd never launch by November.

In start-up environments, daily hiccups are a way of life, and we were no different. It often seemed nothing worked well, from our BlackBerrys to the site itself, which was still under construction. Things broke daily, and this continued for years! Unlike a corporate environment, where there are systems in place to address all prob-lems, we were mostly left to troubleshoot on our own.

Alexis was used to this and had always been pretty unflappable by nature. But it was a wake-up call for Alexandra, who was accustomed to a completely different level of resources and support. She felt as if she were racing against the clock to sign up brands, and these unfore-seen technological difficulties were *not* helping. How could she do her job when nothing seemed to work properly?

Fortunately, at least this initial crisis soon dissipated. She discov-ered she had backed up most of her contacts on her personal laptop and was ultimately able to recover nine thousand of the ninety-five hundred. Those lost five hundred were still disappointing. But it was a good lesson: always prepare for the worst in a start-up, and have a backup plan.

With the bulk of her contacts restored, Alexandra got to work, making phone calls, firing off e-mails, and scheduling dozens of meet-ings to make her pitch to our target brands. Alexandra is a person who loves meeting people and who draws energy from new introductions and from connecting with others. She had kept up over the years with thousands of people. We can't emphasize how crucial this strong pre-existing network of friends and contacts was to the success of Gilt Groupe. Not everyone is a natural networker, and it's OK if you're not. But it still helps to identify early on at least a few people in your network who want to see you do well and may be able to help jump-start your business by providing an introduction, that initial client, or a key partnership. These people are crucial to any company's ultimate success (think of asking for help as identifying the path of least resistance, which is as important as anything). Entrepreneurs often have few resources and little capital, so success can hinge on whether other people are willing to go out of their way to help. In most cases you're only as successful as the people around you want you to be.

Alexandra had been generous with her time over the years; she'd mentored friends' and acquaintances' kids whenever asked, facilitated introductions, sent handwritten congratulatory notes after promotions, and even remembered anniversaries. She'd genuinely enjoyed keeping up with people; she'd never done it with an eye toward what they could provide in the future. And she'd asked for few favors. The result was that almost everyone she e-mailed for help with Gilt—advice, an introduction, a meeting—responded warmly and positively.

---

checklist:
RULES FOR GROWING AND MAINTAINING YOUR NETWORK

1. REMEMBER FACES AND NAMES. After clicking with someone professionally or socially, always politely ask that person for his or her card or contact information, then follow up promptly with an e-mail saying you enjoyed meeting him or her. Within a short period of time, try to invite this new acquaintance to something relevant, either a meal with a few others he or she might be interested in meeting or an event that he or she might enjoy. Catalog all contacts with a note about how you originally met so you can remember and follow up on the details of your first encounter.

2. MAKE INTRODUCTIONS FOR OTHERS. Introductions are crucial in business and so much more effective than cold calls. Make introductions frequently; do it out of the goodness of your heart; do it without thinking what these people might someday do for you.

3. BE A DOER, AND BEFRIEND OTHER DOERS. Think of the people in your life who make others feel good about themselves, who are upbeat, interesting, and entertaining and have a lot going on in their lives. Make plans with them. These are great people from whom to draw motivation and encouragement. Surround yourself with people who inspire you, both personally and professionally.

4. HONOR IMPORTANT DAYS (AND SEND GIFTS). This may seem obvious, but call your friends and family on their birthdays. E-mail them on their anniversaries! Keep track of their kids' birthdays! Send holiday cards, regardless of your religion. If you can't attend a baby shower, send a gift! Enter important dates into your calendar, and update your contacts' e-mails, addresses, and phone numbers regularly. (No excuses.) Finally, make your best effort to attend weddings. These are the sorts of things people never forget.

5. MAKE TIME FOR FRIENDS AND ACQUAINTANCES. In-person contact is always best. But even when busy, Alexandra does her best to pick up the phone (or at least send an e-mail or text) every so often to let people know she is thinking of them.

6. DON'T ASK FOR FAVORS ALL THE TIME. This way, when you *really* need help, your friends and acquaintances will be more likely to lend a hand.

7. BUILD YOUR OWN PERSONAL BOARD OF DIRECTORS. Think of this as an extended list of mentors, champions, and people you respect. Cultivate these relationships. If you need ideas about whom to meet, ask other people you respect professionally to put you in touch with their mentors or friends. These are the people you will turn to when you need unbiased feedback that you might not be able to get from your own employees, coworkers, or actual board of directors. Remember, you'll only do as well as those around you want you to do.

8. BE AUTHENTIC, WITH HIGH INTEGRITY. It sounds so cliché, but be good, genuine, and loyal. Don't screw anyone over in your personal or your professional life because word will spread like wildfire, and it will always come back to haunt you.

There are many approaches to growing and maintaining your circle. Take Jason Binn, the founder of Niche Media Holdings—publisher of upscale local glossy magazines like *Ocean Drive, Hamptons,* and *Gotham*—who is one of the most well-connected people we know. Recently he joined Gilt's team in an advisory role, and we've marveled at his remarkable ability to develop large and diverse circles of friends and acquaintances.

Jason never tries to meet the *right* people; to him, that seems inauthentic and unnecessarily limiting. "Putting blinders on is the worst thing you can do," he says, "especially in a melting pot like New York. You can get so caught up in thinking, who is my customer? That's traditional marketing; it's not relevant today. I've never played that card.

What drives me is being around people who are the best at what they do, whether it's in fashion, art, entertainment, or business.

"To be an ambassador of your brand, you have to get out on the streets," he continues. "Physical interaction between people has become more and more removed. Jann Wenner [the publisher of *Rolling Stone*] was famous for removing all the chairs from the office during lunchtime. It was like 'Get the hint. You shouldn't be in the office during lunch!'"

Jason is also a believer in the power of introductions. When he launches a magazine in a new city, he'll often get lunch with a friend or contact in that city and say, "Tell me about the twenty people I should know who are friends of yours in Washington." Then he'll contact those people. He also immerses himself in a city, living there for up to six months before launching a new magazine.

When Alexandra began reaching out to her friends and acquaintances to set up meetings, she was surprised and delighted by their generosity, especially in the early days of the business. Support came from unlikely corners of her network.

The designer Alvin Valley, whom Alexandra eventually brought on as a brand partner for Gilt's second sale, had been a friend of hers in New York since 2003. The pair, acquaintances through the fashion industry, had bonded over their shared Cuban roots; he'd designed the dramatic Spanish-style red ball gown she wore to her rehearsal dinner.

She met Judith Ripka's husband and sons through her beloved eye doctor, whose sister had married one of Judith's sons. Dr. Jacqueline Muller had initially helped arrange a meeting with the Ripkas back when Alexandra was thinking about leaving Bulgari. Once she moved on to Gilt, Alexandra didn't want to cancel the meeting, so she went anyway and spun what the Ripkas had assumed was a job interview into a sales pitch.

Alexandra met the Rachel Roy team through Morty Singer, a close friend she had gotten to know while working for Marvin Traub during business school. As it turned out, Morty was an investor in Rachel's company. The brand committed to being one of Gilt's first sales. And Laurie Willard of the brand Lorelei, which we sold in December 2007, had gone to Princeton with some of Alexandra's best friends.

Time and again Alexandra's knack for keeping in touch with people produced a key contact or a key meeting. But while her connections often got her in the door, she still had to work hard to convince luxury brands to sell on Gilt. Her jobs at Louis Vuitton and Bulgari had prepared her for the many tough sales meetings she faced that fall. Alexandra had earned her sales stripes working retail, punching in forty hours a week in the Louis Vuitton shop-in-shop at Saks, where she'd developed thick skin, learned to sell to Upper East Side moms and Chinese tourists alike, and become one of the best darn salespeople on the floor. She could usually charm all types of customers, infer what they wanted, and sell it to them. She prided herself on her integrity and refused to sell a customer something she felt was wrong for her—like multicolored monogrammed shoes. Her sincerity was a huge asset to her bottom line.

When she started selling luxury brands on the concept of Gilt Groupe, Alexandra was under a lot of pressure, as she alone was responsible for producing our inventory. But she had confidence in her sales chops and, while somewhat nervous, was really determined. If she could sell five-hundred-dollar Louis Vuitton fountain pens at Saks Fifth Avenue, she could definitely sell something she believed in much more passionately. She was energized by her belief in Gilt's vision and in our team; this time it was *her* company she was selling.

In her earliest meetings Alexandra couldn't even show designers and executives our actual Web site. It was coming along, but it was nowhere near finished; Mike and Phong were still working furiously to prepare for the November launch. So she'd bring along a few screen grabs whenever possible or attempt to draw our visuals on a piece of paper, often just resorting to hand gestures and asking executives to use their imaginations. She was tasked with selling a concept with limited tools.

Her pitch presented Gilt to brands as a discreet, rapid way to liquidate excess merchandise. She explained that it would be easier and more cost effective than hosting a sample sale, which often required brands to close their retail stores and assign all their staff to work the sale for several days, or than building an actual brick-and-mortar outlet, with its high overhead costs.

Alexandra explained how Gilt would be a much higher-end, more enjoyable experience than shopping at T.J.Maxx, Century 21, Marshall's, or any of the other off-price brick-and-mortar channels where designer brands regularly unloaded at steep discounts the merchandise that they'd overproduced. Unlike these retail stores, Gilt would help brands maintain their integrity. Instead of languishing in piles and on messy racks, brands' excess merchandise could be offered to a targeted group of desirable customers in a much more dignified way. We'd invest in top-quality photographers and styling. Customers would have no idea how many of each item were actually available.

Alexandra also highlighted the fact that Gilt's site would be password protected, accessible by invitation only to an online membership. While this had been a subject of discussion in the Gilt offices through the fall, we both had lobbied hard to maintain this feature because of its appeal to our potential brand partners as well as to customers. The reason was simple: a password-protected site was behind a registration wall and not searchable on Google, meaning Gilt sales' items didn't turn up in any searches. Brands wanted discretion; they were concerned with maintaining their high-end market positioning and didn't want their names floating around in cyberspace as deal oriented.

The members-only format, in which users were forced to register before accessing a site, was at the time considered e-commerce suicide. The prevailing view was that shoppers wouldn't actually take time to register when they couldn't first see what merchandise was behind the registration screen. If a customer stumbled upon Gilt while cruising the Internet or received an e-mail from a faceless server, she'd have no way to know it was worth the effort and might be tempted to click away from our registration screen. But here's where our word-of-mouth marketing came in: If she received a personal invite from a stylish friend or heard about how that friend just scored an *amazing designer bag at 60 percent off,* surely one hundred registration screens wouldn't deter her from joining. In fact, the registration screen would seem like less of a nuisance than an indication of the site's exclusivity and desirability.

With this in mind, Alexandra aimed high with the designers she approached in the fall of 2007. We knew we had to make a strong statement about Gilt's identity right off the bat. In order to announce ourselves as a player in luxury retail, we needed a *great* partner for our first sale.

THE POSENS: INSIDE A LUXURY BRAND'S THOUGHT PROCESS

The Zac Posen brand, with which we already had a long history, seemed like an obvious choice. We both were wearers of Zac's clothes, which, though expensive, had been among our favorite special occasion splurges. Zac was known for showstopping party dresses, regularly worn by stars like Claire Danes and Natalie Portman on the red carpet; they sold like hotcakes in the finest international department stores. Though he was still in his mid-twenties at the time, Zac had a strong brand identity, great name recognition, a devoted customer following, the respect of the fashion establishment, and the rapt attention of the media. He had quickly ascended to the highest echelon of American designers, becoming a member of the Council of Fashion Designers of America (CFDA). We knew that launching our site with a Zac Posen sale would create a halo effect; our brand would bask in the reflected glow of his reputation and name recognition, at least at the beginning. The sale would attract PR attention and customers and inspire dozens, if not hundreds, of other key brands to take a chance on Gilt. Perhaps most important, we had a history with his family, so it made sense for us to start there.

Luckily, we'd kept in touch with Zac's mother after we'd graduated from business school. Susan Posen handled all of Zac's business dealings, so she was our primary contact at the brand. Alexandra first arranged to meet with Susan in early October. Let's just say Susan took a *lot* of convincing.

Back then, Zac Posen was a designer brand with fairly limited distribution. It was available only in top stores; it did not sell online; and it barely had brick-and-mortar sample sales. Occasionally, there would be exclusive friends and family events, to which it was nearly impossible to snag an invite. We were asking Susan to take a big leap of faith, and we knew it.

For one of our first meetings, we trekked down to Zac's showroom on Laight Street in Tribeca. Newly expanded, the showroom featured deep black walls with impeccably dressed mannequins lining both sides of the entryway, each lit with a dramatic glow. The theme for Zac's latest collection was "Wheat." It had been inspired by the 1978 film *Days of Heaven*, which was shot in the Texas Panhandle. Yet everyone hustling around the office wore edgy all-black attire and cutting-edge hairstyles. We knew we were entering the white-hot center of the New York fashion scene.

We'd dressed carefully, Alexis wearing Carolina Herrera, and Alexandra in Louis Vuitton. There was a lot riding on this meeting, and we wanted to present the best possible image for Gilt Groupe.

We recently asked Susan what she remembered about this meeting.

"You didn't have a real presentation; it wasn't slick in any way," she said. "But that was fine with me. What struck me was that you had identified a real interesting sort of problem in the industry: what do you do with out-of-season merchandise? As a young designer, one of the greatest pitfalls is excess inventory. Your capital is wrapped up in it, and it becomes, especially in the upper levels of fashion, *dead*. Inventory is spoilable. It's like having lettuce on the shelf."

We learned that Zac and Susan had been cutting to order, which is fashion industry lingo for ordering just enough product from factories and fabric sellers to satisfy actual orders from retailers. But inevitably, they'd still end up with some extra clothes here and there: a retailer would go out of business, or they'd overestimate how many "extras" to order in case their original run sold out in stores and retailers wanted supplemental orders. "A lot can happen in the five or six months between when a retailer places an order and when it's filled," Susan explained.

Season after season, the Posens' extra inventory had grown—to the point where it was not just tying up capital but costing them money to store it in a warehouse.

"You came at a moment when the issue wasn't necessarily extreme for us," said Susan, "but I knew it would be compounded by the fact that our business had grown so substantially that we were going to be required to place fabric orders before we had sales orders. I remember asking you, Alexandra, 'What does Bulgari or Louis Vuitton do?' Somebody had told me they *burn* their old things. And I thought, I can't do that. That was just too painful to think about."

Susan's conundrum was typical of what many top designers faced around the time of Gilt's launch. She cared first and foremost about maintaining the integrity of Zac's brand. "Luxury brand building is a tricky thing," she said, looking back. "If you let your reputation slip, it evaporates very quickly. So we were always very protective of it."

Susan didn't want the inevitable excess merchandise to end up at a store like Loehmann's, where it would hang alongside far lesser labels or, worse, end up on the floor in a heap. She didn't want to host large sample sales herself either. "We just didn't do it," she said. "The thought of women pawing over clothing, throwing it on the ground—the whole thing horrified me. I knew that if Zac saw something like that, he'd die!"

But she also didn't want perfectly good clothing to go to waste when it was possible to recoup some of her costs by selling at a discount, and back in 2007 the company was still too small to consider building its own outlets or even retail stores. "Zac's view is that scarcity is part of the definition of luxury," she said. "But it's a balance. You want people *wearing* the clothing."

Susan saw Gilt Groupe as a possible safety net: "The idea that we could, in a sense, overproduce a little and have an outlet for those goods—that was very attractive."

Still, she questioned us closely about what other brands we were planning to sell. She wanted to make sure Zac would be in good company. She also worried about what Zac's high-end department store clients would think if styles turned up on Gilt too quickly after being offered for two thousand dollars at retail.

Before we sealed the deal, Alexandra headed down to Laight Street again for a follow-up meeting. This time she brought Mike, who was to produce a rudimentary demo version of our site for Susan and her team to review. He was shocked to find that Zac's showroom didn't even have wireless access. Coming from the engineering world, Mike could not get over this! (Perhaps it was a sign of the uphill battle we'd face in getting the fashion industry to embrace the Internet.) He resorted to showing some screen shots he had of the site's logo and design frame—with no photography or images of actual clothing. Alexandra supplemented his efforts with verbal explanations. "We scribbled something on paper," recalls Mike.

"I remember thinking how important it was that you were friends with Susan," Mike adds. "Getting a glimpse of the fashion world, it seemed to operate on pure friendship. They knew you; they seemed to trust you; they wanted to try something new for the business. The Web site was really a detail. They were making dresses; that was their world, not technology and engineering."

Still, Susan is a shrewd businesswoman. While she'd acted motherly toward us in the past, we knew she'd never agree to something she didn't feel was right for Zac's brand. She liked that we had a financial backer in Kevin, and she was impressed by our respective backgrounds. She was intrigued by the data we offered to provide after the sale on the demographics of Zac's customers because it's often tricky for brands to figure out exactly who is buying their clothing (very little information was available from department stores).

"Besides wanting to build a global luxury brand, I always felt that Zac could build a brand that was really of the twenty-first century," said Susan. "Technology would have to be a part of that. I didn't yet know how. But this seemed to be a highly reasonable way to test it."

When she finally agreed to work with us, we'll never forget what Susan said: "We are pioneers in the fashion industry. Zac Posen is a pioneer. Therefore, we would like to be your first brand."

We will always be grateful for her leap of faith.

CHAPTER 6

CHANGING THE LOOK OF E-COMMERCE:

Photos, Curation, and Gilt Groupe's Visual Branding

Want to find a fashionista at lunchtime? Try Gilt Groupe.
The two-year-old company's daily sample sales have made
e-commerce fun and exciting in a whole new way.
—*FAST COMPANY*, FEBRUARY 17, 2010

In New York *friends and family* can mean two things: one, those times of year when retailers from Gap to Sephora offer steep discounts to anyone who happens to get an invite forwarded around via e-mail, and two, the nights, even weeks before an exclusive new restaurant opens, when the kitchen churns out free food for the owners' and staffers' friends and family in order to work out any kinks. While consumers view it as a privilege to be invited to a restaurant's friends-and-family event, it's also a chance for the staff to solicit honest feedback, knowing that these people won't hold mistakes or inadequacies against the restaurant forever inasmuch as they're friends and family (and they're eating for free).

At Gilt Groupe, our friends-and-family event was more like the second scenario. It was late October 2007, and it had been a whirlwind four months since Alexis and Kevin's first meeting. We were ready to take our new Web site for a test drive with a select group of friends and family.

The site looked fantastic, if we do say so ourselves.

Gorgeous and gleaming, the site's visuals were becoming everything we'd hoped for: elegant, sophisticated, discreet, inviting, magazine-like. We'd never seen anything like it—which was the point. Mike and Phong had brought the team's collective creative vision masterfully to the screen, and with streamlined features had created a truly unique online shopping experience. Our now signature black background, in particular, looked visually distinct—authoritative and luxurious but also vaguely sultry. That part had been Alexis's idea. She wanted Gilt to feel like a small, secret Internet boutique to which you were being granted access. She knew that black would make the site more memorable, because virtually no other e-commerce site was using it. She also thought it would lend an air of exclusivity to the collections that other brightly lit, white-background sites seemed to lack, showing off the clothes in a striking way. Colors would pop off the screen. Black would remove all traces of e-commerce's pervasive shopping mall vibe, its almost universal reliance on off-putting and homogenous fluorescent white lighting. We were excited when we later learned black was also the most ecofriendly choice because a black background requires less energy to produce.

We'd worked with a California-based graphics firm to painstakingly construct our stately black and gold logo, which at the time featured a key to signify that the site was locked except to members.

Once inside the site, the spare placement of photos seemed alluring but also decisive. That was very important to us. Our design consciously centered on large editorial images and minimized the use of unnecessary text. During her years working in e-commerce at eBay and AOL, Alexis had learned a lot about how people navigate Web sites. She'd even seen studies that track retinal eye movements as subjects scan a page, and had concluded that photos—and the attitude, brand positioning, and even hair and makeup tips they convey—capture the majority of people's attention. On Web sites, eyes tend to scan from top left to bottom right; they skip around from visual cue to visual cue rather than reading paragraphs one after the next. A large picture might capture 60 percent of the attention a reader

devotes to a given page, while a unique color (say, on the "buy" but-
ton) might command 10 percent. This is markedly different from
magazines, which many people actually *do* read. Viewers experience
Web sites not unlike they do TV (and can you imagine anyone trying
to sell something on TV with a written paragraph?).

On Gilt, Alexis wanted *photos* to be the *content*. She'd go easy on
the text—for example, written styling tips, still common on sites like
Net-a-Porter—and use images to relay that same information. Our
"content," or text, would be limited to straightforward information on
fit, color, and sizing—clarifying details that might help finalize a buying decision.

But in order to make Gilt's images compelling, it was important
that there not be too many of them cluttering the page. From the
beginning, we used a word that seemed to fascinate and surprise people, at least when applied to the Internet: *curated*. This is a common
buzzword now, but back in 2007 the idea that you'd artistically curate
an e-commerce site—that it would have a real editorial voice and
point of view—was all but unheard of. But Alexis believed that consumers no longer wanted "everything," or overly broad selections.
Instead, they wanted just the stuff that was right for them.

If Google streamlined the look of the search engine, stripping away
most of the information contained on a page like Yahoo's, Alexis
believed shopping was heading in the same direction. The Internet
could be intimidating to consumers when it offered too many options
and too many calls to action. The iPod, iPhone, and iPad, on the other
hand, are great examples of how simplicity resonates with customers.
Alexis wanted Gilt to offer a limited, extremely relevant selection of
items that would allow shoppers to get through to checkout in just two
clicks. What we loved about sample sales, after all, was that they were
usually single brand and didn't feature thousands of units of merchandise at a time; instead, they had just enough so that we could

each find something we really wanted. (The staffers continually refreshed the floor with new products.) Shoppers could make decisions in minutes, not hours. We wanted our sales to be similarly focused; we thought that would make it easier for customers to actually make purchases on the Internet, and quickly. Our tightly edited selection would be more visually appealing, but also a lot less intimidating—just the right amount of images and not so much selection that the customer would be paralyzed by the glut of choices, as on the majority of e-commerce sites at the time (in our opinion). Basically, we set out to build the anti-Amazon, where explicitly less became much more.

We wanted to use photography and finished styles—i.e., complete outfits instead of disembodied pants and blouses—to allow our customer a more intimate, relatable experience than other e-commerce sites offered. We wanted her to be inspired by a look she saw onscreen, see herself wearing the look to an event, and get swept up by a desire to purchase it. Gilt's shopping experience was designed specifically to be transformative and, perhaps more important, to provide a coveted escape, if even for five minutes, from one's daily routine.

"We were trying to do what an amazing boutique could do," explains our creative director Leah Park, who came on board in late 2007 and helped us more fully realize our creative vision. "In other words, make you feel like you're the only person there, and you're getting all this attention—that we had hand-selected things just for you. *Not* like you're in this huge, overstocked warehouse full of racks and racks of stuff. And when you click through to the detail shots, it was like going into a dressing room."

We also wanted Gilt, much like *Elle* and *Vogue*, to project authority and for members to see our selections as things we'd personally chosen for them from among the thousands of styles out there by hundreds of designers. A tight selection would emphasize Gilt's high taste level and the exclusive quality of its deals. It would lend the site a subtle confidence. We'd become not just purveyors of style but arbiters.

In order to give our photographs a truly editorial quality—i.e., something that looked as if it might appear in the pages of a glossy magazine, not in a catalog or on a highway billboard—we'd need to make them larger than was typical in e-commerce. But we couldn't ignore the fact that fashion magazines' pictures had one other element largely lacking in e-commerce: *models*. This is why, while it definitely would have been cheaper and less logistically complicated to shoot the clothes on mannequins, we made an instinctive call—after a lot of discussion—to shoot all of Gilt Groupe's apparel (in the fashion industry we call it ready-to-wear) on models. We had no idea what we were getting into. Besides their fees, models need hair and makeup, and we'd need stylists and accessories where appropriate. We just knew that shooting the clothes on actual women would help bring the site, and the items we were selling, to life. They would help provide Gilt's groundbreaking visual content.

At the time, Net-a-Porter featured fine photography, but it used mannequins. Barneys, a fabulously chic and forward-thinking brand, was marketing its clothes online on blue mannequins with cone-shaped heads! Giorgio Armani's site used *headless* models, which we found funny and odd. These images didn't seem to relate to their brands in any sort of unified way and were lackluster and hardly inspirational. They seemed cold and static. They certainly didn't inspire us to buy anything.

Neiman Marcus used models some of the time. That definitely resonated with us. Sometimes it even used architectural, cubelike props, which, if awkward in their own way, seemed to at least be attempting to tell some sort of story. We spent a lot of time trolling existing e-commerce sites, figuring out what we liked and what we didn't, and determining the many important ways that Gilt's photos would be different. And in truth we did not find much we liked.

So we used fashion magazines as a major point of reference. But unlike fashion magazines, we also wanted our photos to allow members to see the clothing in great visual detail, and be as useful as possible. While we were selling an aspiration, which required compelling imagery and creativity, we also wanted to show the merchandise up-close to highlight its detail and craftsmanship. Over time we even started including information about the models' measurements, so that a customer could figure out where a hemline might hit on *her* as compared with a five-foot-ten-inch model. We wanted Gilt to feel not just alluring but helpful. We envisioned the site as a chic best friend providing insider prices and access, rather than some imperious, all-knowing style czar. We decided our site voice would be more friendly than condescending; we wanted to speak to our customer, not down to her. We hoped she would see herself reflected in Gilt and to be encouraged by how easy it was to incorporate into her wardrobe the latest designer pieces. Our styles were glamorous, yes, but so was she, by virtue of her membership.

————

There were plenty of things that weren't yet perfect on the site. But we'd decided that being first to market was much more important than having, say, a functional returns section. We were incredibly excited to have nabbed Zac Posen as our first sale. And we knew that what members wouldn't be able to see—the fact that Mike, our CTO, was running our warehouse, and Alexis, our CEO, was also doing e-mail support—would not get in the way of a great shopping experience.

We decided to stage two friends-and-family sales as dry runs before the big Zac sale, which was scheduled for November 13. The goal was to test whether the payment process worked smoothly and to make sure the site had no bugs. Alexis took charge of the logistics for these sales.

In anticipation of our first test run, she hit a Billion Dollar Babes sale at The Altman Building on West Eighteenth Street to stock up on merchandise to sell to our friends and family. Billion Dollar Babes, a multibrand sample sale company, was the closest thing at the time to an off-line version of Gilt Groupe. It liquidated excess merchandise for popular brands like Catherine Malandrino, Nicole Miller, James Perse, and Petit Bateau, usually amid cocktails, and inevitably attracted a crowd of New York's fashion devotees.

On a September afternoon, Alexis insisted Mike and Phong accompany her to the sale. She needed help hauling her loot back to our tiny Brooklyn warehouse space. It's fair to say that the two men were a bit bewildered when they first entered The Altman Building and saw women furiously grabbing items from the racks and darting into the changing rooms before returning to the floor to quickly shop some more. But Alexis was unfazed; she'd done this so many times before. Like an old pro, she navigated the crowd, scooping up as many See by Chloé tops and dresses and Oliver Peoples sunglasses as she could grab, making sure she beat other women to the best stuff. Mike and Phong looked on, impressed by her obvious skill in this arena. They soon got the hang of it and began making tentative suggestions on what to pull. When asked what he remembers about this day, Phong recalls that he naïvely attempted to help. "I handed a couple of items to Alexis and said, 'This might look nice!'" he says. (She recalls that many of his selections even made the cut.)

These days we have hundreds of people working two shifts daily to photograph the millions of dollars' worth of high-end designer clothing, home furnishings, jewelry, and even caviar that we offer for sale each week. But for our friends and family photo shoot, the crew numbered two: Carolyn Fong, our freelance photographer, and our model, Lauren Remington Platt, who was doing us a favor. Lauren was a tall, striking hedge fund analyst and a friend of Alexandra's who had modeled during college. We had nothing to pay her—we offered

shopping credits on yet-to-launch Gilt Groupe—so we were thrilled
when she agreed to sneak out of her finance job early to model. Alexis
had convinced Carolyn, a former classmate of her sister Lilly Maybank's at Pasadena Arts Center, to photograph Lauren on Carolyn's
East Village rooftop.

On the day of the shoot Lauren called to find out what time she
should show up for hair and makeup. Alexis was confused. What? she
thought. It honestly hadn't even occurred to her to book hair and
makeup, especially for a friends-and-family shoot! "Could you just do
it yourself?" she asked politely. Little did she know that this is unheard
of in the fashion industry, where even minor magazine photo shoots
usually involve several hours of hair and makeup. Rather than com-
plain about our start-up stinginess, Lauren ran first to get a cheap
twenty-five-dollar blow-out at a hole-in-the-wall salon and then to get
a free makeup application at the Chanel counter at Bloomingdale's.
Resourceful—our kind of girl!

Neither of us actually attended the shoot. In hindsight this was a
little crazy; perhaps we figured that Lauren and the photographer
could take care of things on their own. But we were told it was pure
chaos. Carolyn shot the photos against a brick wall—not that elegant,
though it did foretell the edginess of future shoots we'd stage near our
warehouse at the Brooklyn Navy Yard. And when we posted the photos to the site, we completely forgot to translate the Italian and French
sizes to American ones. Oops! The whole experience confirmed that
we still had a lot to learn about the creative process (and that we desperately needed a creative director. We'll get to that soon).

Nonetheless, when the first friends-and-family sale went live, our
friends, siblings, and acquaintances logged on and quickly bought
nearly everything. Maybe it was the prices, which ranged from $20 to
$105 for items that had originally retailed for many times that price.
We ended up having to fix a small glitch in our system that affected
Amex payments, but other than that and the shortcomings of our

photography, the site worked perfectly. After all the merchandise had sold, Alexis, Mike, and Phong gathered to assess areas for improvement before darting out to our small warehouse in Brooklyn to package and ship all the purchases.

Encouraged by our friends-and-family success, we started preparing for the real thing.

CHAPTER 7

DATING, MARRIAGE,
AND HOW TO GET THE RIGHT
VENTURE CAPITALIST TO FALL
FOR YOUR START-UP

Gilt.com went live in November 2007. Matrix Partners put
$5 million of equity funding into Gilt a few weeks later. For
the company name the founders borrowed a debonair "e"
from French (or was it from "shoppe"?).
                    —*FORBES*, FEBRUARY 25, 2008

O
ne of the questions we're asked most often is, how did Gilt
raise money in its early days? While we wish we could say
there's some perfect time to seek investment or some magical combination of words that's guaranteed to make an investor fund your
idea—well, that hasn't been our experience. What we always say is,
raising money is more an art than a science.

As we prepared for our first sale on November 13, we simultaneously began to plan for additional funding. AlleyCorp had funded the
company through its start-up phase, roughly to the end of 2007. Kevin
Ryan, our chairman and the CEO of AlleyCorp, was key in helping us
prepare to pitch Gilt to new investors.

We had come a long way on several hundred thousand dollars;
now Kevin and Alexis estimated we needed five million dollars more
to hire the staff we needed to grow and rent a larger office space. This
would be the amount we'd seek in our Series A round, a term that

refers to a start-up's first round of investment from an institutional firm—i.e., from venture capital, private equity, or a hedge fund. Series A investments are riskier than later-stage investments, given that the company is in its very early days, so these investors usually get preferred stock and rights above those of common stockholders. (Subsequent fund-raising rounds are called Series B, C, etc.)

Adding urgency to our fund-raising efforts was some news we'd heard through the grapevine: two competitors—the sites that became known as HauteLook and Rue La La—were gearing up for their launches. Ideeli, a third competitor, had already soft-launched over the summer and was officially to launch in late December, shifting its model to compete with us directly. We wanted to increase our lead over these sites, and to gain the loyalty of brands and customers before these competitors had a chance to make any impact. We'd put a lot of emphasis on decreasing our time to market. Now we wanted to make sure no one else caught up with us anytime soon.

We were confident about our fund-raising prospects, but also nervous. Despite the fact that we had already convinced several impressive designers to sell on Gilt, the prevailing view among investors (who, it must be noted, are often not shoppers, though their wives are, as they liked to tell us) was that women would not spend real money on things they couldn't first touch and feel and that men would never, *ever* shop for clothing online. Investors' skepticism toward fashion e-commerce seemed to be warranted. Bluefly, a publicly traded fashion e-commerce company that launched in 1998 and sold a variety of contemporary upscale brands, many at discounts of 40 to 70 percent, had seen its share price drop precipitously by October 2007 to around $9 from a height of more than $150 in January 1999, before the tech bubble burst. Despite millions in investments from George Soros, the company had struggled to turn a profit.[1]

---

1.   "Soros Invests Another $1 Million in Bluefly," *The New York Times*, January 30,

Then there was the spectacular failure of Boo.com, an ambitious high-end British fashion e-tailer and "lifestyle destination"[2] that had raised more than one hundred million dollars in the late nineties—including backing from LVMH—and attracted tons of media attention and fanfare before going bankrupt and out of business in 2000. Its founders had been so confident in their idea that they had launched in *eighteen* international markets at once and had six different offices when they folded. Boo.com had become a notorious red flag in the fashion e-commerce space. We knew it could still be in the backs of investors' minds.

Niche e-commerce sites like Net-a-Porter, Shopbop, and Zappos were plugging along at the time of our launch, but they weren't yet receiving the attention they came to enjoy a couple of years later. And LVMH had launched its own e-commerce site, eLuxury.com, but seemed to already be losing interest in it; the site would close in early 2009 as LVMH's various brands debuted their own individual sites.

It may be hard to believe now, but in 2007, we were asking investors, too, to take a leap of faith. We knew that the investment community wouldn't see Gilt as a sure bet, and because of the aforementioned e-commerce failures Kevin and Alexis even discussed that they might have to turn to European investors to secure the funds they needed. Investors there would at least be more familiar with vente-privee's success.

INVESTORS PICK *YOU*, NOT YOUR IDEA

As we prepared for our Series A round, Alexis assumed the title of CEO. This reflected her actual role at Gilt, and it would also assuage

2003; www.nytimes.com/2003/01/30/business/technology-briefing-e-commerce
-soros-invests-another-1-million-in-bluefly.html?scp=6&sq=bluefly&st=cse.
2.   "Boo.com spent fast and died young but its legacy shaped Internet retailing,"
The Guardian, May 15, 2005; www.guardian.co.uk/technology/2005/may/16/media
.business.

the concern of investors, who would want to meet and appraise the person in charge of overseeing their money.

Luckily, Alexis had some useful experience with the venture capital process. Toward the end of her second year of business school, she had started working at General Catalyst, a VC firm in Boston that invests in consumer-based technology companies (she continued to work for the firm full-time for three months after graduation before taking her job at AOL). She'd seen CEOs and ideas pass through the company's conference rooms and developed a sense of what succeeds in securing funding and what doesn't. She'd also observed the gamesmanship involved in getting funding for a start-up and found that she had a taste for it.

Kevin, meanwhile, had had tremendous success attracting investment dollars for previous start-ups, including ShopWiki, Panther Express, Music Nation, 10gen, and of course DoubleClick, and he was known to investors.

Both Kevin and Alexis knew they'd be selling *themselves* as much as their idea—if not more. Kevin remembers learning this lesson years ago, after he initially raised money for DoubleClick from Bain Capital. He recalls that when he later approached his partner at Bain to say, "Look, we know we raised money on this idea, but we really think we want to go in a different direction," the partner said, "That's fine; we never liked the first idea that much anyway." The firm had invested in Kevin himself, trusting that he would eventually arrive at a viable business idea.

In the years since, Kevin has incubated and funded businesses through AlleyCorp, and he's also been on the other side of the fence. He's seen hundreds of entrepreneurs and their ideas pass through his office. He knows firsthand what most attracts the confidence of investors. And as he points out, a majority of start-ups including many of the most successful, like Google and Facebook, are not based on earth-shattering new ideas. "Entrepreneurs think you raise money on the idea," says Kevin. "But VCs invest in the people."

So what makes them want to invest in a person?

"I want them to have a record of success," Kevin says. "It could be academic, extracurricular; it could be that they started a butterfly collection and grew it into the world's best butterfly collection. That, to me, shows someone who's obsessive and wants to succeed."

Nick Beim, our eventual Series A investor, echoes Kevin's thoughts. "More than anything, I seek to invest in incredibly talented, creative, and ambitious people who I think can achieve great things," he says. "They may not have the best idea right away, but generally the best people get to the best idea the fastest." Specifically, Nick looks for "intellectual horsepower, thoughtfulness, drive, domain expertise, impatience, an understanding of the problem they are seeking to solve that is deeper than others', a recognition that they don't have all the answers, and an ability to work well as a team because big problems can't be solved by individuals alone."

Nick wants to invest in geniuses, yes, but geniuses who can get along with others. "Some entrepreneurs are so passionate or driven, or believe so strongly in their own views, that it is difficult for them to work effectively with a team," he explains. "This makes it harder for them to succeed, because it is more difficult for them to attract and retain top talent. I've invested in a few entrepreneurs I would put in this category, and it's been a good learning experience for me. It's very important that an entrepreneur be someone that top potential employees would be excited to work for. Once there is a strong entrepreneur and a strong idea, the art of building a company is primarily the art of attracting and aggregating the best possible talent."

Because there's so little due diligence that can be done on most new start-ups, it's natural that VCs concentrate most on the team involved. Gilt Groupe was young and unproven, so we knew that investors would take a keen interest in the people we had in place and what we'd each accomplished in the past. They'd want to know if they could trust us, if we had high integrity. They'd ask around to find out what our peers and former colleagues said about us. Alexis was acutely aware as she prepared for Gilt's Series A meetings that she'd be convincing investors, perhaps first and foremost, of herself and her ability as CEO to lead the business toward the goals she was setting.

RIDING THE ANTICIPATION CURVE: HOW TO TIME YOUR SERIES A FUND-RAISING

If a good team is crucial to a pitch, timing is also important. These days the speed of innovation has accelerated, and with it, the funding process. Instead of two years passing from when an entrepreneur tests and gets funding for an idea, it might be two months or maybe even less.

Still, many entrepreneurs try to hold off on seeking outside investment for as long as possible so that they'll have to give up less of an ownership stake in their business. This is understandable. If you're raising five million dollars and your business is valued at fifteen million, you'll give up a lot more equity and control than if your business is valued at one hundred million dollars. Yet if we had to sum up *our* position, it would be: raise money sooner rather than later and from the right people.

We believe that raising money early helps protect a business from the inevitable ups and downs ahead in the market. In Gilt's short history, these have included a worldwide recession in 2008 that sent the retail industry into a tailspin and put several brand partners out of business. Because of our business model, this actually worked to our advantage—more on that later—but that won't be the case with most start-ups. In 2008 and 2009 we found ourselves in a position where our infrastructure couldn't keep pace with our growth, and we had to make large capital expenditures in warehousing sooner than anticipated. It was nice to have cash reserves to help us weather the storm.

The point is, you never know when some catastrophic event will cause you to lose customers and leave you in desperate need of cash at a moment when you're not exactly attractive to investors. Alternatively, internal pressures or miscalculations—say, something costs more money to build than you expected, or a supplier disappears— might force you to raise additional money at an inopportune time. If you try to raise money when you're short on cash, or desperate, or when you've just had a setback in your business, you'll be less of an attractive investment.

We've watched plenty of entrepreneurs hold off too long, attempting to move from one million dollars to three million in revenue without investors, for example, or waiting to break even, only to be felled by forces outside their control or things their business plan didn't anticipate. This is why we always emphasize raising money early over maintaining full control or ownership.

We raised our Series A funds on what we like to call an anticipation curve. The anticipation curve refers to that time early in the history of a business when the concept or founders have a lot of buzz, yet little proof exists that the business will or will not fare as predicted. This is a great time to raise money. You have no real results or company track record to vet over weeks or months. At this point you're really just selling the team and the idea, as well as early indications that you're on the right course. Perhaps you've brought on customers or partners, built the site in beta, closed some key deals, or secured a unique marketing opportunity. There are no reams of data to prove to investors that you will succeed, or won't. You're basically saying to investors: "I have a great idea; I've hired the key people who can make it happen; I have some early signs that customers will like it and that we're on an upward trajectory, on the basis of a few recent milestones we have achieved." You have a lot of positive momentum. And no one can prove otherwise—i.e., that it won't work, or that you can't make six million dollars in the first year.

At the top of the anticipation curve, there are a lot of good feelings, both within the company and externally, about what it will be able to pull off. It's a rosy, exciting moment when everything is still possible, and by raising money on the upward slope of this curve, you'll attract your target investment and get cash in the bank before you accumulate a track record that takes months to pore over. You'll also speed the process along and minimize the time you have to spend in market, because investors won't have to get bogged down in as much due diligence.

In the fall of 2007 Gilt Groupe's anticipation curve was definitely surging. We'd signed up brands like Zac Posen, Judith Ripka, and Rachel Roy. We were busily accumulating thousands of e-mail addresses to which we would blast our initial e-mail invite. We believed, based on our instincts and Alexis's experiences at eBay, that we had a viral idea and could grow our membership fast and efficiently. But we hadn't yet hosted an actual sale; we *certainly* had no inkling that we'd have one million members in just over a year and expand into men's, home, kids, travel, food, and so many other businesses. Still, the beauty of the anticipation curve is that no one could say with certainty that we wouldn't. We prepared four key proof points, or milestones, to convince investors of Gilt's potential, to ease their long-standing fears of e-commerce and to assure them the anticipation was real.

First, we'd signed up brands that would help us attract other players in the world of high fashion, including Zac Posen and Notte by Marchesa. These were names with which any fashion house would be pleased to be associated. By aligning ourselves with great brands from the start, we'd carved out a luxurious, high-end reputation in the marketplace that would help us lure exciting new brand partners and more of the right kinds of shoppers. It's hard to overstate the importance of these initial brands in signaling Gilt's potential. Of course, since most investors had never heard of them, we'd have to explain how excited we were about them as consumers.

Second, we had a viral idea and a viable marketing strategy. Our initial marketing push would cost us almost nothing. We knew there was a huge market for Gilt, and that we could grow the site's customer base rapidly and efficiently.

Third, we had a great team of cofounders. Young and hungry, we represented the perfect combination of e-commerce and fashion know-how. We had an experienced and well-respected chairman in Kevin Ryan, who had incubated several businesses and grown Double-Click to the billion-dollar mark. Alexis had been a key player in one of the Internet's largest success stories (eBay), and Alexandra was one of the most well-connected young executives in the New York fashion industry. We had brilliant engineers in Mike and Phong; both also happened to be capable managers and operators. While many others would try, we knew there was no one better than our team to execute this idea.

Finally, there was vente-privee's billion-dollar valuation. Loud and undeniable, this was the proof we needed, from an industry perspective, that off-price event sales were the next big thing. There was a large business already out there in France, one that we estimated could be potentially five times the size in a market like the United States.

Armed with these proof points, Alexis and Kevin took informal meetings with several venture capital firms based in Boston, a city that had a high concentration of VC dollars at the time, and in New York City. These weren't formal pitch meetings—just informal meet and greets to give us a sense of which firms we wanted to talk seriously and to allow word to get out that we were working on a new e-commerce concept (Alexandra attended several of these meetings as well). Informal meetings not only generate buzz but are a great way to socialize an idea to investors without actually asking for cash or starting the clock on a formal fund-raising process. These casual talks offer a window into the key questions that will be asked about a team or an idea in formal pitch meetings and a chance to preview the areas of pushback a pitch may encounter—points in the plan that will be met with uncertainty or skepticism (for example, "Luxury is a niche market; will it hinder your ability to really grow this business?" or "Aren't you underestimating the influence of department stores and other online incumbents?" or "What makes you think you'll be any more successful than Bluefly?"). These doubts are the things that can sink a pitch, so it's best to identify them and prepare responses in advance. Informal meetings also allow an entrepreneur to get a sense for the personality and value various investors might bring to a company as potential board members and how they might improve a start-up's chances for success.

Much like in dating, it's helpful in the VC process to craft an overall air of desirability. There is a lot of group mentality among investors; large amounts of money tend to chase the same ideas. When VCs think their competitors are interested in an idea, they will naturally be more likely to want to take a look themselves. But you never want to meet with *too* many firms because—well, who wants to date the person who dates everyone? The trick is to attract interest from several firms while still making those firms feel chosen and special. Alexis and Kevin tried to emphasize they were just talking to a couple of other firms that were strategic to our business. Two to five firms are usually ideal. As Kevin likes to explain, "I want to go out to the right investors and make them all feel like they have a chance of getting [the deal]."

Sometimes when firms know *who* else is interested, they'll work together to agree on valuation or other elements of the deal. This works to their advantage, but not the entrepreneur's (a lower valuation is in the VC's best interest because the more ownership a VC can buy for its money, the better). Therefore, it's best to be discreet and not share too many details. A CEO might want to drive the valuation up by encouraging multiple suitors, making sure they all think they have a chance to invest, but being coy about the firms' exact names.

It's important to always be honest and forthright when dealing with investors; don't claim you're speaking to "a few" firms when in fact it's just one. But if investors press for specifics on which other firms are interested, simply say something like "We're looking at other early stage consumer-facing technology investors in New York and Boston who have connections in these areas and can help us attract key talent to lead the team." The point is not to mislead anyone; it's to leverage the natural sense of competition that exists between VC firms and to infuse the process with a sense of urgency and excitement.

It can also boost desirability to limit the time spent actively seeking investment. In other words, shorten the time you are in the market for funding. (It's not that different in real estate: an owner never wants to leave a house on the market for too long, lest potential buyers think no one else is interested and lower their offers.) In their informal meet and greets in October, Kevin and Alexis made it clear to investors that we were entering the market in November and aimed to be done within a month. As Kevin explains, "VCs will try to talk to you forever. I generally try to say, 'Look, thirty days from now is when this is going to happen.'" Most investors respond quickly only if there's a stated deadline or clear competition. And the VC kiss of death is when investors become aware that a company has been meeting with the same firms for months with no result. If their competitors aren't excited by the opportunity to invest in a business, chances are they won't be either.

That's why it's important to show positive momentum during conversations with investors. As an example, if you think your company is worth ten million dollars, Kevin would argue, in the interest of keeping "everyone in the mix," that you might want to say something like, "Look, I think it is going to be probably in the seven to ten million range." Following this logic, if you want to raise four million, it might be best to say, "I want to raise two to three million." As Kevin explains, "people want to see, Is the process going well?" It's always better to go back to investors and raise your estimate of the bidding range than to decrease it. "I never want to have to retreat back down," says Kevin. "That's crucial. But I also don't want to overstate it. Some people go in too aggressively and then have to back down." This might cause an investor to question the company's worth or to wonder if there is something he or she doesn't know. Since positive momentum is so important, it never hurts to start out more conservatively.

Of course a thirty-day time frame would not be possible for Gilt Groupe today. The company now has years of operating history, so it typically takes Gilt at least four or more months to raise new capital: every contract and vendor agreement is carefully combed through; every decision we've ever made, analyzed in a rigorous due diligence process. But back then, still riding the anticipation curve, we didn't have much of a paper trail to inspect beyond our personal track records.

Kevin and Alexis were lucky to find a few firms that expressed interest in Gilt during their informal meet and greets. Oddly enough, one of the only firms that didn't seem impressed was a female-led VC firm based in New York. It was the only firm they knew of with a female partner—and not just one: it had four! Kevin and Alexis were disappointed when the partners appeared unconvinced of our team's ability to pull off our idea. We knew some firms would find our team too young and unproven, or fail to be convinced that we could execute; this was inevitable. And although it was hard not to take it personally, Alexis tried not to dwell on their decision for too long.

———

Kevin thought it was important to start the formal pitch process with each firm at the same time, to get them off the starting blocks in unison so that none would be further along in the process than the others. After weeks of meet and greets, he and Alexis narrowed down their target investors to three Boston-based firms and tried to schedule pitch meetings with each on the same day, during their regular Monday partner meetings. Most VC firms host these meetings; these are usually when the biggest, most promising pitches are presented. Because these meetings are so pivotal, Silicon Valley partners tend to join by videoconference, and vice versa (East Coast offices join the West Coast's partner meetings). Alexis knew the pressure would be on. One added bonus of scheduling the meetings for the same day was that it would add to our aura of desirability to mention that we had to leave one meeting in order to rush off to another.

---

checklist:
ELEMENTS OF A SUCCESSFUL VC PRESENTATION

1. AN ELEVATOR PITCH YOU CAN MAKE IN FIVE SECONDS (THIRTY SECONDS IS WAY TOO LONG!). Concepts must be bite-size, memorable, and easy to explain to your grandparents. Gilt's concept was simple: *an invite-only online sample sale featuring designer goods at prices up to 60 percent off.*

2. INFORMATION ON THE TEAM AND ITS BACKGROUND. In other words, the people that VCs will ultimately be investing in. Our pitch included detailed information on the background of each member of our team, from Alexis's success leading prior start-ups within eBay to Alexandra's work at Louis Vuitton and Bulgari to Mike and Phong's prowess as engineers to, of course, Kevin's well-known success at DoubleClick. We knew we needed to describe our team thoroughly in order to convince investors we were the right people to back.

3. SPECIFICS ON THE OPPORTUNITY. How large is the market you are addressing, and how much of it will you capture? In other words, would people buy designer fashion online, and if so, how much of it could we sell? How large could we grow the business? We needed to demonstrate that consumers would in fact shop this way—this seemed to us like a no-brainer, but we brought some market research to back it up—and that we could secure the inventory to meet the demand. We pointed to the popularity of sample sales and to the viral marketing techniques we planned to employ, and emphasized the brands we'd lined up for our initial sales.

4. A DESCRIPTION OF THE BUSINESS CONTEXT. Investors will probably ask questions such as: Are there competitors who will come in and threaten your success? Will incumbents in the marketplace, like department stores, try to block your growth? Are there regulations or legislation that will make growing the business difficult? Gilt was not subject to any government regulations that would affect its growth. And our speed to market would give us a clear advantage over our (inevitable) competitors. Although there were no guarantees that incumbents and other e-commerce players wouldn't copy us (in fact almost all of them eventually did), we would at least have a lead over them.

5. LAST, THE TERMS OF A DEAL. What's in it for the investor? Every VC will want to know exactly how much money you are asking for, how you're planning to use it, and what rights it will get in exchange for the money—share of the company's equity, voting rights, a board seat, and/or preference over other shareholders in recovering money if things do not go well. We'd settled on five million dollars as our target investment, because we knew that was what it would take to build a team, expand our logistics and office space, and get to the next level. For us, five million was the number that could truly make a difference. We wanted investors to believe that their funds would be extremely impactful and would carry us at least until we reached additional critical milestones, with enough buffer room for mistakes.

The first meeting Alexis and Kevin scheduled on that November Monday was with a firm called Matrix Partners, known for its success investing in early-stage businesses. The firm had produced some of the highest returns on its investments not only in the boom years but throughout tougher periods in the early aughts. Kevin already had a good relationship with one of the partners at Matrix, Nick Beim, who had been following AlleyCorp for some time and had a long-standing interest in working with Kevin. Alexis had also met and connected with Nick in her Spinback days. After a few informal discussions it was clear that Nick was actively pursuing us. And we definitely reciprocated his interest.

If the VC process is a lot like dating, then entering a Series A agreement is like getting married. Investors don't tend to give an entrepreneur their money and then leave that person alone to spend it however she sees fit. Instead, a start-up typically gains a new partner, who comes to the office, sits on the board, and becomes a core member of an intimate team, perhaps even calling weekly or more to check in. That's why it's often not so much choosing the right firm that makes a difference as choosing the right partner. It's important to honestly evaluate what that individual brings to the table because it's pretty difficult to get a divorce after entering a funding agreement. Maybe an investor will bring contacts that will be helpful in business development; perhaps he or she knows talented engineers or other key people you will need to hire. We knew that Nick had a strong finance background and could offer valuable insights into tackling business problems and scaling our operations and technological platform. But on the basis of his ties to a large network of talented executives, we also thought he could help us find and recruit top talent.

Most important, he was (and is) thoughtful, gracious, and a sheer pleasure to work with. From the beginning, his feedback was always strong and direct but delivered with genuine humility. He never presumed to know more than anyone else. He was at the core someone we wanted to be around, someone we could definitely see strategizing with over long dinners.

During the few weeks of informal discussions we had with Nick, he had dinner in New York with Alexandra; it was important he meet all key players before making the decision to invest. Alexandra remembers making a special effort to dress up for the occasion because she wanted to show this venture capitalist that she did indeed have some fashion sense. They had a long dinner at Brasserie, on East Fifty-third Street, and Alexandra liked Nick immediately. He was easy to talk to; he asked lots of questions and seemed genuinely interested in Alexandra's answers and perspective on Gilt.

Alexandra got the impression that Nick was worried Gilt might limit itself by targeting exclusively high-end luxury designers. "Could you ever see Gilt Groupe selling more mainstream fashion?" she remembers his asking. She quickly reassured him that she definitely could, but that in order to convince luxury brands to sell on Gilt, it was important that the initial group of brands be at the high end of the spectrum. Besides, our viral marketing push would be predicated on the site's perceived exclusivity. Gilt Groupe would have to be positioned as a luxury brand first before it could consider expanding into less expensive categories of merchandise.

Alexis and Kevin connected with two other firms through personal contacts that they ended up seriously considering. They liked what they learned about these firms in their meet and greets, and they liked the partners with whom we'd be working. But going into their formal Monday meetings, Alexis and Kevin considered Matrix the clear front-runner.

On a Sunday in early November, Kevin, Mike, and Alexis traveled to Boston. Alexis stayed at the home of Liz Larowe, a college roommate and dear friend, and she proceeded to tweak the pitch into the wee hours of the night.

She awoke the next morning with a huge jolt of energy, not unlike the adrenaline rush she used to get before a big lacrosse game in college. She drove to Matrix's offices in Waltham, near where several other investment firms and technology companies were headquartered. There she met up with Kevin and Mike. They walked together into Matrix's polished building and waited a few moments for an earlier presentation to wrap up before entering the conference room.

They were greeted by Matrix's dozen or so partners, all men, packed tightly around a conference table. There was also a woman, Sheila Marcelo, who was not a Matrix partner but the CEO of Care .com, a business the firm had backed the previous year. VC firms often invite knowledgeable outsiders to pitch meetings to provide a point of view they may be missing. Sheila, as a successful female entrepreneur, would be asked to weigh in on our idea from a woman's perspective, as well as to give her thoughts on the team.

The presentation lasted about an hour, during which time Alexis and Kevin did most of the talking. Standing in front of those men (and woman) in her Carolina Herrera jacket and four-inch heels, Alexis knew she faced a fundamental dilemma: How could she build trust in our idea and respect for her leadership while admitting that she was willing to drop everything for a Dolce & Gabbana or Fendi sample sale? How could she admit to this audience that she loved something so seemingly frivolous as shopping for designer clothing? She wanted to be honest about how exciting she found Gilt's business model (because she represented its target customer) without risking being taken less seriously as a businesswoman and as the CEO of the business. How can I get them to see how excited people will be without sounding like a dingbat? she thought. It was a delicate dance. Coming from low-key eBay and before that the male-dominated world of investment banking, Alexis had certainly never waxed on about her shopping habits in front of a roomful of middle-aged men clad in blue shirts and khakis. She knew a big part of a VC partner's job is to assess people's judgment; they don't tend to be fond of frivolity. Yet our business would live or die on the basis of people's passion for fashion—our members' love of a deal. Alexis had to convince the VCs of this *and* to project "CEO." Both were equally important.

She decided not to hold back; her passion and enthusiasm for the Gilt business could only help her pitch, she figured.

Alexis boldly predicted Gilt would bring in six million dollars in revenue during its first calendar year. To be honest, we thought this was incredibly aggressive; making this much money right out of the gates would be a huge feat. But Series A projections are often ambitious. When you're raising capital, it helps to paint a picture of what you are striving for—within reason, of course. Alexis didn't just pull the six million–dollar number from the air; instead, she calculated our projected costs and considered the marketing tactics we would undertake. She also took into consideration typical ranges for click-throughs on e-mails and industry conversion rates for people making purchases when they reached a site.

Despite thinking it slightly bullish, we decided to put the six million–dollar figure out there. Who's to say we can't do what we say we're going to do? Alexis thought. There is no evidence to prove us wrong. (Of course she had *no* idea how conservative the estimate would ultimately be; we ultimately cleared twenty-five million dollars in revenue in our first year.)

The Matrix partners, for their part, didn't seem put off by Alexis's projections. The excitement and engagement level in the room was high. The partners asked informed questions, and for each, Alexis,

Kevin, or Mike had an answer ready. They wanted to understand our cash flow model better. Alexis assured them we paid for goods *after* we sold them; this is known as positive working capital. They had no familiarity with Zac Posen or Notte by Marchesa, as was to be expected, so Alexis did her best to assure them that women like her would jump at the opportunity to buy these brands at a discount, even, and *especially*, from the comfort of their homes or desks in the middle of the workday. The partners asked whether we'd sign exclusive agreements with the brands. Alexis responded that she was open to pursuing this, but not hopeful it would work because the fashion industry operates on handshakes and gentlemen's agreements. Instead, Gilt would rely on its superior luxury branding and attractive customer base to keep brand partners loyal. The partners asked Mike about his decision to code the site in a new, unproven programming language, Ruby on Rails, pushing him on how the site would accommodate dramatic increases in traffic.

As they quizzed Alexis, Mike, and Kevin, the partners stayed focused and managed to keep their BlackBerrys off the table. Importantly, Alexis felt that she managed to appear passionate while still exhibiting poise and eliciting confidence. She'd entered a zone; she was *on*. When it was over, she walked out of the room on a little bit of a high.

Afterward she happened to run into Sheila Marcelo in the ladies' room. "You guys did a *great* job," Sheila said emphatically. "You should feel proud." It was Alexis's first clear indication that the pitch had gone over as well as she thought.

Buoyed by their first successful meeting, Alexis, Mike, and Kevin darted off to their next formal pitch meeting. Unfortunately it couldn't have been more different from their experience at Matrix. Many of this firm's partners joined via videoconference from the West Coast, and believe it or not, once Alexis got going, they muted the volume and continued their conversations, obviously far more interested in their BlackBerrys and in cracking jokes to one another than in hearing about Gilt. She could swear several even laughed and rolled their eyes! Perhaps our concept seemed too frivolous for them. Alexis remembers looking at Kevin incredulously and thinking, Is this really happening? Can we please get up and walk out of this meeting right now?

Instead, she, Kevin, and Mike kept moving through the pitch for the benefit of the people around the table in Boston, and Alexis tried her best to block out the teleconference screen at the head of the table. While there were plenty of awkward pauses, she fought the urge to confront the VCs' rudeness directly, or, even better, tell them off before walking out of the room. After all, she didn't *really* know what they were talking about on mute. While they certainly didn't appear interested in Gilt, she knew she had to dig in and complete the pitch in the most professional manner possible.

Needless to say, she, Kevin, and Mike all but discounted this second firm after that meeting. It was obviously not a team we would want to take money from, lest its partners behave with similar disrespect during our board meetings. We never got direct feedback about why they'd seemed so rudely uninterested in Gilt's concept, but we also knew we didn't want to spend any more meaningful time with them.

The third meeting happened later that week, and was much better; the VC team reacted with extreme interest and urgency. But in recent days Alexis had completed a little of her own due diligence and heard some troubling feedback about the partner we'd be working with at this firm. Although she did not let this derail the conversations, it remained in the back of her mind and was ultimately a red flag we couldn't ignore.

On the basis of our knowledge of and instinctive good feelings about Nick, we'd decided that Matrix was still our first choice. (Not that we wanted Nick to know that, at least not *yet*.)

MAKING A COMMITMENT (WHILE KEEPING A FEW OPTIONS ON THE BACK BURNER)

Alexis and Kevin talked to Nick soon after they got back to New York, and he was candid about his fellow partners' interest and enthusiasm.

Twenty-four hours later, on Tuesday, Nick called and told us to expect a term sheet shortly from Matrix (this is a short document that lays out the terms of the agreement; it's usually negotiated heavily by all parties before being signed). We were all elated. But we didn't yet tell the other firms; instead, we kept them warm while we waited. We made sure Matrix knew we were still talking to others too, so we could maintain that sense of competition and keep our options open in case something went wrong.

But just like Nick had promised, the Matrix term sheet arrived on Tuesday, and by Thursday it had been finalized—just days after our meeting. The anticipation curve enabled us to go into market on a Monday, have term sheets that week, and close all due diligence and legal work a short three weeks after that. This was a rapid process by any standard.

The VC world can be insular, so word of our term sheet with Matrix got around quickly. We found it hilarious when it sparked a whole new round of interest in Gilt. Suddenly several other VCs were calling and saying they wanted to be included. "It's in your best interest to get a better price," they said, or, "Why not benefit from having the backing of two firms and their respective networks?" But we were committed to working with Matrix and Nick.

Matrix had spoken to a few of our brand partners and looked through our financial projections; Nick had met with key members of our team and toured our warehouse space. He'd done all the due diligence he could do, which wasn't much. And the firm valued us in the double-digit million range. We can't overstate what a huge deal this was for us as a brand-new company. All proof points aside, we'd attracted a great valuation for a business that basically amounted to a Web site and PowerPoint presentation with just a few sales under its belt and a great team. Matrix's five million–dollar investment would give the firm a sizable, but not onerous, ownership stake in Gilt. And we'd welcome Nick to our small board, joining Kevin and Alexis.

We recently asked Nick why he and his partners at Matrix had chosen to invest in us.

"There were a lot of things I loved about Gilt's pitch," he said. "Most important, I thought the team was really impressive. You'd all been top performers in your respective fields, and you had very complementary backgrounds: Alexis in e-commerce, Alexandra in fashion, Mike and Phong in high-scale online transactional businesses, and Kevin in building successful start-ups and running a successful Internet business through its hypergrowth phase. All were extremely bright and ambitious, and you worked well as a team.

"The business model was also very intriguing in several respects," he continued. "It had a high potential for virality and, consequently, the opportunity to grow very rapidly and aggregate members at a zero effective marginal cost—something that is very unusual among Internet companies.

"It also brought a very effective excess inventory solution, and ultimately a marketing solution, to an industry that was structurally inefficient (lots of small and midsize designers, few of whom sold online, with little innovation coming from major retailers who sold their items).

"Finally," said Nick, "Gilt had the ability to expand into other verticals, since high-end vendors in almost any sector are reluctant to discount in a public manner on the Internet, a factor which greatly expanded its addressable market size."

When it was all done, it was interesting to see how the other firms that had been lobbying us so hard at the end positioned their interest in Gilt to the outside world. We heard through the grapevine that they'd said things like "Oh, yeah, we took a look at Gilt Groupe. It was too expensive for us" and "We decided to pass." Given its abundance of adrenaline and ego, the VC world is obviously as much about solid financials as it is about reputation and jockeying for position.

As we said, it's more art than science.

CHAPTER 8

FROM COLLEGE FASHIONISTAS
TO URBAN IT GIRLS:

Planting the Seeds of a Viral Phenomenon

> We were aiming to create a viral business model, but it
> depended on getting an initial critical mass of loyal style
> mavens to become members of our company. We thought
> that once they joined and hopefully quickly became
> obsessed with Gilt Groupe, they would in turn spread the
> word to all of their nearest and dearest.
>
> —ALEXIS MAYBANK AND ALEXANDRA WILKIS WILSON,
> BLOGGING ON THE *HUFFINGTON POST*, JUNE 16, 2009

It was Halloween night 2007. While the Chelsea neighborhood in New York celebrated in typically outlandish fashion—we could hear the clamor of the annual West Village parade half a block away, with bands playing, transvestites sashaying up Sixth Avenue on floats, and crowds dancing and singing loudly for hours on end—we (Alexis, Alexandra, Mike, Phong, and our two newest recruits: Rachel Wolkowitz, our director of marketing and communications, and John Auerbach, our director of finance) sat at our single long L-shaped desk on West Nineteenth Street, preparing to launch our membership, or send out thousands of e-mail invitations with links people could forward around or use to log on and actually join the site. We'd worked out all the kinks in our friends-and-family dry run.

These e-mail links would, we hoped, kick off our word-of-mouth marketing campaign in advance of our Zac Posen sale, scheduled to happen in two short weeks. We'd entered all the names and e-mails we'd been doggedly accumulating for months into our database.

We were delirious from lack of sleep. That night Gilt Groupe seemed anything but glamorous.

In fact Mike remembers thinking Alexis was crazy to have scheduled our Zac Posen sale for two weeks after our membership launch. "I thought you were nuts," he says. "We were going to start the membership campaign for a launch thirteen days later, and you thought we'd have enough members to buy anything? I just did *not* think that was going to happen." (Still, "I trusted you," he admits. "And you were right.")

We were obsessed with launching in November, well ahead of the holidays and our competitors. And much like an invitation to a party, Alexis believed we could not send the e-mail too early, lest potential attendees (shoppers) forget about it and lose their excitement over too many weeks of waiting. Besides, we had faith that our e-mail invitations would produce enough members to make our first sale a success. We'd compiled a list of more than twenty thousand e-mails. These included thousands of our personal contacts, from our nearest and dearest friends and family members to casual business acquaintances from Silicon Valley, Boston, New York, high school, grad school, and beyond. It also included thousands of virtual strangers whose contact information we'd amassed through sheer determination and resourcefulness, by seeking out communities of passionate shoppers, students, businesswomen, and fashionistas who would be naturally incentivized to forward our e-mail along to friends.

As we prepared for the launch, we thought of the "buzz" campaign for the 1999 movie *The Blair Witch Project*, which was one of the most successful indie films of all time. Instead of a traditional marketing campaign, with movie posters and commercials, the filmmakers subtly sparked discussion on the Internet by planting the idea that the events recounted in the film were true. This got everyone talking, urgently asking friends about it. The buzz the filmmakers generated did their marketing for them, cheaply and effectively. Instead of picking up marketing messages about the film from television ads or movie posters, most people heard about it from friends, or via word of mouth from trusted sources, which is much more powerful. Though Gilt had little in common with *Blair Witch*, it had the potential to be similarly viral, since it offered exclusive, fleeting deals on amazing merchandise, something members would be naturally excited to share with friends. With our Zac Posen sale coming up, we had a feeling word would travel fast.

Alexis had also seen firsthand the power of a great viral marketing campaign at eBay. She and members of her team had traipsed all over the West Coast, trying to get the word out about the business by reaching the right circles of collectors, people who were passionate about buying or selling one thing in particular. They found these people on news groups and Listservs (precursors to blogs) and at all the stamp collecting and *Star Trek* conferences, not to mention the aforementioned South Dakota motorcycle rallies. These grassroots efforts targeted large groups of like-minded people with similar obsessions and effectively attracted these dedicated hobbyists to the site; once they discovered the wonders of eBay, the collectors were naturally incentivized to spread the word to friends with similar hobbies and interests. Again, people who are passionate talk about what they're passionate about and are natural viral marketers. They made eBay one of the greatest viral success stories of all time.

Our first hint that news of Gilt would travel fast was that off-line sample sales were extremely viral. Long before they were posted on sites like DailyCandy, these sales were advertised primarily through e-mails or word-of-mouth invites from one New York fashionista to another. We knew how quickly these e-mails got around—like wildfire! *We* talked and e-mailed about sample sales constantly, with each other and all our friends; we also dutifully forwarded invites to as many acquaintances as we thought might be interested. Surely our friends and friends of friends would do the same—to an even greater degree—if the sales were online and accessible to friends and family who didn't live in Manhattan. By 2007 it had become easier than ever to share viral information with friends, since blogs and social networking sites had devised increasingly innovative ways for people to talk to one another. Some of those ways (Facebook, blogs) even made conversations semipublic, for hundreds or thousands of other "friends" to see.

And fashion, like movies and like car collecting, was something many people naturally talked about among friends. Sports are another example. It's no surprise that fantasy sports leagues are a huge word-of-mouth phenomenon. If your business deals with something that friends don't easily discuss over dinner, cocktails, coffee, or walking down the street—like medical information or personal finance—chances are it won't grow virally (can you imagine: "You'll never believe the amazing new remedy I just found for my eczema"?). But things like fashion and sports come up in casual conversation among friends all the time. Women ask one another what brand they're wearing and where they bought it; they also shop together as a social activity.

We knew from experience that women, at least women in the United States, especially loved to discuss great finds on fashion. "Oh, this? It's actually H&M by Karl Lagerfeld." Or, "You'll never believe the deal I got on this at the Barneys Warehouse Sale!" Talking about shopping bargains wasn't just information sharing; it was a source of pride for women we knew (ourselves included) and reinforced one's savvy and know-how. There seemed to be great psychological rewards to knowing where to find the best value for your money. We noticed that these psychological rewards snowballed as you shared evidence of your cleverness with a friend or, even better, told her where she could get this kind of deal herself. There was an element of social reward, a sense of maintaining or increasing your social status by being the first to know about something interesting, cool, or useful. YouTube was wildly viral purely because people are inclined to be the first to share outrageous stories (and clips) with their friends, and TV, movies, and humor are natural parts of entertaining conversations. We expected that our customers would want to tell their friends about Gilt because doing so would provide a so-called altruistic reward, the satisfaction of knowing you'd helped a friend get a bargain.

Though we hoped our customers would reap social and altruistic rewards from telling their friends about Gilt, we also wanted to offer a monetary incentive. That's why we'd decided to offer a twenty-five-dollar shopping credit to anyone who invited a friend to join when that friend made her first purchase. This was hotly debated internally because it seemed like a rich sum. But Alexis recalled that eBay's lifetime value of a customer was forty-nine dollars. This amount shaped what eBay could spend to get that customer's attention in the first place. And if the eBay shopper could be expected to be worth forty-nine dollars to eBay in his or her lifetime, Alexis guessed—on the basis of her own buying habits—that the Gilt shopper would be worth more. She and Alexandra were the target customers after all. She had a feeling Gilt could achieve a lifetime customer value perhaps even four times that of eBay's. So, twenty-five dollars seemed just right.

Keep in mind, though, that if people don't think something is good for their friends in the first place, they won't share it, no matter how much you incentivize them. A monetary incentive does not replace a social incentive; it just rewards it. A business still needs to involve something people are talking about already in order to go viral.

Also increasing Gilt's word-of-mouth potential was that it was easy to explain. We could do it in one phrase: *an invite-only online*

sample sale featuring designer fashion at prices up to 60 percent off.
While many investors and men didn't initially get it, the women we
were trying to reach in the beginning knew exactly what we were
talking about. The language, if not the business model itself, was
familiar.

Finally—and this is key for any potentially viral business—we
could reach our target customers cheaply and easily. While Alexis
hadn't been naturally hooked into the stamp collectors she'd sought
out during her eBay years, we both were definitely hooked into *our*
target customers. They were our friends, family, acquaintances, and
former coworkers. We knew tons of women who regularly bought
designer clothing and shopped at sample sales. And we knew tons of
women who lived for a bargain on these items. We had big networks
of potential customers already in place and hundreds of thousands
more within a five-mile radius of our Manhattan office.

Since Alexis's days at eBay, "tribes" of like-minded enthusiasts had
also become easier than ever to identify without leaving one's computer. The rise of blogs, Facebook pages, and Twitter has given people
with similar interests more places to congregate and disseminate
news to one another on the Internet quickly. There are thousands of
blogs targeted to lovers of handbags or even to a designer like Marc
Jacobs alone. Fashion was a subject with broad appeal, so there were
also hundreds, if not thousands, of women's professional and educational organizations already in place on the Internet whose networks
we could tap.

Bloggers, specifically, are hubs through which viral information
spreads because they thrive on being in the know; this knowledge is
the basis of their currency and reputation. We knew they'd love being
the first to tell their readers about Gilt.

Of course you don't need a blog to be someone through whom
information naturally spreads. Think of the person in your life who is
always the first one to tell you about the hot new restaurant or an

amazing new band you'll love, who seems to magically acquire news and gossip before everyone else in the group, and who derives personal satisfaction from sharing it all. In *The Tipping Point*, Malcolm Gladwell refers to these people as mavens. They're individuals who, either online or in real life, have access to large groups of people that look to them for information and who are inclined, whether for monetary gain (i.e., to grow a blog) or not, to spread the word about things that matter to them.

But being passionate is not the same as being a maven. Passionate people talk to their good friends about things that excite them. Mavens talk to much wider circles, and this is why they're key to any successful viral marketing campaign. We needed women who were just as excited to get access to a brand-new Diane von Furstenberg dress at 60 percent off as they were to tell every guest at a party—or perhaps their thousands of Facebook friends—how *they* too could score such a dress. In launching our membership, we'd tried to identify the talkers, the entertainers, the social media mavens, those who could connect not just one to one but one to many. Once we introduced them to our concept, we hoped they'd become so engaged and enamored with our brand that they couldn't wait to tell their friends.

Mavens are pretty easy to identify inasmuch as they tend to assume positions of leadership, whether on college campuses or in personal and professional organizations. So we contacted the heads of multitudes of women's groups, ranging from the Garden Club of America to the National Association of Realtors. We scoured the Internet for local groups in key cities, like moms' clubs in Pasadena and Tribeca, attorneys in Bel Air, university and business school alumni groups, sororities, and museum groups in first- and second-tier cities. At the very least the women and men atop these organizations had the attention of their own members, and often, they knew leaders of other relevant organizations too.

In building our e-mail list, we also concentrated heavily on a less well-heeled but naturally viral demographic: college kids. Though most don't have the disposable incomes of young professionals in cities, college and grad students live in one of the most innately viral environments in existence. They have a lot of time on their hands to converse with their friends, and at their age, being in the know, the first ones to tell friends about something cool, proffers even more social currency. Colleges are densely populated by mavens and people routinely spreading the word to one another over meals, at soccer games, and even during class. Schools are also hotbeds of social networking. They're petri dishes of ideas that replicate and spread quickly. We knew that schools with strong Greek scenes or with traditions of dressing up for sporting events, formals, or parties—in other words, places like Tulane, Vanderbilt, UVA, and USC, where students don't wear sweatpants and last night's makeup to class— would be natural audiences for Gilt.

Luckily, college kids identify themselves readily online. After flipping through *U.S. News & World Report*'s annual rankings of the top hundred colleges, Alexis gathered e-mail addresses for the presidents of every women's, fashion, business, retail, technology, and entrepreneurial student group at the undergraduate and graduate level through each school's Web site. Later we followed up with personal e-mails. "Hi, I'm Alexis. If you think your members might be interested, please pass on this invite to join our new site!" Then we pasted a link to register (www.gilt.com/alexis) to highlight that the invite was in fact coming from another person and that it was offering special access to our sales.

We also had plenty of connectors in our own extended networks. We reached out to any friend with a big personal network or a large number of Facebook friends, appealing to her or him for access to his or her contacts. For Alexandra, these included the international marketing and PR maven Susan Shin, who had access to lists of relevant contacts. It also included Alexandra's brother Alan, who lives among creative types in Brooklyn and has a large network of friends with a decidedly different vibe from Alexandra's (you could call them hipsters). These people became key for us, spreading the word far and wide. Many, such as Alexandra's friend Heather Lynch McAuliffe, vice president of public relations at J.Crew, and Doug Wurtz, an acquaintance of Alexandra's who works in finance and invited hundreds of friends in his network, helped kick-start our word of mouth completely unprompted. Alexis meanwhile reached out to her sister Fleur Keyes, a decorator in New York City who was tapped into New York's and Boston's twentysomething scene, and to friends and family in San Francisco and Los Angeles, and childhood friends and family in South Carolina.

Before we sent out our e-mail blast on Halloween night, Alexandra made some final entreaties to the team. "Didn't you stay in touch with any friends from college?" she asked the engineers. "Don't you have more acquaintances you can invite?" She'd already begged Kevin to come up with more names in the preceding weeks, and he'd produced almost two thousand. We were impressed!

Of course, we were also aware that blasting out an e-mail invite was only the first step. It was one thing to attract these women and men to our site for the first time or to convince them to sign up for membership. But a truly viral business—unlike a movie, which most viewers might be expected to see only once in the theater—keeps customers coming back for more. It does this by providing ongoing fodder for conversation: new tidbits of information and products for sale or access to new services or features. Gilt would keep customers talking by lining up a constant stream of exciting sales. Unlike department stores' Web sites, which often seemed to offer the same merchandise for months, updating only seasonally, our site would be entirely different from day to day. We'd start with three to five new sales per week, a number that eventually grew rapidly across many categories into the hundreds. We'd advertise our sales on the site a few days in advance and send out e-mails to all our customers in the minutes leading up to each sale. Because the sales were fleeting, there would be an urgency further propelling the spread of information, a feeling of "I have to tell my friend about this now before she misses out." We'd constantly offer new styles and ideas for friends and social groups to discuss, prompting an e-mail, a phone call, a dinner conversation, or a Facebook message to share the news. We'd even give specific bloggers a sneak peek of, say, five looks in a sale we knew would appeal to them. This would make them feel even more in the know and encourage them to keep spreading the news to their readers.

---

checklist:
DOES YOUR BUSINESS HAVE THE POTENTIAL TO BE VIRAL?

1. DO PEOPLE NATURALLY WANT TO TALK ABOUT THE TOPIC AMONG FRIENDS? If it's not a subject that people already discuss casually and socially, it will be unlikely to benefit from word-of-mouth marketing.

2. IS YOUR ASK TO CUSTOMERS CLEAR, COMPELLING, AND EASY TO EXPLAIN? We made our message clear and simple to understand. Customers could remember that Gilt was an online luxury sample sale and easily explain it to their friends.

3. ARE CUSTOMERS REWARDED FOR TELLING THEIR FRIENDS? Friends who tell friends about Gilt still feel a special thrill: it indirectly reaffirms their social standing or recognition among circles of acquaintances because they're sharing something useful that will actually benefit their friends. We call this altruistic motivation.

A business can increase this motivation by giving customers who refer new customers soft rewards. For example, they might get information a day in advance of other customers, be invited to test a product or service before it goes live, or be granted five minutes to shop early. These nonmonetary rewards make customers feel like valued insiders. Hard rewards, or monetized incentives, can also speed or further reward the customer's inclination to share and can be a good way for a company to say thank you. (Though we believe soft rewards and social rewards exceed all else.)

4. CAN YOU IDENTIFY AND REACH GROUPS OF YOUR TARGET CUSTOMERS QUICKLY? If they're not people you know already, do you know where they are? Do organized groups exist that can help you spread your message? Never assume that the most enthusiastic customers will just find you; you need to find them and communicate with them regularly. We had huge personal networks in place of potential Gilt members and also knew how to leverage existing networks of shoppers online, through blogs, or in local cities or on campuses.

5. ARE YOU GIVING THEM A SUSTAINABLE REASON TO COME BACK AND KEEP THE CONVERSATIONS GOING? From the start, our members posted on their Facebook accounts with news of exciting sales we were hosting, sent one another texts, and communicated the news over dinner or drinks, thereby doing our marketing for us. Bloggers also eagerly pointed out their favorite items from their favorite brands, driving their readers to our site. And we *always* had new sales to keep the conversation going.

Shortly after our e-mails started going out through the server that Halloween night in 2007, we began to excitedly monitor activity on our site in real time and waited for people to receive our link and sign up to become members. Of course, some members of our team stuck around longer than others that night. "I remember to this day, Alexandra, that you said very, very clearly that you were going to have everything done in advance," Mike remembers. "You were *not* procrastinating, and no matter what, on the eve of the launch, you were going to go home at a normal hour instead of staying with the rest of the procrastinators. And you did."

Mike, Phong, and Alexis, on the other hand, stayed in the office until 5:00 A.M., finishing up their work and watching live online as people opened their invitations and registered for membership, slowly but surely. It was incredibly encouraging. We knew we were asking something unprecedented, at least as far as e-commerce went: we wanted our customers to register for membership, and to give their personal information, to a site they wouldn't be able to see and inspect first, a site that wasn't selling anything yet. At the very beginning, we counted on the personal entreaties we'd made to motivate people to sign up (and we had also published on our site the names of the designers we'd secured for our first four sales: Zac Posen, Alvin Valley, Judith Ripka, and Rachel Roy).

But despite the hundreds of people who signed up for membership on that first night, it didn't take us long to realize, through feedback from friends and the underwhelming "open" rates we had access to, that many of our e-mail invitations must be going straight into spam folders. We had *not* anticipated this problem, and it was highly stressful. We had to think and act fast.

Phong quickly began to brainstorm alternative delivery tactics so that e-mail from Gilt Groupe would not end up in spam folders. While he figured out a more permanent solution, he decided that one way to get people to receive our e-mails *now* was to send them from our personal e-mail accounts. So in the days before the Zac Posen sale, we began furiously firing off a new round of e-mails from our personal accounts, instead of from the Gilt Groupe servers, explaining the concept of Gilt Groupe and inviting friends to join and spread the word. In these e-mails, we included personal invitation links (like gilt.com/alexandra and gilt.com/alexis). Again, these links reinforced the fact that the invitation was coming from a trusted friend and was not spam.

Mike and Phong continued to work on other ways to elude customers' spam filters. "We had to quickly build up infrastructure to separate out the IP addresses," explains Mike. "We decided to send the invitation e-mails out over one channel (or IP address, as it's technically called). The normal, daily stuff—e-mails about various sales—would go out on a different channel." In other words, by separating the two types of e-mails, we ensured that customers who placed orders would not risk having their purchase confirmations sent to spam folders. As Mike explains, "We started breaking things down so spam would not affect *all* of our e-mails." Phong also worked on white-listing the IP addresses of our mail servers so that different e-mail providers, from Gmail to Hotmail to Yahoo, would approve the gilt.com servers as legitimate mailers and deliver our e-mails to customers' in-boxes. White-listing—think of it as the opposite of blacklisting—is an unscientific process. Either you build up your reputation as a company so that these e-mail systems recognize your legitimacy over time, or you personally approach each of the different e-mail providers one by one to ask them to accept your mailings. Either way, it takes time.

In addition to working on our spam issues, we hit the pavement to sign up more members. Alexandra became obsessed with blanketing the city with flyers for Gilt. She darted in her sneakers up and down Fifth Avenue from the Upper East Side to our Flatiron offices, shamelessly distributing a flyer to every woman who looked as if she might vaguely fit our target demographic (young, professional, time-starved, style-conscious). Every time she worked out at the Equinox on East Eighty-fifth Street, she'd leave a stack of flyers in the women's locker room. She also stacked them in five-star hotel bathrooms around midtown and in the fitting rooms of designer boutiques. Once she even hit a Billion Dollar Babes sale to hand out Gilt Groupe invitations to the women walking out with the most overstuffed totes!

When either of us was invited to a brunch or a friend's birthday dinner, we'd bring along a stack of paper invitations for Gilt Groupe, and we'd also e-mail invitations to the CC list. Throughout the fall of 2007, most of our friends probably received the invite at least several times. And just as we'd hoped, they told *their* friends. Guerrilla marketing tactics, as they're known, effectively help spread the word to identifiable clusters of interested consumers and galvanize word of mouth.

Our last-minute push and the thousands of personal e-mails we sent ensured that our invitations actually reached potential customers and ended up making the invitations doubly potent. By the end of November the two of us had personally sent almost twenty thousand e-mails inviting people to join Gilt.

And by the date of our first sale, despite the challenges, we'd managed to sign up thirteen thousand people as registered members. It was fewer than the twenty thousand we'd hoped for, and we admit we were a little disappointed. But most of these people had come from our personal networks.

In hindsight, the number wasn't so bad!

CHAPTER 9

THE GROUND GAME:

Insider Marketing and How to Keep
a Growing Business Exclusive

Valentino may be the undisputed star of Matt Tyrnauer's "Valentino: The Last Emperor," but the designer had stiff competition for the spotlight at the documentary's New York premiere at MoMA on Tuesday night. Madonna, Gwyneth Paltrow, Martha Stewart, Blythe Danner, Anne Hathaway, Claire Danes and Hugh Dancy were just some of the A-listers on hand for the Gilt Groupe and Quintessentially-sponsored evening, which included a sit down dinner at the Oak Room of the Plaza Hotel.

—*WOMEN'S WEAR DAILY*, MARCH 19, 2009

Things were going better than we ever expected. We managed to beat Gilt's future competitors to market by launching in a swift four months. Just as Alexis and Kevin began taking meetings with venture capitalists, we staged our membership drive and signed up our initial thirteen thousand members; less than two weeks later, we hosted our hugely successful inaugural Zac Posen sale, selling a stunning $9,565 worth of merchandise.

Throughout November, Gilt racked up more successes: on November 19 we hosted our second sale, of Alvin Valley pants, tops, and suiting, which also produced exciting traffic. Next came Judith Ripka, an undoubtedly riskier event, since Judith's jewelry had higher price points and seemed like something our customers might want to see and inspect before purchasing. It was Alexandra who insisted we sell fine jewelry on Gilt, because she knew from her days at Bulgari that it was a high-selling category on QVC and HSN. While Judith's wares sold more slowly than Zac's or Alvin's, they still sold, and it was exciting to see customers buying eighteen-karat gold online!

By early 2008 we'd managed to accrue more than twenty thousand members just by tapping our own networks and the hundreds of preexisting groups we found online. But our Matrix funding would allow us to take our viral marketing campaign to a whole new level. Even the largest networks—and ours were large—are finite. To keep a viral business growing, you eventually need to seed new nodes, turning new geographies and other people's large networks into self-sustaining hubs from which information about your business spreads to additional circles of friends.

Our own networks were concentrated in New York, Boston, San Francisco, and Miami. Perhaps because of the East Coast concentration of our friends and acquaintances, we'd also managed to attract a lot of members in New York's spillover cities, like Washington, D.C., and Philadelphia. In certain other important locations—Los Angeles, to name a big one—we didn't know as many people and hadn't managed to create much buzz with our initial membership efforts. As yet we hadn't seen the proportion of purchases coming from L.A. that you would expect from a luxury site. This was troubling; we knew women in L.A. would love Gilt's sales.

To reach these women (and eventually men), we needed to tap into others' networks. We needed to actively find and meet people like ourselves in L.A., Chicago, Dallas, Atlanta, and other key cities and get them talking about Gilt to all their friends. And we knew it would take more than sending out lots of e-mails to make this happen. We needed a ground game, a political term Alexis liked to use that meant we'd be adopting grassroots tactics to spread our message. By borrowing lessons Alexis had learned at eBay and calling upon our own instincts and experiences, we crafted a plan to infiltrate local markets one by one—to reach on-the-ground groups of people our referral invitations could not.

If our viral campaign had so far been akin to a runaway weed, spreading outward from our networks to convert thousands of people in other cities whom we'd never met, we thought about the next phase of our marketing campaign as creating carefully planned, self-sustaining local ecosystems. Within these ecosystems, news of Gilt would take hold and propogate, fed by word-of-mouth referrals from influential tastemakers and the chatter generated by our exciting sales.

Seeding these local ecosystems would involve:

- Targeting underrepresented geographies

- Reaching out to relevant tastemakers (mostly females in their late twenties to early forties) and partnering with them to discerningly tap their networks

- Creating newsworthy yet cost-effective events

- Attracting local print, TV, radio, and blog attention, using our event as a hook

- Returning to the market within a period of months to keep the buzz going

We knew it wouldn't have necessarily helped us all that much to take our message to a mall in South Dakota. Instead, we needed to identify the geographies, locations, and groups of people most relevant to our brand, to size up the strongest metropolitan areas for fashion, where plenty of women already aspired to own cutting-edge designer brands like Alexander Wang and 3.1 Phillip Lim and were predisposed to be interested in our business. As a bonus, we knew that buzz marketing in urban areas naturally spreads to surrounding suburbs. When a group of friends starts chatting about a cool new concept in San Francisco, it's likely to catch fire and spread throughout Berkeley, Palo Alto, and Marin County and maybe even throughout neighboring cities like San Jose. When it comes to viral marketing, focusing on cities is usually a great way to get more bang for your buck.

We prioritized urban markets where we had yet to establish a foothold, as well as those where we expected any local competitors to emerge. For example, we already had a strong presence in Boston. We'd both lived there for years, through college and grad school. We had generated healthy membership numbers and were well positioned to leverage the Harvard communities. Normally, we wouldn't have focused on Boston because Gilt was doing well there. But we'd heard that SmartBargains, a different type of online designer discounter, was in the midst of changing its business model to compete with us more directly; it would soon rebrand itself as Rue La La. As a local Boston company Rue La La surely had its own strong local networks and would attract local press and goodwill once it launched. This immediately made Boston a higher priority for us. We had to cement the loyalty of our existing members and attract new ones before Rue La La made an impression.

Then there were cities like L.A., where Gilt had yet to really make a splash. Celebrity culture has made Los Angeles a very important city for fashion, as red carpets and tabloid weeklies disproportionately influence what Americans buy and wear, as well as increase their awareness of celebrated new brands. While Chicagoans certainly like to shop and may influence many smaller midwestern cities, trends that start in L.A., even more than those originating in New York, inevitably spread throughout the country. We knew that failure to gain a foothold in and around Hollywood would be a major setback for our business.

Word had also reached us that one of our competitors, Haute-

Look, was gearing up for a launch. Its founder had close ties to L.A. and the garment industry, and we knew our personal networks couldn't compete with those of an entire L.A.-based team. Similarly to Boston, this made the city an even higher priority.

Working with our small but growing marketing and communications teams, we developed a detailed plan that we repeated in each important market. Instead of just searching for women who were interested in fashion, we aimed to discover the true influencers, or mavens, most likely to tell others about Gilt Groupe, the social fixtures who knew broad swaths of local men and women. These tastemakers would become essential parts of the local ecosystem, sharing membership links or local event invitations in a highly targeted manner and helping the news take on a life of its own.

To encourage these tastemakers to engage with the Gilt Groupe and support us, we needed to meet them in person. We'd fly to each city and host a series of pressworthy events, perhaps movie screenings or fashion shows, followed by cocktails and a party, or perhaps even a dinner. We'd offer something hard to access, like an early screening of a fashion-themed movie like *The September Issue* or a fashion show. We'd invite some of the local tastemakers to join us on the host committee. We knew it was important that Gilt be associated with excitement—both online and off—and what better way to spark buzz than to find the local movers and shakers, throw a glamorous party, and ask our well-connected cohosts to invite all their friends? (While such events are common in New York, they are much more unusual, and therefore buzzworthy, in smaller cities.) Gilt would debut in high style, its name embossed on a sought-after invitation alongside names of the most well-respected, recognizable local influencers, the people everyone wanted to know. This would lend instant credibility and a feeling of exclusivity to our event and by extension our site. Not unlike on Gilt itself, invitees would feel special, chosen, and in the know. Tastemakers would, we hoped, leave the event primed to let all their friends in on the secret of the Internet's most exclusive new sample sale. Gilt's name would start to have stand-alone cachet and luxury currency in its own right, independent of its high-end brands.

In each city, we'd also meet with bloggers because they are natural viral marketers who pride themselves on being quick with information and disseminating it to their readers. We wanted them to be enthusiastic about Gilt and to help us build loyalty by posting regularly about our upcoming sales. In any viral marketing campaign, it's important to reach people more than once—preferably again and again, with new information each time. Customers need to have a reason to *continue* e-mailing, visiting the site, and talking about your business. Bloggers would help ensure that their readers—by nature a savvy, self-selecting group already interested in fashion—received breathless news about Gilt's specific amazing sales on a consistent basis. They would augment the work of our local tastemakers on the ground, each component of the ecosystem supporting and feeding the others. A tastemaker who'd attended our event might later read about an upcoming Gilt sale on a local fashion blog and be more likely to repost the news to her Facebook page or even send an e-mail or a text to friends.

The initial buzz generated by bloggers and by tastemakers chattering about Gilt to their friends would also be reinforced by local media attention surrounding our event, such as online pictures of our exclusive party. In some cities, our PR team would secure local TV appearances for us; we'd get the chance to speak on-air about Gilt, and we usually offered viewers a limited window of time to join the site, which we explained was members-only. A potential customer who heard about Gilt from a friend and *also* read about the site on her favorite blog and *also* saw it mentioned on a morning show was much more likely to sign on and become a member than someone who just saw us on the morning show. Hearing about Gilt from multiple trusted sources would help prospective customers remember the brand and feel inclined to register and support us.

To help reinforce our initial buzz, we knew we needed to keep the excitement and blog chatter consistent over several months—to keep anticipation high for Gilt sales and to give people newer and fresher reasons to tell their friends about us. We decided to return to each city a few months after our first visit to host yet another event, being careful to keep our new contacts warm in the interim. Our follow-up event would ratchet up the excitement around our brand and promote the sense among tastemakers that Gilt was an exclusive, though friendly and appealing, club of fashion insiders that brought them access to unique local events. They'd learn that Gilt was consistently in the vanguard, whether granting access to high-end designer brands like Vera Wang and Thakoon or exclusive events they'd never otherwise get to attend locally. In fashion and other arenas, we'd reinforce that we had the inside track. Over time Gilt itself would become the tastemaker, our brand shorthand for the well-connected friend everyone wanted to hang out with and to whom everyone looked to for VIP access.

After one event, we'd be on to the next. As we look back now, it feels as though we spent a year on airplanes, darting from one city to another, with barely a moment to catch our breaths!

SMASHBOX, SCIENTOLOGISTS, AND THE CHATEAU MARMONT: GILT GROUPE HITS LOS ANGELES

In March 2008 we kicked off our elaborate national grassroots push by sponsoring L.A. Fashion Week at Smashbox Studios in Culver City. As we mentioned, L.A. was a critical market for us; we wanted to make an impression before HauteLook got off the ground (by late

2007 HauteLook's home page said "Coming Soon"). While L.A.'s Fashion Week wasn't nearly as widely recognized or well attended by the fashion industry as New York's or Paris's, it was exciting to the city itself and attended by local fashionistas—a weeklong bonanza of parties, celebrity sightings, and photo ops that seemed fresh and notable.

In addition to local fashion shows, our L.A. PR team arranged for us to host an after-party for Whitley Kros, an up-and-coming young design duo comprised of Marissa Ribisi—wife of the singer Beck— and her friend Sophia Banks. The designers were firmly entrenched in the L.A. scene and had attracted the attention of a small but loyal cadre of celebrities; they'd also been described as "ones to watch" by *WWD*. Clearly, they were influencers in both the local fashion and Hollywood scenes.

Unfortunately, we didn't know in advance that many in their crowd were Scientologists who didn't drink alcohol. So on the evening of Gilt Groupe's first glitzy party, as we sipped champagne and worked the room, we noticed that almost everyone else was drinking water. But the event attracted plenty of celebrities, including Erika Christensen, Juliette Lewis, and Jenna Elfman, and garnered attention on local blogs. Gilt didn't exactly make the cover of *Los Angeles Magazine*, but we were encouraged.

And though we didn't understand its inner workings the way we do today, we both liked the energy and sunshine of L.A. We spent time getting to know Booth Moore, a well-known fashion writer for the *Los Angeles Times*, and met several influential bloggers. We enjoyed buzz in the press around our sponsorship of L.A. Fashion Week and, more important, introduced ourselves to tons of people who seemed excited to hear about Gilt. Some had even heard of the site already!

By the time we caught our plane back to New York, we were exhausted but exhilarated. (Of course, from the vantage point of the press machine that Gilt has become, this whole trip seems a quaint memory.)

Over the next year and a half, we perfected our formula, hosting dozens of events in key cities across the nation. Critical to this push was Christian Leone, a former vice president of public relations at Giorgio Armani who joined the Gilt team in June 2008. Christian, who now reports directly to Alexandra as vice president of brand relations, was a maven writ large, universally adored in the fashion industry and astoundingly well connected in nearly every key city we targeted. After our own networks had become tapped out, Christian joined Gilt with a fresh perspective and a huge Rolodex of friends and business relationships across the country. In Chicago, Christian's hometown, we arranged a screening of the movie *The Duchess*, followed by an after-party at the James, a hip hotel, cohosted by Christian's friends. In Dallas we hosted a screening of *Bride Wars*, followed by a cocktail party at the Joule Hotel that he packed with Dallas It girls who were his friends or friends of his friends. Christian always knew the right people to call, whether we were in L.A. or Dallas, or even on Nantucket, and inevitably got these local tastemakers excited to introduce Gilt to their friends.

Each event we hosted tended to fuse elements of Gilt's brand— excitement, timeliness, luxury—with a local feel, to help make the site seem like an intimate club. In Atlanta, Candi Naboicheck, our beloved events director, enlisted nightlife guru Bevy Smith, a larger-than-life local TV personality and exclusive dinner party host, to help us throw one of her Dinners with Bevy at Spice Market at the W Hotel, attracting a group of influencers that spanned television, music, and fashion, including music industry types like Bryan-Michael Cox, Sean Garrett, and Keri Hilson.

We always dressed to the nines for our events, wearing pieces we'd bought right off our site. Because the crowd would inevitably be attractive and meticulously styled in the latest designers, both high and low, we wanted to project the right image for Gilt—stylish, savvy, exclusive, yet also approachable. How better to do so than by wearing our own merchandise? Did we mention we were (and still are) Gilt shoppers?

The culmination of more than a year's worth of events took place right at home in New York City, where we hosted a premiere at the Museum of Modern Art (MoMA) in March 2009 for the much-discussed fashion biopic *Valentino: The Last Emperor*, followed by a dinner at the Oak Room at the Plaza Hotel. We partnered with Matt Tyrnauer, the *Vanity Fair* editor who'd directed the Valentino documentary. And thanks to Christian Leone's powerful connections, we managed to attract an A-list group that included not just socialites and fashion designers but Hollywood A-listers like Gwyneth Paltrow, Anne Hathaway, and Claire Danes. Anna Wintour also attended the screening and sat directly behind us.

As we entered the Plaza greeting a seemingly endless parade of our brand partners, customers, and supporters, we suddenly saw Candi, our events director, and our public relations manager Amanda Graber waving frantically for our attention.

Madonna had shown up, all but unannounced! And . . . we had no seat for her.

The seating arrangements for dinner had been painstakingly finalized days prior, and there were no more seats at Mr. Valentino's table. Luckily, no one had yet sat down to eat, so Candi and Amanda scrambled to squeeze another seat in anyway, *discreetly*, between Mr. Valentino's and Gwyneth Paltrow's. Let's just say that table looked very cozy.

Toward the end of the night, we bumped into Madonna and Gwyneth as they were being escorted out of the Oak Room by Giancarlo Giammetti, Mr. Valentino's longtime business partner. "Would you be so kind as to take a photo with us?" Alexandra inquired of Madonna. Clearly tired and ready to go home, Madonna started to make a face. That's when Alexandra added that we were the cofounders of Gilt Groupe and that we had sponsored the screening and dinner. The Material Girl's face lifted. "Well, in that case, sure!" she said.

In the photo, we are smiling widely: Madonna, Gwyneth Paltrow, Mr. Giammetti, and us.

The ultimate goal of our grassroots campaign was to build not just buzz but lasting trust in our brand by building trust in *us*, Alexis and Alexandra. Before launching Gilt we'd agreed, at Kevin's suggestion, to put ourselves forward as the faces of the business. We'd even discussed this over that fateful dinner the three of us shared at DB Bistro Moderne before Alexandra officially joined the team. We'd all noticed that vente-privee's e-mails were sent by a fictitious character named Cecile de Rostand. How fortuitous that Gilt had two very *real* women at the helm, who were relatable and accessible and who shared the tastes and passions of our customers. We could speak to our members and potential members directly and genuinely, without having to invent characters. And in doing so, we hoped we could also forge a much more personal bond with our shoppers than other e-commerce sites—most of which were run by middle-aged men— had managed to forge with theirs.

We knew that putting ourselves "out there" in the press would have its downfalls—we'd have to undergo media training, for one, and be subject to increased scrutiny. It would also be a huge investment of time. But all three of us knew that increasing A&A's visibility would help us personalize and build trust in the brand. Gilt wouldn't be remote or aloof, a faceless corporate behemoth like most online retailers. Instead, it would have a friendly human face, despite being a brand most customers interact with only via their computers.

As we started hosting events, our strategy seemed to be validated. After meeting one or both of us or attending an event we sponsored, members generally increased their activity on our site. Even if we didn't immediately see a dramatic spike in spending, we noticed that these customers stayed with us longer, shopped more over time, and invited more of their friends to join. Over the years, they became our loyal advocates—our teams on the ground, so to speak. We believe that this is partly because we're two young females. We were easy for our members to relate to. Not unlike the instinct to "buy American," our members seemed to like supporting a business helmed by approachable female entrepreneurs, and best friends to boot. They actively wanted us to succeed. After all, we weren't that different from most of them.

Whenever and wherever we traveled, we invited loyal shoppers to join us for coffee or a meal. Over time, we became friends with hundreds of our customers. We were careful to follow up after each trip with personal e-mails or handwritten notes to many of the bloggers, tastemakers, members, and even potential local brand partners we'd met in our travels.

To introduce ourselves to our thousands (now millions) of members we'd never actually get the chance to meet in person, we also put ourselves "out there" on the Gilt site by making our bios and e-mails available online. From the beginning, we personally answered as many e-mails from members as we possibly could. In January 2008, we began sending the daily e-mails alerting our members to sales from an account bearing our names. We thought this would help us speak directly to our customers—to create a sense of personal connection that is too often lost online. We wanted to personalize our business and to make customers feel that we were the ones curating the sales, just for them (and we often were!). We even started a blog that highlighted our personal "picks" from the day's sales. And beginning in January 2008, we included in each Gilt package a note (written in gold script) thanking our member for his or her purchase and signed "Alexis & Alexandra, the Founders."

The more we put ourselves out there, the more members felt personally connected to the company. We became almost proxies for the brand—two friends with insider access to deals and tips. We took pains to stay versed in other subjects of interest to our members, because they often asked us for restaurant recommendations, hotel ideas, and even reading suggestions. They looked to us to help sift through the overload of information, brands, and services out there. Becoming tastemakers ourselves was key not just to branding Gilt, but to helping us develop real authority in the marketplace and eventually expand into new categories. When we introduced a new brand members hadn't yet encountered, they were more willing to give that brand a chance because we were suggesting it. They trusted not only our integrity, but our sense of style. Gilt sales that had an element of service or advice—for example, suggestions for layering pieces or weekend wear—were (and are) some of our most popular.

In late 2009 we even designed a special category for our most loyal customers: Gilt Noir. Constituting the top Gilt shoppers on the basis of dollars spent and duration of membership, Noir members receive special early access to preview our sales. While they can't actually purchase anything before noon eastern time, they can troll the sale's offerings fifteen minutes in advance and strategize to beat others to any marquee items likely to sell out fast. Noir members are also given access to special sales not available to other members (for example, an exclusive sale of pieces by the acclaimed brand Rodarte). If Gilt is an invite-only club, Noir is a doubly exclusive group: a secret, private back room. We regularly host intimate dinners all over the country for Noir members, which make them feel even more like valued friends to us and of the Gilt brand.

When we started meeting our Gilt Noir members, we were surprised that they would rarely ask about when we'd sell a certain brand. Instead, we'd find ourselves peppered with questions about who we were and how we had started Gilt. Our customers never ceased to amaze us: They were accomplished, intelligent, cultured men and women, often career professionals. They were lawyers on international tribunals in The Hague focusing on the genocide in Rwanda, the head of the SCUD missile program during the Reagan era, or the top defibrillator implant surgeon in Florida (yes, these are actual Gilt customers. The latter even inspired us to create our successful iPhone and iPad apps so that she could run out of the operating room during a break, add items to her cart, quickly press "buy," then run back in—sterilized, of course).

Again, we noticed that after we directly interacted with these members, their spending increased over time, as they transitioned from fashionistas shopping their favorite designers' collections to "friends" with a personal interest in our success. We were careful to provide these shoppers with even more meticulous and personal levels of customer service.

These tactics helped Gilt maintain its intimate, exclusive feel, even as the site grew exponentially.

CHAPTER 10

CUBICLES, CAPPUCCINOS, AND HOW WE BUILT AN EFFECTIVE START-UP TEAM

> If you want to work for Gilt, [Alexandra Wilkis] Wilson says she hires people "who have a fire in their belly, a passion, a lot of joie de vivre," along with a stellar résumé and will work, enthusiastically, more than a nine-to-five workday, which pretty much all Gilt employees do.
> —*NEW YORK MAGAZINE*, OCTOBER 26, 2010

When we look back now, it seems we spent much of late 2007 and early 2008 camped out at Tarallucci e Vino, an adorable little Italian café on East Eighteenth Street, near Union Square, interviewing a steady stream of candidates for the long list of jobs we were trying to fill. The Matrix deal had made it possible to add to Gilt's team in a way that would have been previously unthinkable. Suddenly we were hunting down the top talent in the market to fill critical positions, a task we took very seriously (and still do).

Our small but committed team was putting in long hours at the office getting Gilt off the ground. Alexis, Alexandra, Mike, and Phong had become a surrogate family. The four of us were completely invested in Gilt. We ate, breathed, slept it. The start-up environment was truly all-consuming. Hunched over our computers, we feasted on Mexican food from Uncle Moe's and salads from the deli around the corner. Even Alexandra, who was so scarred by three years of investment banking that she insisted on going home to eat dinner each night with her husband, later picked up right where she'd left off, at home on her laptop.

We were always dashing to meetings, firing off e-mails from cabs, leaving frantic messages for one another at all times of the day and night.

When we did sleep, we often found ourselves awakening in the night with ideas about how to grow our membership or the name of some long-forgotten acquaintance who could put us in touch with a key designer. Our friends (at least most of them) assumed we'd dropped off the face of the earth. They stopped asking what we were doing on the weekends.

Luckily, unusual among start-up teams, we never bickered. From the start the four of us trusted one another and valued one another's expertise, all of which was different and vital to our success; none of us was above pitching in to do whatever was necessary for the good of the business. It wasn't easy to imagine working with anyone who didn't share this level of dedication.

Yet we desperately needed more bodies. And one of the main advantages of being part of a business in its infancy is getting to choose exactly with whom we'd spend our days in the office (because they'd clearly be long). Alexis, in particular, had always loved the challenge of hiring, of thinking about the personalities around her and what types of people might best complement preexisting team members. We now had the chance to shape our team from the bottom up. We'd get to create, one person at a time, the kind of culture we wanted at Gilt Groupe.

We knew that one way to make everyone feel like an owner—in other words, as invested as we were—was to *make* everyone an owner. So we decided to give all new hires options in the company. In addition to ownership in the business, we wanted new employees to feel ownership over their own projects and initiatives and to let them help shape our company culture and values. During the hours we spent at

Tarallucci that fall, we drew on some of the lessons Alexis had learned from Simon Rothman of eBay, a truly masterful judge of talent and her longtime mentor. Simon had always ensured that new hires meet as many members of a team as possible during the interview process. This helped the team feel empowered to shape the group and, more important, caused members to feel a joint responsibility for that individual's success. Simon even had juniors assess potential seniors and peers assess peers. In Simon's mind, getting these people on board with a hiring decision was important because they would be *especially* critical to the new individual's success.

As we brought on new people, we insisted Mike and Phong help interview buyers, that Alexandra meet young engineering talent. Then we'd all compare notes. We wanted to make sure new hires had not just the skills but the personalities that would fit with our small group and the corporate culture we were establishing. We figured that if we all were excited about each new addition, we'd be predisposed to help him or her succeed. Alexis, who has no tolerance for office politics, especially wanted to vet out people that would not meld with the team or, worse, stir up problems that could cause unnecessary inefficiencies and waste time. Mike and Phong, too, vetted for personal fit and ethics before even digging too deeply into an engineer's skills, and were involved in almost all key hires at the beginning, just as we were involved in key engineering hires. Phong, an introvert by nature, always had a great read on job candidates, from their interests to their values. As a result, he became our office "radar," the person we relied on to identify personality fits above any other.

As we met person after person, we tried to get a sense not just of the candidate's experience but of the candidate as an individual: what types of people she liked to work with, what type of environment she most thrived in, how she would go about building a team to complement her own strengths and weaknesses. It was always revealing to compare an interviewee's answers with the information we gathered checking references (self-awareness and the so-called emotional intelligence quotient were always important to us).

We were especially careful to find new employees we thought would be well suited to a start-up environment. Unlike in a more established corporate office, roles in a start-up inevitably change over time, sometimes very quickly (at Gilt, they sometimes changed once or twice a year). Gilt needed people who were flexible and adaptable. We were always completely blunt in stressing to applicants that they'd have to wear multiple hats, that their jobs would change, and that on paper the scopes of their responsibilities would even appear to narrow over time, though they would actually take on more responsibility (in terms of people or budget managed, for example). This is true of any role in a growing company, but particularly true when the company is growing fast.

During Alexis's time at eBay, the company had grown from forty to four thousand people. While it was obviously succeeding beyond anyone's wildest hopes, she'd seen many people on the early team become disgruntled with the narrowing of their roles, or fight against more layers being added to the organization and their perceived decrease in responsibility; these people eventually left or found themselves replaced. It was one reason Alexis was eager to manage expectations out of the gate at Gilt and to attract people who would continuously seek new opportunities to thrive—in other words, enjoy the wild ride ahead. Replacing an individual, especially when the business is growing rapidly, is incredibly costly, so it's always best to manage prospective employees' expectations up-front, and let them choose if they are ready to embrace a company's pace of growth. We'll be the first to admit that growing a business from the start-up phase is not for everyone, and this is OK. But it's better to discover this in the interview process than a year into a person's tenure. We wanted agile, adaptable, multitalented coworkers who would be comfortable taking on new roles as we grew and expanded, people who could be happy and effective building teams from scratch but also strong enough to run larger teams and meet larger targets.

We also didn't want to have to replicate the hiring process again and again as the business grew. In Gilt's first year, we eventually hired one hundred people, most of whom at least one of us (Alexis, Alexandra, Mike, or Phong) personally interviewed. So if you assume we met three to five people for each position, we spent a *lot* of time recruiting. We wanted to bring on board a set of people who could grow with the organization, not hire one set of employees for one stage of growth only to be forced to hire a different type of employee at a later stage. This is a common mistake start-ups make, one that destroys cultures, morale, and momentum. It's more cost-effective to invest in optimizing your hiring practices from the beginning than to flush out early stage employees in order to hire a more "mature" team. (We're happy to say that today most of our key initial hires remain with the company in roles of importance, even as our team balloons to more than nine hundred people. In fact, eleven of Gilt's first fifteen employees remain integral to the company.)

One of our most important hires in the fall of 2007 was Leah Park, who had had a long tenure at Bergdorf Goodman's magazine. Leah came on board to be our creative director, a position she holds to this day. We'd been searching for a couple of months for a real creative talent to elevate our visual branding, which is so crucial to attracting both brand partners and customers. As much as we both loved fashion, our early photo shoots had forced us to admit we were far more adept with spreadsheets than with aesthetics. At one of our first shoots for Alvin Valley, we didn't even get around to hiring a clothing stylist; we figured we could just style the looks ourselves. This left us to hem seams, iron clothes, and even pin pieces on the model to make sure they fit. It was a nightmare, and clearly we were not the best suited to these tasks. Phong, meanwhile, served as

the photo technician for the shoot. Although we marveled at his flexibility and ingenuity, this was *not* the most efficient use of his time!

That was why we were incredibly relieved when we found Leah—
or rather, Leah found us. She contacted us through our Web site to
say she was looking for a new challenge, loved our business concept,
and was impressed by the team we'd assembled. Alexis met her late
on a Friday afternoon in our office on West Nineteenth Street and immediately insisted that the rest of the team drop everything and interview her as well. Her portfolio, her passion for our concept, and her
ideas for elevating the branding and creative elements of the Web site
blew us all away. Leah was talented yet humble, and even better, she
seemed truly passionate about joining the crazy world of a start-up.
She was also the type that looked equally stylish in Manolos and
Chuck Taylors—an effortlessly chic fashion savant.

For Leah, the creative elements of the site came easy, and when
she started at Gilt, she got to work radically elevating the site's visuals. She banished the key from our logo, proclaiming it cheesy. She
also fidgeted with the font, adjusting the color, adding increased shad-
owing, and streamlining and simplifying it. The changes themselves
weren't dramatic, but the cumulative impact was shocking.

She also took the photography up several notches. Leah was intimately familiar with the level of editorial photography we'd been trying to achieve with our non–art school backgrounds. Though Gilt's
limited budgets were a major adjustment for her, coming from Bergdorf's, she knew exactly where to find good photographers and how
to produce a shoot. She created visual and style guides for our shoots
and brought on top photography and styling talent—at prices palat-
able to a start-up, purely through her personal relationships. Sasha
Pflaeging, our first and principal photographer, began working with
us through Leah and today remains a member of the team (later he
shot Alexis's wedding).

At first, it was hard for Leah to churn out the volume of pictures we needed. Her freelancers (photographers, stylists, hair and makeup) were not used to shooting more than a few "looks," or images, per day (at fashion magazines, creating three or four pictures often takes a good twelve hours). Leah began by shooting twenty or thirty looks per day for Gilt, which she thought was amazing. "This is three times more than we've ever done!" she'd say. But for us, it wasn't enough. "Can't you just add a few more?" we'd ask. "And a few more?" The creative team members didn't think in terms of pricing efficiencies, the way people from finance backgrounds did; they wanted first and foremost to put forth the most beautiful work possible. But if we were going to shoot every item we sold on the site ourselves, we had to come up with a more efficient way to do it. And *fast*.

It didn't take long for Leah to speed things up to a level beyond even her wildest expectations without compromising quality. Within six months she'd managed to bring conveyor belt efficiency to high-end photography and, in the process, almost single-handedly revolutionized the look of e-commerce. Soon our brand partners were calling to ask for the names of certain models or photographers we'd used, and some even tried to buy the images we took of their merchandise for their seasonal "look books." Competitors started trying to secure the same models and photographers. Over time, Gilt's well-oiled photography machine grew to its present productivity of about sixteen shoots per day, with photo teams occupying eight studios on double shifts and turning out sixty "looks"—and about 180 images for the site—per shoot. These days, of course, our photographers down at Brooklyn's Navy Yard might be shooting ready-to-wear by Helmut Lang, coffeemakers by Bodum, or a vegan zucchini loaf being offered by BabyCakes NYC. Regardless of the product, we believe Gilt's photos are still the best on the Web, and as competitors flooded the market, they remained a key differentiator. We owe a lot of this to Leah.

But she didn't just concern herself with our Web site visuals. In elevating Gilt's visual branding, Leah considered even seemingly minor details like our business cards. "The most important thing is presentation," Leah now explains, "*especially* when you first build a business. That's where you want to put your investment. If you have a semi-nice business card and you're all about luxury, that's a huge problem. Even if you haven't yet tapped the luxury market, you want to make sure your business card is amazing, and to spend money on things that will affect people's first impressions of you." And so our flimsy gray business cards with images of three-dimensional keys were swapped out for dark, heavy cardstock with shiny gold print. "It was important that everything we did be about projecting fashion and luxury and exclusivity," Leah explains. When building a brand, everything the consumer sees matters, from site visuals to business cards, packaging, and e-mails from customer support. Leah understood that no detail was unimportant.

One distinct hiring challenge we faced from the beginning, and that many start-ups face, was building our engineering team. As technical cofounders, Mike and Phong were critical to attracting other world-class engineering talent to our team. Once you have one outstanding engineer, you can more easily find others. Talented engineers tend to travel in packs.

So if you have a great business idea, how do you find an engineer to help you realize it?

"Hang out at MIT?" suggests Mike with a laugh. And while he's half-joking, he does have a point: Go where the engineers are. Urban tech meet-ups, conferences, and events at engineering grad schools are great places to network with engineers. Another strategy is to develop an informal "engineering board," or a person or group of accomplished engineers you know and respect. Ask these people for recommendations or for help vetting candidates.

Beyond that, "when you're starting a company, the most important thing is probably leadership and charisma," says Mike. "Think
about engineers as creative people. What you really need to do is
build a culture where people believe they're part of building something great and are empowered to do what's best for the business and
the idea."

The possibility of being tasked with very challenging problems is
one of the best hiring carrots you can dangle in front of an engineer.
At Gilt, we were building something from scratch, which was exciting. Although the business model itself was quite simple, the site was
actually quite complex, since so much of our business takes place in
the same ninety minutes each day. We needed an engineering team
that could tackle the challenge of growing our technological infrastructure to the size of Amazon's for roughly an hour and a half
beginning at noon, when two hundred thousand women might try
simultaneously to buy the exact same shoe. This was a traffic issue not
unlike the ones that have plagued Twitter, a site that has suffered outages when news or world events cause hundreds of thousands of people to tweet at the same time. Rather than investing in more server
hardware, Gilt's engineers would have to take advantage of cloud
technology.

Many people ask us, and Mike and Phong, if they should out-
source their engineering needs. To them we say: "Is engineering core
to your business?" If you're selling handmade paperweights largely
through stationery stores and all you need is a Web site, then the
answer is probably no. But for an e-commerce business like Gilt, engineering is no secondary concern. That the site be fast, trustworthy,
and compelling is of paramount importance. Also, as Phong notes,
"The code will be written much better by someone on staff—who's
going to need to maintain it—than by someone who knows they're going to work on it for two months and then that's it, they don't have to
see it anymore."

Mike and Phong developed some smart ways to make Gilt appeal to top engineers—and to keep them happy. Some of these tactics can be used to hire talented employees in any department.

---

checklist:
GILT'S TECHNICAL COFOUNDERS, MIKE AND PHONG, ON HOW TO HIRE AND RETAIN TOP ENGINEERS

1. PRESCREEN. Mike and Phong developed a one-hour written test for developers (it's still online at Gilt.com/tech) to help make the interview process more efficient. Candidates completed the test before being invited to the office to interview. The goal was to assess speed, experience, and technical skill, but also to find "people who were honest enough to say 'You know what? I have no idea what's going on there,'" says Mike. "That was a big part of it."

2. HIRE FOR CULTURAL FIT, NOT JUST TALENT. "I remember lots of times I'd meet someone I knew could do the job, but they weren't quite somebody I'd want to hang out with at night or on the weekends," says Mike. "We made a lot of decisions to pass on people who could have solved problems and made the next three months better. We waited to meet people who could make the next two, three *years* better." Adds Phong, "When I was interviewing, I approached it as fifty-fifty in terms of how good they were technically and how well I got along with them."

3. CREATE AN EXTERNALLY VISIBLE TECHNOLOGY BRAND. In attracting top engineers, it's important that Gilt be seen as a place where top engineers already work, solving exciting and relevant problems. "We needed to sponsor and speak at the right conferences," explains Mike. The Gilt engineering department even started a tech blog, *Gilt Technologie*, that helps highlight the quality of engineers already employed and showcase the challenging tasks they are undertaking in their work. "Over time, that shifted the types of people who were applying to Gilt," says Mike. "They were coming because they were excited about the kinds of things we were doing . . . [they were] learning that people at Gilt were really smart, and wanting to work with smart people."

4. FIND CREATIVE WAYS TO GET TOP TALENT TO YOUR OFFICE.
"The best engineers are never looking for jobs," says Mike. "Most have never interviewed in their lives." Sometimes, it helps to lure them to the office by inviting them to give a talk or to just come meet some of the Gilt engineers. When Mike and Phong set their sights on an engineer known for his mobile apps (they first met him at the Apple Worldwide Developers Conference), they invited him to come "hang out and meet some of the team," recalls Mike. "He had no idea he was coming to interview. He was just chatting with people. And by the end of the day he figured out, 'Hey, wait a minute. . . '" This engineer is now a key developer at Gilt.

5. GIVE THEM TIME TO CREATE. Or, as Mike says, "take every obstacle out of their way." At Gilt, this has meant regular hackathons (one was even covered by CNN) during which engineers can work for hours without interruption and devote time to a product that they're interested in developing.*

Note from Alexis and Alexandra: We've noticed that free food is also extremely effective in motivating engineers. When, in a cost-cutting measure, Gilt eliminated free sodas in favor of a vending machine, we practically had a riot on our hands. The free sodas have since been reinstated.

At a daylong off-site meeting Alexis arranged in early 2008 with an executive coach named Barry Carden, we discovered that our initial team was weighted heavily toward similar Myers-Briggs personality types: extroverts and intuitive thinkers. (Myers-Briggs is a tool that classifies individuals by personality type and helps them understand more about the ways they prefer to use their perception and judgment. How do they work? How do they experience the world? Analyzing these preferences can be highly valuable to managers and coworkers.) While extroversion and intuition are common in entrepreneurs and others who join start-ups, it's also true that people tend to unconsciously connect with and prefer others like themselves. We discovered that for the most part we had hired people just like our founding team. *Uh-oh.* This meant that we lacked balance. Alexis, Mike, Alexandra, and Kevin were all similar Meyers-Briggs types, which signaled a problem. Aside from Phong, our lone introvert, the others we'd hired were also just like us. Barry encouraged us to actively seek out someone who made fewer judgments based on gut instinct and questioned the validity of new ideas, instead of just loving each one more than the last. Perhaps this person would be even a bit more of an introvert or a quiet listener.

It was this feedback that led us to Jennifer Carr-Smith, who became our chief operating officer (COO) in spring 2008. An experienced operator and taskmaster, she'd worked at Polo Ralph Lauren and Drugstore.com and brought much-needed experience (and a focus on processes, operational infrastructure, and the bottom line) to an idealistic, creative team that was in general far more focused on growth and ideas than on implementing the systems we needed to help us realize them. It soon fell to Jennifer to impose infrastructure on our improvisational company.

We asked her why she took a chance on Gilt. "I was just so excited about the opportunity," she said. "I felt passionate about it. You have to be two hundred percent passionate about joining any start-up, because you're going to be there all the time.

"I felt good about the team"—she continued—"after we met for maybe the fourth time, I thought, OK, I have to do this, because they have all the other pieces in place and it's so obvious that I am the missing link.

"We had Mike running the site on his laptop," she recalled. "We had no process; we had no systems." JCS, as we called her, made an immediate impact, improving our operational efficiency and instituting processes. Take our RTVs (returns to vendor): "Until that point, if a piece of fine jewelry hadn't sold during a sale, getting it back to the vendor was a manual, logistical nightmare," recalled JCS. "We had no process in place. Hopefully, someone would eventually get around to plopping it in the mail" (fully insured, of course). JCS saw that this wouldn't do and developed a process, as she did for everything.

She also examined our operational practices in the warehouse and ensured that we were prepared for successive quarters of seismic growth. She implemented a human resources team and benefits. She built out our accounting systems. And she elevated our facilities and our office space. These things were all necessary, but we'd been so focused on growth that we hadn't paused to think about things like HR, even as we increased the pace of our hiring. Bringing on an experienced operator to handle these details, which Alexis tended not to gravitate to and weren't in Alexandra's tool chest, was a huge relief.

Of course, JCS faced plenty of challenges. "In that kind of start-up environment, everyone wants to make big changes quickly," she said. "I remember that Kevin always wanted to do things overnight. I had to be the one to say, 'Okay, I hear you and want to get you there, but we're running a *business* now. We can't do all those things immediately.'" JCS was detail-oriented and relied on experience and facts more than intuition. She brought a healthy dose of reality, and sometimes skepticism, to the abundance of new ideas that constantly streamed through our offices.

But while she brought a new set of skills to the table, Jennifer was also an amazing cultural fit; she naturally understood how to work with creative types whose jobs differed greatly from her own. "I so admire creative skill sets, and I made it a point to let everyone know that," she said. "That what they did was valuable, and I did *not* want to change that, just make it more efficient. I tried to put it in terms that mattered to them, like allowing them to be more creative, and to use their time on more fun things. This was actually very similar to the approach I took with Mike and the engineers."

———————

In January 2008 we moved into our first permanent office, an airy two-floor space on West Twentieth Street with lots of light that's now used by Jetsetter, our travel business. We were careful to maintain an open floor plan so we could sit in cubicles right in the center of the action. This way we'd all be approachable and partaking in the same energy as the rest of our team. Like a trading floor, there would be no hierarchy—no haves (those with offices) and have-nots (those without). Information would flow easily. And because our business was so far defined by growth and change, this would also prevent people from getting attached to their corner offices. They'd be more willing to move, and often, inasmuch as they'd just be trading one cubicle for another.

As new hires trickled into our office, we had fun observing the melting pot environment we were creating. Few, if any, of our employees had ever worked in an environment quite like Gilt's. We were at once a forward-thinking fashion *and* engineering company; we hired engineers from the best schools and tech start-ups and buyers from top department stores and fashion brands.

It didn't take the engineers long to figure out that their new coworkers would be a boon to hiring. Soon they were parading new recruits through the office to observe the scenery. "And here are the women in merchandising! And here we have PR!" Strangely, an excess of female team members walking around in five-inch heels seemed to help Gilt's engineers close the deal on some of their more promising recruits. When they noticed that Leah's team held model castings on Wednesday mornings in the office, they started scheduling interviews during that time so that prospective hires would walk into Gilt, come face-to-face with a parade of Amazonian models, and think, *this* is the place for me!

CHAPTER 11

IN WHICH WE FACE A SUPPLY CRUNCH, ARE MOMENTARILY TEMPTED TO COMPROMISE OUR INTEGRITY, STRUGGLE TO SATISFY THE APPETITES OF A GROWING MEMBERSHIP, AND COME FACE-TO-FACE WITH A WORLDWIDE RECESSION

> The concept seems tailored to recessionary times. Any guilt that consumers feel over spending thousands of dollars on unnecessary items can be replaced by bragging rights for finding a killer bargain, like a $4,500 diamond necklace that was recently on sale for $2,250 at Gilt.
> —*THE NEW YORK TIMES*, DECEMBER 6, 2009

Shortly after our launch, we were interviewed by a reporter for *The New York Times*'s *T Magazine*. We were excited that our first print coverage would be in a venerable and respected publication based in Gilt's hometown. The journalist was lovely, and she seemed to ask all the right questions; we waited excitedly for the story. But it never appeared, and we never found out why. That was a huge disappointment. For a while we wondered if we'd *ever* get media coverage. Fashion glossies, perhaps scared by how their advertisers would react to an off-price luxury fashion site, seemed to be avoiding us.

A few months later, another New York paper came calling: our trusty, salacious local tabloid, the *New York Post*. We gamely showed up for a photo shoot in our offices but were alarmed to see both of us had chosen animal print ensembles for the occasion. How mortifying! We feared we'd look like two blondes lost in the Serengeti, one of us in a black and white Alessandro Dell'Acqua giraffe print jacket, the other in a leopard print Alvin Valley blouse—two Janes of the urban jungle! When the piece appeared on January 8, 2008, the headline read FUROR OVER FASHION "FIXERS." (Luckily, the frocks weren't *too* frightening.) We still remember exactly what the piece said because it was so on point: "Gilt is the Soho House of sample sales. If you are not signed up, you cannot attend. And it takes a friend or a friend of a friend to get you on the list." This initial coverage opened the floodgates, and we were soon contacted by dozens of print and broadcast media outlets that had hesitated to feature Gilt Groupe. Our local events helped galvanize this coverage. Appearing more often in the media helped reinforce our word-of-mouth efforts, keeping Gilt top of mind for savvy shoppers and encouraging them to tell more of their friends.

You could say things were going a little *too* well. We were about to face our first supply crunch.

Although Alexandra had had much success convincing highly coveted designers to sell on our site, and more were signing on as they recognized the clear marketing benefits, we quickly learned that few of these brands had enough extra inventory lying around to satisfy our growing membership. Many of our early brand partners, for all their buzz and acclaim, were still small businesses. Also, at the time brands as a rule sought to limit the excess inventory they produced, meaning we were dependent on their margins of error. We were unable to predict how much product would be available in the coming months. For a fast-growing business, we didn't exactly have a reliable supply chain, and this was scary.

Meanwhile we hadn't placed a limit on how many members we'd

accept or on how many friends each member could invite to join. As early as January we heard from devoted customers who logged onto the site promptly at noon eastern time, only to be beaten to the items they wanted to buy—repeatedly. "This is frustrating," they wrote to us in e-mails. "Do you really have inventory?" Some scarcity was essential to our business model because it helped create that sense of competition and excitement and drove members to our site at the same time each day, reinforcing the notion of appointment shopping. We confess we almost hoped that new members might get beaten to a choice purchase once or twice because this way, when they eventually did land a coveted item, they'd feel even more exhilarated and triumphant (and be more likely to make Gilt part of their daily routine). But if a member was beaten three or four times, she might just get frustrated and possibly give up, never again to return to Gilt. She was supposed to be an *insider*, after all. What good was membership in an exclusive club if it provided no special advantage?

The customers who were actually buying meanwhile had become incredibly good at it, to the point that new members were truly at a disadvantage. On the one hand, this only increased the thrill of gamesmanship that our best customers felt, the sense that they'd beaten others to a rare, incredible bargain. But we didn't want this to come at the expense of acquiring new customers.

Mike and Phong tried to make some small technical changes to buy us time while we sourced new inventory. A month after we launched, they responded to customer feedback and added a shopping cart feature that allowed shoppers to exclusively reserve an item for ten minutes before purchasing it (our initial shopping cart function didn't actually reserve an item, meaning dozens of members could place the same item in their carts, each thinking she'd be able to purchase it, only to find it sold out while she continued shopping). We also added a policy that allowed members to receive free shipping on items they purchased within an hour of one another; that way, they wouldn't feel pressure to do all their shopping before their ten-minute cart limit expired. We wanted to promote gamesmanship, but it was essential that Gilt be a game in which one could actually triumph, at least some of the time, with a little skill and savvy. We wanted members to feel the rush that comes from gambling and winning and *not* that the deck was stacked against them.

While Alexis spent time spearheading our marketing and the viral growth of our membership, Alexandra, as our chief merchandising officer, spent the first months of 2008 trying to bring on brand partners who could potentially provide larger volumes of product—the Tory Burches, Kate Spades, and Diane von Furstenbergs of the world.

In February, Alexis left the office to spend a week for her father's seventy-fifth birthday in Patagonia, completely out of cell phone range. The timing wasn't ideal—our start-up was less than eight months old, and she was CEO—but Alexis's loyalty to her family and her total confidence in Alexandra and the team had persuaded her to make the trip. Even when working around the clock, Alexis had always been incredibly calm as a leader, never sweating the small stuff. She had a healthy dose of perspective at all times. And things were going so well at Gilt that it seemed unnecessary to put off celebrating with her father. This was one of the benefits of having partners she truly trusted. Surely Alexandra, with Mike and Phong, could hold the fort down for a week.

Alexandra was—and is—more high-strung than Alexis, so she found Alexis's trip mildly stressful. But she told herself hopefully that nothing would go wrong.

Naturally, it was during this week that Giovanni Cafiso, who was in charge of ready-to-wear sales at Valentino at the time, called Alexandra. Through helpful introductions, she'd been carefully cultivating a relationship with executives at Valentino, one of her favorite brands, for months but had yet to convince them to sell on Gilt. Now

Giovanni wanted to talk. Thrilled to hear his voice, Alexandra, who had been leaving for work and was still in her apartment building's lobby, stopped dead in her tracks and sat down on a bench. The connection was bad, but she remembers the conversation vividly. Giovanni explained that he had a large volume of Valentino inventory—about two hundred and fifty thousand dollars' worth—bound for Loehmann's, one of the brand's then regular liquidators. He was willing to offer it to Gilt instead, on the condition that we provide a cash commitment instead of our preferred consignment agreement, in which we essentially borrowed the clothes or jewelry, paid for only what members bought, and returned whatever wasn't purchased. "You need to tell me within one hour if you want it," said Giovanni. "*All* of it. Otherwise, it goes to Loehmann's."

Alexandra was speechless.

Nowadays two hundred and fifty thousand dollars' worth of merchandise isn't a particularly noteworthy haul for Gilt. But at the time Alexandra could only think, oh . . . my . . . God. We'd sold seventy-five thousand dollars' worth in single sales only a couple of times in December—still impressive, considering that we had just over thirty thousand members (our early members were obviously die-hard shoppers). Two hundred and fifty thousand dollars' worth of merchandise would be a huge amount of inventory for us. Even with our membership increasing daily, would we really be able to sell it?

Furthermore, Alexandra and her two buyers usually cherry-picked all the items we sold on Gilt. We never took *every* item a brand wanted to liquidate, just every item we thought our members would love. We approached the art of buying like department store buyers, except that we weren't usually working with current-season merchandise. We had to photograph all the items we featured, and that was expensive because we had such high-quality production, using top photographers and ready-to-wear models. So if we didn't think we could make a profit on a given style, it wasn't worth the investment to photograph it.

Even when we'd occasionally paid up front, we'd at least hand-picked all the items ourselves. But Giovanni was adamant that we could have all or nothing. We were a young company and preferred not to take on that kind of financial risk. But Alexandra knew that this made it hard to compete with Loehmann's and other liquidators, who could take *everything*. She also knew that once we sold Valentino, other European luxury houses were sure to follow or at the very least take a meeting to learn more about Gilt Groupe. This was important because we didn't want to attract only New York–based designers. We needed big, desirable international brands with plenty of devoted fans and large volumes of inventory. Valentino was the most illustrious brand we'd yet been offered, a globally recognizable European house with a rich heritage in couture and a robust celebrity following. It would make our members feel even more excited and privileged.

Alexandra's mind was spinning. How could she pass this up?

She dialed Alexis's cell phone in vain. Voice mail. She knew there was no chance Alexis would receive an e-mail—even a desperate one—within the hour either.

Still sitting on the bench in her lobby, Alexandra frantically called one of our buyers to run the deal by her. The buyer expressed deep reservations about the fact that we wouldn't even be able to *see* the inventory before committing to buy. What if it was too "piecey"? Gilt didn't want to be stuck with a large volume of merchandise containing just one or two items in each style; this would increase our photography costs per item, destroy our margins, and possibly leave *us* with excess inventory that we'd need to somehow liquidate. Alexandra admitted that Giovanni had offered very little information whatsoever on the merchandise. The buyer said, essentially, "How can we commit to this then? This is ridiculous."

Alexandra knew she was right; it *was* ridiculous. But her gut told her to buy it anyway.

With minutes to go before her allotted hour expired, Alexandra called Giovanni. "Yes," she said, adrenaline surging through her body. "We'll take it."

When they arrived, the clothes—beautiful gowns, cocktail dresses, coats, jackets, and suits—were gorgeous, and Alexandra's fears immediately dissipated. Many of the looks were from Valentino's last collection for the fashion house that bears his name and had even been sashayed down the runway during the showing of his final collection. They were so plentiful that we parceled them out and sold them over several sales in the spring and fall of 2008. These sales were a wild, smashing success for Gilt Groupe, in terms of both revenues and, more important, branding. As Alexandra had predicted, the merchandise was gobbled up by our excited members. She was relieved she hadn't underestimated their shopping prowess.

The Valentino sales also provided loud, definitive proof that we could move a *lot* more product if only we could gain access to more quality inventory. But how to open up our supply chain?

Alexandra redoubled her efforts to reach larger brands with devoted followings. Diane von Furstenberg, a quintessential New York designer whose famously flattering wrap dress, conceived in the seventies, was enjoying new heights of popularity, had been on Alexandra's radar for months. DVF hosted popular brick-and-mortar sample sales in New York that lasted for days and inevitably attracted lines snaking around several city blocks. We'd been attending these sales for years and had observed up close the enthusiasm and loyalty the brand inspired. We also guessed that these sample sales must divert a lot of resources, even for a mid-size company. Even if they weren't persuaded by the marketing angle, we hoped DVF executives would agree that selling on Gilt would be easier and more cost effective.

Alexandra had sent several e-mails to a couple of executives at DVF but had received little response. This was probably because she had no solid contacts there and was essentially cold calling. Then, early in 2008, she was surprised to notice a DVF sale on Haute-Look, a flash sale site that had gained a foothold selling mostly contemporary—or more mass-market—brands and denim. Alexandra could hardly believe it! Wouldn't DVF prefer to sell in the company of our impressive brand partners? For many high-end brands, this had been the first question: who else is selling with you? This was one of the most important tenets of retail after all: location, location, location. It's why brands paid top dollar for space on Fifth Avenue, near Tiffany and Bergdorf Goodman. We'd assumed this maxim would apply to Gilt as well.

When Alexandra finally succeeded in arranging a meeting with DVF executives, they were tough: They explained that all our competitors had paid them visits and that they'd agreed to sell with Haute-Look because they believed that site's customer was less likely to already shop in the DVF stores. DVF was far less expensive than Valentino after all—a wrap dress usually retails for a little more than three hundred dollars—and the brand's executives worried that by selling on Gilt to upwardly mobile urbanites who might otherwise be able to afford to pay retail, they'd cannibalize their own business. At least their brick-and-mortar sample sales were localized, rewarding and energizing loyal New York customers without making bargains available all over the country.

Their concerns were surprising, and ones we hadn't yet heard. For the first time, a brand saw our savvy, style-conscious members as a *problem*, not as an appeal. Alexandra listened carefully but put forth her own (persuasive, she hoped) rebuttal: that selling on Gilt only enhanced customer demand for a brand, both online and in retail stores. In addition to creating a day of pandemonium around our brand partners, we funneled excess merchandise directly to the kind of customer DVF wanted to attract: well connected, brand conscious, affluent. It's possible many weren't yet loyal DVF customers, but they would be after triumphantly scoring their first pieces on Gilt. Our sales might just help whet a customer's appetite for the brand—especially because unlike brands like Dolce & Gabbana, DVF *was* attainable to her at full price.

Then there was the fact that our membership was larger; we could move more merchandise than our competitors.

Eventually, with persistence and assurances, Alexandra managed to prevail over the DVF team. In late February, April Uchitel, vice president of global sales at the time, called and said, "OK, how much can you absorb?" The brand was adamant about being as discreet as possible and insisted that we not publicize the sale to any media outlets. It was fine with our members gaining access to the deals, but it didn't want the entire Internet buzzing about them. Alexandra readily agreed. Then she gave our buyer explicit instructions to buy as much inventory as she possibly could. We needed to prove to DVF that we could handle serious volume. We offered to take fifteen hundred units of apparel, a huge amount for us at the time.

When the sale went up in March 2008, we achieved over 96 percent sell-through in total, meaning we sold almost every item. We sold more than a thousand pieces within the first hour alone, tremendous for us. We immediately wished we'd bought even more!

We were so excited by the sale that we quickly forgot our promise not to publicize it to the press. In an interview with the *Wall Street Journal*, Alexandra accidentally mentioned a DVF statistic when the journalist pressured her for details on some of our most successful sales to date. In hindsight, this was understandable; she wanted Gilt to look as good as possible, and the name just slipped. But the DVF team was justifiably upset to read about its Gilt sale in the *Journal*.

It didn't help when it discovered that our HR team had also included DVF in job descriptions posted to our Web site, as in "Gilt

Groupe sells high-end brands from Doo.Ri to Diane von Fursten-berg." *Oops.* Alexandra had forgotten to stipulate internally to our recruiters that DVF wouldn't want to be mentioned in this way. We promptly apologized and assured the brand it wouldn't happen again.

THE VIEW DOUBLES GILT'S MEMBERSHIP OVERNIGHT

In early March 2008, our team got a call from Michael Fazio, who runs a well-known luxury concierge in New York for both hotels and private clients and is the author of the book *Concierge Confidential*. Michael was also a frequent guest on *The View*, where he discussed topics pertaining to style and luxury. He was calling to ask if we'd mind if he mentioned Gilt in an upcoming *View* segment. Obviously, we were thrilled and immediately consented. Our public relations team even offered to provide a special link viewers could use to become members, gilt.com/theview. We figured the segment might attract a few thousand new members.

We had *no* idea.

Alexandra recently asked Michael why he had approached us. "First of all," he said, "when Gilt started, I had the same envy that I had about Gmail. As in, how'd you get that?' I really had to work to get my invite to Gilt. Such brilliant branding, in hindsight. And I really thought *members only* meant you wouldn't even want to do it! You seemed so quiet, exclusive, and under the radar. When you agreed to provide a link for viewers, I thought, oh, my God, I got Gilt! As a concierge, it felt like the biggest coup. Like I'd scored an inside table at Union Square Café."

On the day of the segment we sent over some Dolce & Gabbana pieces and an ostrich jacket by Alessandro Dell'Acqua that had the unfortunate habit of shedding feathers everywhere. Michael recalls that backstage *The View*'s cohosts "treated your merchandise like a sample sale! They were like 'Let me see that. What is in that box?'"

The segment was brief, but Michael showed off our merchandise and excitedly discussed Gilt with the show's cohosts. Then he revealed that all of the day's viewers were invited to sign on and become members, and our link flashed on the screen.

In the next twenty-four hours, *fifty thousand* people signed up to become members, doubling our membership overnight. A previous television segment in Philadelphia had brought us ten thousand new members, so it's safe to say we were totally unprepared for the power of national TV. To this day, *The View* remains the most impactful media segment in Gilt's history.

Alexis remembers being in our Brooklyn warehouse with Mike that day, preparing for a possible uptick in orders and ensuring that nothing went awry. After Michael Fazio had finished talking, we stopped what we were doing, leaned into Mike's laptop, and watched, stunned, as Gilt's membership numbers ticked higher. They climbed by two thousand, four thousand, and then ten thousand. They kept climbing. And with them came the sales. Orders were streaming in at a dizzying rate, and the servers were having trouble keeping up with them all; they were beginning to falter under the pressure of so many surfers, members, and new customers inundating the site. After a moment of slow-motion disbelief, Mike (who, in addition to engineering, was still leading the charge on warehouse logistics) lurched into overdrive, hacking away at his laptop to address the sluggish service our new customers were experiencing as a result of this onslaught. Alexis meanwhile worked to get the logistics team ready for its largest day ever of outbound orders.

Ultimately, we did *not* manage to box all of the day's purchases by the end of the day, as had always been our goal; we didn't even succeed in packaging them by the end of the following day. Clearly, we had warehouse capacity issues to address. But our brief mention on

The View had offered more solid proof of shoppers' passionate interest in our site.

But it was a bittersweet triumph. The next morning in the office we felt mainly stress, even a bit of terror. With our team, we now had to produce enough inventory to satisfy the demands of fifty thousand new members.

WHY WE TURNED DOWN ACRES OF AMAZING EUROPEAN DESIGNER CLOTHES— AND FELT GREAT ABOUT IT

That spring Alexandra faced another tough supply challenge that was to have far-reaching implications for our inventory but would also help define who we are as a company. Just before leaving New York to attend a trade show in L.A. with one of our buyers, Alexandra got a call from a man who said he worked for a company that we will call Club Sunset. Let's call him Angelo. He said he had current-season merchandise from several top European fashion houses that he could offer at an amazing price. Intrigued but slightly nervous, Alexandra agreed to pay him a visit while she was in L.A.

Needless to say, this sidetracked her and the buyer from attending the trade show. After landing at LAX, they spent a day and a half combing through Angelo's warehouse in downtown L.A., riveted. The selection was astounding: in-season, brand-spanking-new merchandise from Dolce & Gabbana, Missoni, and Valentino, all with impressive depth (in other words, a wide range of sizes and units in each style). Angelo transported the ladies via videoconference to his larger warehouse in Italy, where they saw hundreds of rolling racks stocked with thousands more luxury pieces. All current. All clearly authentic. All with tags. All capable of fetching thousands of dollars in department stores or boutiques. Alexandra's mouth was watering.

Especially after Angelo offered to let us have our pick of this bounty, at *85 percent off retail*. Alexandra had been negotiating directly with executives at Dolce & Gabbana about buying merchandise that was a year older, for a price closer to 75 percent off retail. Angelo's offer seemed too good to be true.

But while Alexandra was momentarily tempted to scoop up as much product as she could, she couldn't ignore the bad feeling in her gut. Where did Angelo get this incredible selection?

In her previous jobs at Louis Vuitton and Bulgari, she'd never been exposed to the murkier underbelly of retail and to the elusive characters commonly known as jobbers. Our buyer, who hailed from the discount world and knew its intricacies well, had to explain to Alexandra that jobbers are sometimes shady middlemen who operate in the margins between brands and discounters. You're never quite sure where they get their inventory. Usually, the story is something like "My sister's husband's uncle owns a warehouse in Italy and is best friends with one of the Ferragamos," or "My brother has an agreement with Roberto Cavalli to take on merchandise that doesn't sell." The tales are convoluted but slightly believable at the same time.

All Alexandra knew was that the merchandise was obviously authentic and that our customers probably wouldn't care where it came from, as long as it was real.

"I'm working with all your competitors," Angelo assured her. She didn't doubt that he was. "Come on," he urged her. "Let's make a deal."

Alexandra called Alexis in New York. "I wish you were here to see this," she whispered into the phone. Alexis listened as Alexandra attempted to describe the quality and quantity of the merchandise all around her. It seemed she'd stumbled upon a pot of gold at the end of the rainbow—the solution to all of Gilt's problems. The brands we were working with just didn't have anywhere near this kind of extra volume. Their product was rare and specialized; that was part of its appeal. We'd been buying as much as we could, and it would disappear almost immediately when the clock struck twelve, leaving frustrated members in its wake. We were in a race against time to find more product for our members, and *fast*.

Angelo seemed like an easy solution and one that our competitors had obviously taken advantage of. Would we be able to compete in the rapidly evolving landscape of online luxury retail if we didn't follow suit?

On the phone with Alexis, Alexandra shared her excitement but also her hesitation. Alexis too had the thought, this doesn't make sense. She didn't have a good feeling about the situation. Like Alexandra, she doubted the legitimacy of the product and its origins. How had he obtained the items?

Alexandra left L.A., telling Angelo she'd be in touch. When she returned to New York, we had one more conversation about it, reviewing details of Angelo's amazing merchandise. But we were in total agreement that the situation was suspect. We placed a very high value on the trust we had built with our customers and our brand partners. We wanted to build real, long-term relationships with brands, not go behind their backs for short-term infusions of inventory. Buying Missoni out of a suspicious warehouse in L.A. was *not* our vision of how we'd work with one of the most exclusive brands in the world. From the start, we'd aspired to make Gilt Groupe exciting and captivating and to develop a reputation that would make top brands proud to sell on our site. "If anything went wrong," Alexis said, "would we want this information on the front page of *The New York Times*?" We both knew emphatically that the answer to this question was no.

Over the next few months Angelo and other jobbers called us occasionally to check in, each time offering deals that sounded even more amazing. Although we saw much of this inventory appear on competitors' sites, we knew we'd preserved our integrity and taken the long-term strategic view; that made it easier to turn them down. The incident had forced us to clearly define how we'd conduct business as a company. We'd drawn a line: the only way we'd ever *consider* working with a third party was if we had written consent from the brand itself. Sure, this decision certainly made things harder for us as a fast-growing young company that was crunched for supply of products. But we've never once regretted it. Our brands and customers respect the fact that we have integrity as a company and that Gilt is directly authorized to sell everything on our site by the brands themselves.

After we turned down Angelo's offer, we had Leah Park and our in-house counsel create a seal of authenticity that we now display alongside every item we feature for sale:

Authenticity Guaranteed:
We guarantee that Gilt is authorized to sell this product.
Every brand that we sell is the label it promises to be.

But since we weren't taking jobbers like Angelo up on their offers of inventory, we had to find other solutions. Our board meetings, which were held every two months, typical for a start-up, were celebratory but also increasingly tense. On the one hand, Alexis was constantly upping our revenue goals for the year. "Nick, Kevin, I know we projected six million dollars," she'd say, "but I'm now raising that estimate by three million." Delighted yet startled, Nick and Kevin would urge her to be careful about overpromising. Nick wasn't accustomed to CEOs *raising* revenue estimates, especially during a business's first few months. But as a viral business we had grown quickly with very little expenditure. Our marketing was so highly efficient that we'd get one customer and he or she would quickly bring us five more. Toward the end of our first year, we raised our original revenue estimate more than fourfold and exceeded even this projection. But our inventory problems were only getting worse.

We began to examine every inch of our supply chain. Our business model had been designed to purchase brands' leftovers. But what if we bought earlier in the production cycle? Where were the links in the supply chain where we could potentially get our hands on more product? We didn't want to always be dependent on the booms and busts of the marketplace or to be left dry in months like August, when there is little excess inventory to buy.

We started reaching out to brands to try to buy into their current-season merchandise—in other words, place our order at the same time as department stores and full-price retailers. We figured that this would help brands drive their costs down (because manufacturers typically charge less per unit for larger orders). We were right: many brands were eager to work with us as more of a partner, instead of just giving us their excess inventory. We promised not to sell their merchandise at deep markdowns until it had been put on sale on the department store floors.

But buying at the beginning of the season was not the same as buying leftovers. For one thing, we were not able to secure nearly as big a discount off the wholesale price. Merchandise produced specifically *for* us, rather than products taken off designers' hands at the end of the season (at which point they were essentially sunk costs), was just never going to be as cheap.

We knew we were making ourselves slightly vulnerable because placing our orders six or nine months in advance didn't exactly allow us to be nimble or to anticipate changes in fashion trends or in our membership growth. We'd even start having leftovers of our own to liquidate, in "final" sales, at even steeper discounts (luckily, our members loved these sales).

We also began discussions with certain brands about the possibility of producing capsule collections exclusively for Gilt. This would guarantee our brand partners more orders, allowing them to meet factory minimums, drive down their costs, and increase their margins.

Some of the earliest brands that agreed to work with us on capsule collections were some of our most exciting emerging designers—Doo.Ri and Behnaz Sarafpour, for example.

While these capsule collections actually decreased *our* margins, they allowed us to build a more perfect supply, because we could buy more intelligently for our members, specifying exactly the number of size sixes we wanted or taking into consideration the fact that our members showed a preference for specific silhouettes, materials, colors, and prices (for example, our sweet spot for a contemporary dress was around one hundred dollars). We'd no longer have to rely exclusively on the end-of-season inventory; now we could actively shape our supply to meet our customers' preferences. Gilt's forward-thinking solutions to our supply problem laid the groundwork for the company's rapid growth.

LURING MEN TO FASHION E-COMMERCE

In the summer of 2008 we started selling children's products and home goods. But we also gained a whole new audience of shoppers to buy for: *men*. Our initial plans had called for us to break into the men's business a year or so after our launch, but it quickly became clear that was too slow. Ever since Gilt had launched, we'd had male members, mostly friends and friends of friends we'd attracted through our own networks or spouses of the tastemakers and devoted shoppers we'd wooed in other cities. Most had signed up to check out the site, assuming we'd eventually sell men's clothing. But a few months into our existence these men were growing impatient. They were receiving our daily e-mails, but there was never anything for them to buy. We got a slew of personal e-mails from male friends; our customer support e-mails also registered complaints: "When will you sell to dudes? If you're not planning to, I'm going to unsubscribe." The opportunity to buy gifts for the women in their life was evidently not enough to keep them interested.

But our board remained unconvinced. At one meeting early in the year, while we could sense the *teensiest* bit of excitement in the room—Nick and Kevin might soon be able to shop for themselves on Gilt!—we remember hearing doubts about whether we were really just targeting women by branching out into men's and if we expected the bulk of our sales to come from female members buying for their boyfriends and husbands. We didn't think so, but who was to say? We knew that stores' e-commerce sites, like Brooks Brothers', probably sold 50 percent of their merchandise to women. But we also couldn't ignore the surprising number of young twenty- and thirtysomething men who were practically heckling us to offer sales for them. There must have been many more who hadn't taken the trouble of personally e-mailing us. Perhaps young men were just bored with brick-and-mortar retail or had never taken to it in the first place, and no one had yet thought to cater to them online. If department store Web sites overwhelmed women with their choices, we could only imagine what they were like for men.

Besides, there was as yet no competition in the men's category. If we were able to lure large numbers of men to Gilt, we knew we'd have them all to ourselves.

John Auerbach, then our director of finance, raised his hand and offered to spearhead Gilt's men's merchandising, working under Alexandra. (He later became general manager of Gilt Man.) Fortunately, pitching Gilt to men's brands was very different from pitching it to women's. Many of the men's brands were more receptive and open-minded from the get-go. (Also, the fact that we were already selling women's fashion paved the way for our men's business.) It turned out that reaching male consumers in their twenties and thirties was also one of the hardest things for a brand to do. For men, shopping had never been a pastime or a communal activity with friends, as it was for women. In general, they weren't as motivated by new trends, and they definitely didn't want to look as though they spent a lot of time getting ready to go out. Retailers had traditionally relied on magazines like *GQ* and *Details* to reach target male demographics. But it was hard to gauge the effectiveness of this advertising.

The first men's brand we sold, in April 2008, was John Varvatos, whose rock-and-roll branding is so thorough that the company even took over the legendary New York music club CBGB and turned it into a flagship store. By the time of our Varvatos sale John Auerbach had also lined up brands like Trovata, Earnest Sewn, Diesel, Dolce & Gabbana, and Rag & Bone. In advance of the men's launch, we e-mailed members to alert them of our new men's tab and mentioned it in a few TV appearances and newspaper and magazine interviews. Because our team was stretched so thin already launching new businesses and solving our inventory problems, we decided to make the rollout of our men's category a soft launch and focus on a larger marketing campaign later.

But on the day of the John Varvatos sale, our fledgling men's business announced its potential loud and clear. We achieved an astonishing *97 percent* sell-through rate. Almost every single piece we'd featured sold! Men immediately approved of our model. It made sense. All the things women loved about our site were even more likely to appeal to men: our selections were well edited; we presented six great choices, not six hundred mediocre ones. We required almost no patience or time investment. Like a very stylish friend, wife, or girlfriend, Gilt told men what to buy, except we made it easy for them to do so from their desks, without wasting time in a store. Rather than a trend-driven business, we emphasized practicality: on Gilt, men could get all their shopping done in under ten minutes.

Our subsequent men's sales were equally successful. And even more astonishing than how fast they sold out was that an average of 75 percent of purchases were made by men themselves (over time this climbed to more than 90 percent). Clearly men had been gunning to shop for clothing online, like they already shopped for electronics, and just hadn't found a compelling place to do so before Gilt.

We learned over time that men, even more than women, were drawn to the gamesmanship of Gilt. They loved winning an item on the site even more than they loved the discount. Alexandra's husband, Kevin, would call her from the trading floor at the bank where he worked to comment from time to time on how Gilt was popping up on screens all around him.

Four years later Gilt Man is a daily online lifestyle destination for millions of men.

THE RETAIL APOCALYPSE AND HOW GILT CAME TO THE RESCUE

As we grew rapidly throughout 2008, a storm was brewing in the background. When we'd launched in 2007, the luxury business was still booming. But as Gilt grew, the American economy started to do the opposite.

September 15, 2008, was an incredibly dramatic day in New York City. The financial firm Lehman Brothers filed for Chapter 11 in the largest bankruptcy filing in American history. Meanwhile, Merrill Lynch, Alexandra's former employer, sold itself to Bank of America in order to avert the same fate. We knew these events would have deep implications for New York City, for the fashion and retail industries, and for Americans in general. We wondered, How would this impact our nation, our customers, our business, and our investors? Even though our prices were great, fewer people would probably want to shop when the economy was crumbling and everyone they knew was losing his or her job. August 2008 had been a slow month for Gilt, so we initially worried that this was a sign that our members were cutting back.

Throughout the fall each day's news seemed to be worse than the last. Friends lost their jobs; unemployment spiked. Soon after Lehman's collapse, *The New York Times* declared that "sales at the nation's largest retailers fell off a cliff." Luxury brands, department stores, and retailers right down to Gap started offering astonishing discounts earlier than ever in an effort to move merchandise they'd ordered in flusher times. We assumed this was bad news for us because these stores' aggressive discounts would put pressure on *our* discounts and margins too. The *Times* quoted industry analyst Marshal Cohen: "This is the year the consumer has been given a holiday gift beyond belief," he said. "You can get anything, anywhere, at any price."

We watched with concern as New York's fabled department stores and boutiques descended into chaos. Alexandra remembers vividly a picture texted to her by one of her best friends of the normally beautiful Saks shoe floor, 10022-SHOE, in utter disarray; actually, it looked as if it had been looted. "You'd think I was at Loehmann's," read the text. "But this is the shoe floor at Saks. I just bought several pairs of Louboutins at 80% off!" Brands were frustrated that these stores seemed to be discounting their merchandise practically as soon as it hit the floor, thereby diminishing the integrity of the brands' pricing structures and causing customers to question what any luxury good was actually *worth*.

Department stores across the country also started canceling orders left and right and issuing returns to vendor, forcing brands to take back merchandise they couldn't sell. Meanwhile smaller specialty stores went out of business at an alarming rate, further threatening our brand partners' fragile businesses. Morale in the industry was lower than we'd ever seen it. Designers were scared. On one occasion, we met with a high-end women's apparel partner in that brand's showroom in the dark—we can only assume it was because it hadn't paid the electric bill.

It was during this time that our phones started ringing off the hook.

We hadn't predicted the recession, but we'd inadvertently produced, in Gilt, the perfect solution for panicked brands. Soon buyers at Saks, Barneys, and Bergdorf Goodman were sending their beleaguered vendors our way, telling them, "Just call Gilt." Designers that had been saying no started giving us the green light; they had a lot of extra inventory on their books and were desperate to cut their losses. We were there and ready to support them.

On the Monday before Thanksgiving, Alexandra got a call from the manager of Allegra Hicks's Madison Avenue store. Allegra, a London designer popular with the celebrity and jet sets, was admired for her exquisite prints, caftans, and home furnishings. We'd sold her dresses a couple of times on Gilt, and the sales had done well. Now the manager was calling to inform Alexandra that the ten-year-old company was going "into administration" (we learned this was the British way of saying "out of business") and that the store would be closing *that Friday*. Would we like to buy its entire inventory?

Alexandra immediately grabbed one of our buyers, Katherine, and hailed a cab uptown. The store's home inventory—candles galore, trays with intricate handles and detailing, pastel-colored tabletop linens—was strewn in piles all over the space, and it was gorgeous. Alexandra and Katherine decided to buy it all on the spot. But since most of Gilt's team had already left the office for Thanksgiving, our warehouse was closed. Unable to think of any other solution, Alexandra and Katherine called the moving service The Man With A Van and soon found themselves helping two movers haul boxes of heavy candles, trays, and tablecloths to Alexandra's apartment. Never mind that Alexandra was scheduled to host family for Thanksgiving that year. Several days later, when her in-laws arrived, Alexandra's living room had a large Allegra Hicks section. But the candles smelled so good they didn't mind.

And so, as an entire industry teetered on the verge of collapse all around us, we were able to develop and cement new brand partner relationships by being there in a pinch to provide a welcome safety net. We literally helped some of our brands keep the lights on throughout that frightening fall. For others, we helped make the bottom lines a little less ruinous. Our supply problem evaporated almost overnight; there was more excess product flooding the market than we could even absorb.

And despite the dour economy and our slow August, our customers didn't slow down their buying one iota that fall. We had an incredible amount of pent-up customer demand that we were finally able to meet with an amazing lineup of new sales. Like most shoppers, Gilt members were increasingly obsessed with value and avoiding conspicuous consumption in the stores. And if Gilt represented a discreet way for brands to cut their losses, it was an equally discreet way for shoppers to spend money in a time when it was seen as gauche to stroll on Fifth Avenue or Madison Avenue with shopping bags (Kathy Fuld, wife of Lehman CEO Dick Fuld, was famously caught leaving Hermès with an unmarked shopping bag full of holiday purchases). Gilt was a way to take advantage of the fall's markdowns quietly, in the privacy of one's home or office.

As 2008 sputtered to an ignominious close, our first-year revenues climbed, as we'd predicted, to an astonishing twenty-five million dollars; that was *nineteen million* more than we'd put forth during our fund-raising process (bullishly, we'd thought). It made us wonder what our revenues could have been if we'd had more inventory available to us during our first eight months!

But underlying our relief at having (momentarily) solved our inventory problems was a deep fear about what the future would bring. We'd cemented important new relationships, yes, but we had a feeling that brands would cut back on production to shore up their businesses after a traumatic fall and winter, and that scared us. The retail supply chain would correct to reflect consumers' newly strapped bank accounts. Therefore, our new initiatives on capsule collections and beginning-of-season purchasing helped us prepare for an uncertain 2009.

Still, we were proud that throughout the great retail slump of 2008, the site generated much-needed energy and excitement for a depressed industry. Only on Gilt did shopping seem fun, and because of our amazing value, it wasn't anything to feel guilty about.

CHAPTER 12

HOW WE DEVELOPED OUR OWN LEADERSHIP STYLES— EVEN AS GILT GROUPE GREW AND OUR ROLES EVOLVED

Gilt Groupe Founders: The Most Powerful People In Fashion?
—*FORBES*, NOVEMBER 9, 2010

It was June 2008 when Alexis first started to feel just a little bit antsy. Her job as CEO had already changed a lot over the twelve months of Gilt's eventful existence. She'd spent most of her time hiring, managing, marketing, strategizing, and fund-raising. But Gilt was pushing seventy employees and on its way to closing out the year at twenty-five million dollars in revenue. Alexis's life had lately become a string of meetings, sometimes stretching from 9:00 A.M. to 9:00 P.M., all aimed at communicating messages to larger teams of people and hammering out the processes and logistics of this growth. She led discussions on operations and HR practices; she reviewed financial details and site release plans (the painstaking procedures we used to release new code to the Web site). And though she was at the center of a fast-growing business, she kind of felt as if she weren't actually *doing* anything—just sitting in meetings! Alexis knew in her gut that she enjoyed the creative, early stages of a business much more than its later stages, when emphasis necessarily shifts to the implementation of processes and controls.

Alexandra's job had changed too, but to a lesser extent. Though she was now managing a merchandising team of close to twenty-five, all of whom she'd personally interviewed and hired, she was still constantly traveling all over the world to meet with brands and designers, and she regularly experienced the thrill of closing the deal on a coveted new brand. She continued to be involved in the exciting work she'd been doing from day one.

Alexis, on the other hand, felt a slight but growing impatience with her role. She'd learned that launching a nimble start-up is very different from running a large business with many different teams and moving parts.

She couldn't exactly share her restlessness with colleagues at Gilt—not even Alexandra. As CEO you can't go up or down within your organization to seek advice. She did not want to discuss her restlessness with anyone until she was ready to make definitive changes, lest it cause uncertainty and anxiety in the organization. It was important she appear confident, strong, and in control for the benefit of her employees. And this was obviously not the type of conversation to have with one's board—at least until one is *ready* to have it.

It's been said that CEO is the loneliest job in the world. For certain quandaries Alexis faced—like managing a board of directors, or restructuring teams, or planning her own next step—she could get hard, unbiased advice only from impartial outsiders. She learned the importance of developing her own informal advisory board, a set of shrewd people in her life who could offer the best, most pertinent thoughts and feedback.

One helpful source of feedback was an organization called Creative Good, which brings together CEOs of high-growth businesses—all under $150 million in revenue—in noncompetitive industries. This allows the various CEOs to be blunt about the decisions they're facing. "I'm having a major problem with my board. Can I get your advice?" or "Is there any great software you've discovered that could help me solve this problem we're having?" In addition to two major daylong sessions annually, the organization facilitated regular phone calls that helped Alexis develop key outside sources of feedback, CEOs in similar positions at noncompetitive businesses she could consult when she faced specific decisions.

But that June Alexis called Simon Rothman, her longtime mentor. She knew that success could be addictive and that it was tempting to stay too long in a position because you thought you *should*, even if that position was no longer making you happy. Alexis knew that Simon would give her unbiased and reliable feedback and perspective.

Simon knew Alexis well; he knew what she loved to do and what she was good at. At eBay, he'd seen her excel in the adrenaline-fueled early stages of a business, when the pace of growth was fast but the company had not yet reached the point at which focus necessarily turns to fine-tuning processes. He knew she loved the conceptual stage and the getting-things-done stage—problem solving, idea generating, innovating, working closely with a nimble team, and pouring all her ingenuity and scrappiness into figuring out how to get a great idea off the ground. She wasn't a so-called steady-state leader, one who thrives on making slight changes that eke out small-margin impacts on a large business. The feeling of being in the trenches motivated her. She thrived on risk and uncertainty and adrenaline. She could be impatient with details.

Simon listened thoughtfully as Alexis explained how her role had changed at Gilt. He didn't mince words in telling her, essentially, "Alexis, you need to start thinking about how long you want to stay in this role."

Alexis wasn't surprised. She already knew, deep down, that Simon's words were true, and she started to think about her next move within the business.

TWO DIFFERENT PEOPLE, TWO
DIFFERENT LEADERS

The best managers and CEOs we've observed in action have had their own trademark leadership styles, ones that were both *natural* and effective. This is why, as Gilt has grown and we've taken on new roles and managed larger teams, we've tried above all to be authentic and consistent.

Though both of us are women and roughly the same age, our teams know that working for one of us is completely different from working for the other. As CEO of Gilt, Alexis was a free-thinking, dogged, big-picture problem solver; she motivated with *vision* (her team believed in her and wanted to join her for the ride). Alexandra has always been more meticulous, a fast-moving, detail-oriented executor with a sophisticated emotional radar; she motivated with *empathy* (her direct reports were inspired by her example, and her team knew she "saw" and cared about them).

Maybe it's because we felt so much pressure early in our careers to act a certain way that we feel so strongly that a good leader must be genuine and embrace the characteristics that make him or her *different*. We both started out in male-dominated work environments. Alexandra remembers, early in her tenure at Merrill Lynch in London, being filmed by a professional coach who had been hired to give the analysts constructive feedback. The coach, a woman, told Alexandra that she needed to use more masculine language and gestures in order to succeed in the business world. ("You roll your hands too much," she said. Also, "When you walk into a man's office, keep your communication simple and to the point. Men like to hear things in threes, so count your points off, 'One, two, three.'") And this was in 2001! Alexandra knew that the U.K. wasn't as politically correct as the United States, but she was still a little shocked.

As one of four women in her incoming class of analysts at

Alex.Brown, Alexis also felt pressure not to act too feminine or too young. She initially tried to dress as if she were thirty or forty to deflect attention from her age, wearing androgynous suits and putting her hair in a tight twist every day, as if a ponytail would cause her to be taken less seriously, making her appear younger and carefree.

But Alexis hadn't been at Alex.Brown for long when she had an aha! moment. For the eighth weekend in a row, a group of male analysts was organizing a game of touch football, and though they were discussing it loudly in the office, shouting across cubicles, no one offered her an invitation. This was particularly ironic, she thought, because she was the only Division I college athlete in the whole group. While she was doing everything right and her team liked her, it hit her that she was probably *never* going to be invited to that game of touch football.

If acting like a rough-and-tumble financier isn't going to make me more accepted, I might as well be myself and therefore different, she thought.

Alexis stopped taking cues from the people around her and learned to let her actual personal traits—femininity, directness, calm confidence, and yes, a dash of sportiness—shine through more at the office. To her delight, this got her much further than blending in ever had. After moving out of finance and into her time at eBay, she wore heels and let her hair down; she dressed her age, regardless of whom she'd be meeting or how many years younger she was than the people she was managing. During her time at eBay Motors, she regularly addressed conference rooms stuffed with men in their fifties who worked in Detroit's automotive industry, not to mention Silicon Valley men in their swashbuckling forties. Instead of being nervous that these older men would discount her on the basis of her dress or gender and that she might allow herself to feel the pressure to alter her appearance, Alexis spoke with the same conviction in her ideas and authority she used with her friends, family, and colleagues back at eBay's offices.

She was surprised at how much her youth, femininity, and confidence seemed to throw them, usually earning her 120 seconds of uninterrupted airtime with which to convey her thoughts. She discovered that being herself, especially in male-dominated arenas, actually gave her an edge.

At eBay, Alexis was also influenced by the leadership style of CEO Meg Whitman, who conformed to none of the damaging and prevalent eighties or nineties stereotypes about highly successful women. She wasn't power-suited or tough-as-nails; she hadn't been hardened by years spent navigating a sexist workplace. Instead, she managed everyone from marketers to engineers with a stern but maternal style; tall in stature, confident, casual in dress, she was strong, quick-witted, and often warm. She commanded respect from consumers, engineers, journalists, analysts, and politicians alike. Her presence was felt immediately when she walked into a room. As the first woman for whom Alexis had ever really worked, Meg was a revelation; she confirmed that you didn't have to just emulate the leaders above you (her bosses had surely been mostly men). Meg took her cues from no one. She got respect by being herself.

————————

We don't want to imply that leadership is just about being masculine or feminine. What works for one woman won't necessarily work for another, and on this point we're Exhibit A. We believe that good leaders identify their own unique traits and work to really emphasize them. It's OK to be lopsided—instead of well rounded—when highlighting the elements of your personality, appearance, or convictions that truly make you one of a kind. Neither of us is good at everything, but we're both very good at *some* things. We've had success when we've brought our real selves to the table, whether this meant admitting our love for fashion, pursuing a goal and not taking no for an answer, going out of our way to mentor a struggling junior employee, or giving hard, unflinching feedback.

As CEO of Gilt, Alexis, who likes to wear four-inch heels and presents a feminine affect, actually had many traits traditionally associated with men, and this is part of what made (and continues to make) her leadership style unique.

Unlike many women, she is not a multitasker; she prefers to focus on one project or problem until she's seen it to completion, examining it from every angle until she can crack the code. She jumps into each task or new role with gung ho enthusiasm, sweeping others up into her vortex and inspiring what Alexandra has always thought of as a sense of "we can change the world and accomplish anything" camaraderie. Alexandra believes there is no one better than Alexis at inspiring and motivating start-up teams.

Alexis was also cool as a cucumber, whether presenting to the board or giving a television interview on Bloomberg TV. Alexandra still vividly remembers the time Alexis forgot to bring her wallet on a business trip to Washington, D.C. Instead of having a panic attack at the airport that we'd miss our meeting, Alexis managed to talk her way through security using nothing more than her Equinox gym card and one of our press kits, which featured her name and image.

Alexis has never been overly concerned with everyone's liking her; that's an impediment to true leadership, she believes. Alexandra still marvels at how Alexis can make tough decisions for the good of the business, regardless of how unpopular they might be. At one point, in a move that was understandably viewed as risky by our board, she instructed our Gilt Home merchandising teams to cut a quarter of their sales. She had intuited that the sheer volume of offerings was overwhelming the customer and limiting the growth of the business, and that the team had strayed from one of Gilt's founding principles: *less* is *more*. The sales calendar was absolutely packed with brands, perhaps too many. Alexis was adamant that Gilt members didn't have forty-five minutes to peruse all our offerings; they wanted to be in and out in ten! The Gilt Home team had kept piling on brands until they were providing no extra benefit to either members or our bottom line.

And sure enough, by trimming the number of sales and brands offered, Alexis was able to markedly increase both revenues and customer satisfaction. Gilt Home became one of Gilt's fastest-growing businesses, but also one of our most profitable. Although cutting the sales calendar was not a popular decision, and seemed to defy logic, Alexis made the tough call—then she waited a couple months for the business to stabilize and watched revenues begin to grow faster than ever before.

Alexis is careful to listen to all voices, entertain all views, and review all available data, but her decisions are always based on a gut instinct about what's right, what's fair, and what's best for the team, group, or company. She doesn't delay decisions just because she lacks complete information; decisiveness is important to Alexis. But she's also always prepared to be 100 percent accountable when she's wrong.

In building the Gilt team, she also had no problem admitting when she was wrong in a hiring decision and "removing" from the team people who, while skilled, were not cultural fits (or, worse, threatened to be spoilers or sour apples). Any company growing as fast as Gilt was is bound to make a few hiring mistakes. When Alexis found out that an employee on her marketing team was complaining openly about other employees, spreading false rumors about compensation, and even attempting to pit her colleagues against one another, Alexis verified her sources and—despite the fact that the employee was extremely talented from an analytical perspective—moved this person out of the organization within a couple weeks. Alexandra, on the other hand, required coaching from Alexis and an HR manager before for the first time in her career she was able to work up the nerve to let someone go in the spring of 2008.

One of Alexis's obsessive focuses as CEO was creating the right kind of company culture in our office. The scrappy, collegial, collaborative culture of start-ups had always motivated her, and she wanted to find ways to create this vibe at Gilt and nurture it as the business grew. Alexis partnered tightly with Mike, who also felt strongly about creating an office environment that fostered ideas, sharing, and transparency (but also one where it was safe to admit failure or take responsibility for bad decisions). Mike took on a special responsibility for establishing and documenting Gilt's culture norms, or operating principles, and Alexis took seriously the task of setting the tone for her team.

She knew she definitely wanted to create an office in which everyone felt comfortable being as straightforward as she was, a culture in which employees address one another directly instead of working around one another or "raising issues up the flagpole" (i.e., addressing issues directly to a person's boss, not to the individual himself). She knew that side conversations hindered productivity and degraded trust, tearing at the fibers of a team.

But she soon realized it wasn't enough to just set a good example. By late fall 2007 there were some petty dramas festering among certain members of our team that Alexis was determined to stop dead in their tracks. While she's the first to admit she's not the sensitive type, Alexis made one of her most important decisions as CEO: she brought in the executive coach Barry Carden on a recommendation from Sheila Marcelo. In early 2008, when we all surely had more urgent things to attend to, Alexis insisted we slip away for a two-day off-site at Soho House, in the meatpacking district. There were some who rolled their eyes. After all, we had brand partners to meet with, inventory to photograph, people to hire.

Instead, we spent two days sitting in a circle in a conference room and discussing what was working and, more important, the issues that were threatening to derail our new company. Barry led us in exercises designed to help us discuss all our tensions in a safe environment. Over the course of the day everyone got hard, honest feedback on his or her performance, and we also learned how others viewed us. Alexis learned that she can sometimes be a pacesetter and should occasionally slow down to better communicate her goals to the team.

The day got so intense that after hearing hard feedback, one of our buyers had to momentarily leave the room to collect herself. But we practiced tackling even hard topics head-on and communicating them in a nonthreatening way, and it turned out to be precisely what was needed. All of us were surprised—in a good way—by how direct we were able to be and how much everyone listened and took a keen interest in what was being said, even when we were being told to change. The day helped set the tone for Gilt's highly participatory company culture, and showed team members that there was no risk in addressing concerns to colleagues head-on. The Gilt office became a place where you could—and should—speak your mind, risk free, provided you could do it in a respectful and constructive way. Bringing in Barry was crucial to helping create the office environment our small founding team so desperately wanted to nurture and maintain. He has subsequently done many more sessions with Gilt over the years, even coaching our senior executive staff to this day.

By refocusing on our relationships with our team members and pausing to establish open communication and trust, we were able to move a lot faster in those first two critical years. We knew one another's strengths and weaknesses and where we stood with each other. We wasted less energy trying to vet one another and assess if certain people were trustworthy.

checklist:
ALEXIS'S LEADERSHIP STYLE

Keep your eyes on the big picture.

1. BE DECISIVE. Be willing to make a decision, even if it's not popular. This applies to everything from personnel decisions (if you waste too much time questioning whether a candidate will fit into your workplace, then he's not the right person, and in the meantime you've frustrated both the potential hire and your recruiters) to product decisions (nothing is worse for a team of engineers than building something and then being forced to start over because of a leader's indecision). It's important to solicit feedback from key parts of your organization, to listen and learn, but also to develop your own gut instinct. Second-guessing paralyzes an organization.

2. LEAD BY EXAMPLE: BE CALM AND BE CONSISTENT. When Alexis is stressed, even Alexandra rarely notices. She's careful not to take out her stress on her employees because a team mirrors the behavior of its leader. If you have a tendency to berate others, for example, or to be overly competitive with a peer, don't be surprised when your employees do the same. But even more than calmness, Alexis believes consistency is the best quality a leader can embody. Employees want to know what to expect. They are more comfortable moving forward toward a specific goal when they know your emotional inclinations won't change on a dime, for example. If you're constantly revising your strategic objectives, employees will start hedging their bets or even delay getting started on the tasks at hand. And if you're emotionally inconsistent, they might fear coming into your office to discuss important matters.

3. SQUASH OFFICE POLITICS. In order to foster an environment where people deal with one another in a straightforward manner, be honest and straightforward yourself; be the honest broker. Key to keeping an environment free of distracting politics is ensuring that communication is open and direct, that there is trust, and that a direction is clear and unambiguous.

4. SET VERY CLEAR PRIORITIES. Alexis doesn't like it when strategic priorities are vague or, worse, nonexistent. This means much time is wasted discussing projects not core to the success of the business. When Alexis took on the challenge of revamping Gilt's home business, her priority was to make the home décor category more exciting to our customer, and this guided all her decision making. She began by asking herself, Who is our customer and what is he or she looking for? She learned by analyzing results of previous sales that our Home customer wanted fashion in her home, accented with unique international finds that represented a sense of discovery and adventure. She looked at our product lineup to analyze how it was (or was not) meeting this customer's needs. Gilt Home would no longer waste any time with products or price points that customers' didn't find relevant; we'd stop focusing on adding new brands, which was not helping our bottom line. Identifying her strategic priority helped her determine what her team would not focus on, and eventually led to her decision to cut 25 percent of the sales schedule.

5. CIRCULATE INFORMATION; MAKE TEAM MEMBERS FEEL LIKE OWNERS, NOT EMPLOYEES. Alexis believes that making employees privy to as much information as possible promotes higher engagement and a sense of fiduciary responsibility. When employees know what is happening and what their efforts are resulting in, they feel like part of a greater mission, as if they are crucial to and invested in the business's destiny and success—and they make decisions accordingly. As CEO, Alexis instituted a weekly all-hands meeting, during which we all remained standing, so as to be energetic and engaged. We opened the floor to anyone who wanted to share updates, introduce new employees, disseminate financial results, celebrate the previous week's big wins, discuss an important upcoming article on the company, or share any other relevant information. It was, and remains to this day, a great way to help keep an open flow of information across all of the company's various businesses and departments.

If Alexis was (and is) a more visionary leader, Alexandra's leadership style has always been based more on communication and grounded in her natural ability to maintain and grow strong, trusting relationships. Though she was never CEO of Gilt, her ability to relate to others and to intuit and respond to a person's feelings made her a powerful force in Gilt's offices from the company's earliest days, someone to whom many people look for direction, support, and information. As Alexis likes to say, Alexandra quickly became the glue that held Gilt Groupe together.

She also became Alexis's unofficial sensitivity adviser. Alexis, who could sometimes be strong-headed as CEO, always sought Alexandra's advice behind closed doors about how she could present tricky topics to the board or to employees and how she could more accurately intuit organizational dynamics. She relied on Alexandra, who was uncannily aware of any underlying sensitivities, to help keep her informed of what certain teams at Gilt were feeling and alert her to any blind spots. Were the engineers feeling underappreciated? Did merchandising balk at the new incentive structure?

As an expert communicator, Alexandra could give hard feedback in a loving, supportive way that encouraged and motivated an employee, rather than frustrating her. These conversations were difficult for Alexandra, but she was, in Alexis's opinion, the best at them. A person could always be certain that anything Alexandra said came from a position of caring.

She also regularly reached out to people at varying levels within Gilt—especially in merchandising, marketing, and public relations—to hear how they were doing and what was new with them outside the office. This was a great way to take the temperature of the organization and to keep her pulse on their thoughts about the company and its direction. She also invited her merchandisers to her apartment for dinner, helping instill a sense of cozy camaraderie.

But she was also a taskmaster, never failing to deliver on what had been asked of her—and this, too, made her an effective leader. She could break down and attack a challenge with ruthless efficiency, and the high standards to which she held herself inevitably rubbed off on her employees. In the beginning, Alexandra worked like crazy and expected no less focus and dedication from her team. She was a speed demon, talking, walking, and e-mailing fast from her BlackBerry from meetings and cabs all over town. Her pet peeve was when someone on her team wouldn't respond within twenty-four hours to an e-mail she'd sent; everything seemed urgent in those early days! Alexandra was careful to always keep on top of her own e-mails, voice mails, and to-do lists, and she expected others to do the same. If she had a shortcoming, it was patience. She preferred people and projects to move as fast as she did and didn't always respond well to slow-moving situations. Over the years she learned from Alexis's ability to remain calm at all times. She also worked consciously on being more empathetic when people moved slowly, instead of automatically assuming laziness or even incompetence.

checklist:
ALEXANDRA'S LEADERSHIP STYLE

Be the kind of person you'd want to have as a boss.

1. BE WILLING TO LEARN FROM YOUR EMPLOYEES. When Alexandra started at Gilt, she had a lot of experience working with luxury brands but no formal training as a buyer. She never tried to hide the fact that many of her new hires knew more about the buying process than she did. She asked for their perspectives every day and valued their opinions. She made it clear they were working *with* her as much as for her. It helped that Alexandra has never been above any task, large or small, at Gilt. She never expected her team members to do things she wasn't willing to do herself, from cold-calling brands and generating ideas to making buys alongside them. They saw she was capable of doing—and doing well—the things she expected of them.

2. PRACTICE EFFECTIVE COMMUNICATION. Alexandra follows up verbal communication with an e-mail to reinforce what has been said and/or agreed upon. She knows how to get a message across so it is understood. She taught Alexis that communication involves more than just saying something once: you often must communicate to employees verbally *and* in written form, repeating yourself to reinforce your message. In fact hearing something once almost never sticks.

3. GIVE JUNIOR EMPLOYEES A TASTE OF THE TOP. Alexandra has always tried to bring younger staffers in on the action as soon as they're ready: to meetings, trade shows, fashion shows—the "good stuff." This is not only educational but motivating and something she's benefited from in her own career. In February 2008 we hired a new merchandising assistant (MA). On her second day, we invited her to the tents at Bryant Park for the Vivienne Tam fashion show, and when the lights went down, we spied an extra open seat in the front row. We invited the MA down. It was an exciting moment for this new employee. Subsequently she became the hardest-working merchant Alexandra had ever hired.

4. GO OUT OF YOUR WAY TO BE A MENTOR AND TO CHAMPION PEOPLE WHO DESERVE IT. Since we started Gilt, Alexandra has made it a priority to be accessible to junior employees who want her advice or expertise. She'll coach them on how to have a hard conversation with a colleague or how to ask for more feedback. When she sees people in a rut, she takes the initiative to reach out to them and help guide them out of it. She is a good listener. She opens up to younger employees by sharing stories of low moments from previous stages in her career.

5. DON'T ALWAYS KEEP THINGS PROFESSIONAL. As Gilt grew, Alexandra regularly reached out to people at varying levels within the company—especially in merchandising, marketing, and public relations—to find out how they were doing and what was new with them outside the office. This was a great way to take the temperature of different groups of Gilt employees and to keep her pulse on their thoughts about the company and its direction. Alexandra also hosted dinner parties from time to time at her home. In the summer of 2008, Alexandra even rented a small van and took the entire merchandising team to the outlet mall Woodbury Common for an impromptu scouting trip. She thought it would be an opportunity for bonding, and a chance to research our brand partners in an outlet context. Needless to say, the merchants were thrilled. From the beginning, we were never afraid to foster a collegial atmosphere at Gilt. This was part of our culture, and it made people excited to work for us.

SUDDENLY SUSAN: WELCOMING GILT GROUPE'S NEXT CEO

In the summer of 2008 our board member and investor Nick Beim began talking to a well-known and extremely well-respected executive named Susan Lyne about joining our board. Susan, who at the time was the CEO of Martha Stewart Living Omnimedia, and before that the president of ABC Entertainment at Disney, happened to be a neighbor of Nick's parents up in Bronxville, New York; Nick had been friendly with her for years. She was a trustee of the New School in New York and on the board of the financial firm CIT. We considered Susan a dream "get" for Gilt's board.

Susan was reportedly being courted by Harpo to run Oprah's new cable channel, OWN. But she was intrigued by what Nick told her about our company and our growth. She was familiar with Gilt and had on occasion shopped on our site. Unbeknownst to us, she was also at a point in her career where she was looking for a change; she'd helmed large media companies and was interested in doing something more focused on growth and technology, where she'd be tasked with managing 100 percent year-over-year growth (i.e., when a company grows 100 percent in the space of a year) rather than trim her staff to account for shrinking revenues.

When it became clear that Susan would consider taking an even more active role at Gilt, the internal conversations quickly shifted from board member to CEO. It would be beyond our wildest dreams to attract an executive of Susan's stature to Gilt.

Nick introduced Susan to Kevin Ryan, who convinced her of Gilt's tremendous potential and was instrumental in bringing her on board.

That is how, one year and three months after cofounding Gilt Groupe, we found ourselves preparing to welcome the former CEO of none other than Martha Stewart Living Omnimedia to lead our overachieving start-up. That an executive like Susan saw something

exciting and promising in Gilt was not just validation for us personally but a stamp of approval that would reverberate throughout the
business community. *Gilt meant business.*

The more we learned about Susan, the more we knew that she
would be perfect for the job. She had deep experience in turning brands
into household names, from *Premiere* magazine, which she'd launched,
to *Desperate Housewives, Lost,* and *Grey's Anatomy*—all shows she'd
green-lighted as president of ABC Entertainment. She commanded
respect as a person who had led public companies. She could forge
large, strategic partnerships with Fortune 500 businesses that could
help us emerge as a leader in the competitive world of e-commerce.

Perhaps most important, her references were universally positive;
people really loved working with Susan. She could help Gilt recruit a
lot of great talent.

Alexis and Susan e-mailed throughout the last two weeks of
August to arrange a time to meet for coffee and get to know each
other. In these e-mails, Alexis gleaned exciting tidbits about Susan's
life, such as the fact that she'd just returned from Rwanda, where she
was doing charity work. On the day of their first meeting in August,
Alexis remembers sitting at a sidewalk café called Orsay in Manhattan, catching up on e-mails—shockingly, she was *early*—waiting for
Susan to arrive. When Susan breezed up to the table and sat down,
Alexis immediately felt her positive energy. Confident and poised,
Susan has a genuine openness that makes everyone instantly want to
talk to her; she is Clintonesque in her ability to engage people and
make them feel that they are the *only* persons of interest in the room.

By their second meeting Alexis and Susan were examining financial documents, board meeting decks, detailed information about our
customers, our preexisting team, and the thought processes behind
certain decisions we'd made. Susan had dozens of questions; she
wanted to know all about our relationships with the board and with
various brands, and planned areas of further expansion. Alexis was
typically blunt about our challenges and emphasized our company

culture and the fact that employees would respond well to a CEO who was available and accessible, not tucked away in a corner office. Our scrappy, innovative, all-in-it-together vibe was what had attracted many of our most talented team members. Alexis explained that we all sat in cubicles in an open floor plan to foster collaboration and the free flow of information and that as founders we'd done our best not to separate ourselves from the rest of the team.

Alexis was delighted when instead of being turned off by this— after all, at this point in her career, she *did* deserve some perks— Susan seemed genuinely enthusiastic.

Alexandra also met with Susan in August, at the casual sandwich spot 'Wichcraft near our Flatiron offices. Before their meeting, Alexandra couldn't help looking up Susan's Gilt account; she'd started doing this with all potential hires because she found immediately suspect anyone who claimed she wanted to work for Gilt but hadn't yet bothered to join our site as a member. But Susan was indeed a member and in a short period of time had actually become a valuable customer, having purchased a number of fashionable items from great designer brands.

In person, Alexandra was as captivated as Alexis had been. Susan was humble, personable, and a good listener. She asked Alexandra all about our brand partners: how she'd convinced them to sell in this new way; what excited them; what concerned them; how she was working to open up our supply chain and solve our merchandise problem. She quizzed Alexandra about what was working well within our company and what needed more attention. Susan clearly cared deeply about the people she would manage and asked detailed questions about our team. Alexandra shared her thoughts and even concerns freely, opening up about the dynamics of the existing management team. "Will you be all right with sitting out in the open with the rest of us?" she asked Susan. Alexandra could only imagine the plush offices that Susan had in prior roles; surely returning to a cubicle would be a shock! But Susan was a good sport and assured Alexandra that details like a corner office were not important.

It was decided that Susan would start as Gilt's CEO after Labor Day.

Now Alexis just had to tell our team.

We knew we'd need to handle the transition carefully for the benefit of our employees, and we had a lot of discussions among ourselves, including Mike and JCS, about how best to do this. We decided to tell the team the Friday before Susan started in September. This would minimize time for speculation and worry.

In the days leading up to our announcement, we shared our concerns only with one another. Would Susan radically change the culture we'd worked so hard to build? Would she bring in big changes to the team? Would the atmosphere in the office become more serious and more corporate? Would our contributions be diminished? We had confidence in Susan, but we couldn't help being a *little* bit nervous, no matter how unlikely these scenarios seemed. Gilt was our baby, and we felt very personally invested in its growth and success and in the well-being of its employees.

Besides, Alexandra would now be reporting to a new boss instead of to her dear friend and confidante; that would be significantly different and much more formal, no matter how wonderful Susan turned out to be.

As usual, Alexis sought Alexandra's advice on how our team might react to the news: would employees worry that people would be hired over them? That they'd have to re-prove themselves and their worth to the organization? Alexandra had never been more proud of Alexis as she watched her handle the transition to a new CEO with grace, poise, and diplomacy. She'd seen Alexis do this before, set up an organization for success and then hand over the reins before moving on to something new. But Alexis worried that the team would be disappointed in her or think she was abandoning them at a time when the business was flourishing. One of her largest motivators for success had always been to serve the people well who had taken leaps of faith to join her; above all else, she never wanted to let these people down. Would employees now perceive that in transitioning away from CEO, she was backing down from a commitment she had made to them?

As we prepared for the announcement, we tried to anticipate any concerns and think hard about how we'd address them honestly but in a way that rallied the team behind Susan. We wanted to make sure to position Susan's arrival as the huge coup it was and to set a positive tone for her tenure at Gilt. We knew it was important that we present a united front to our employees, that we show strength and confidence and genuine enthusiasm and make everyone feel good about the change.

We decided to make the announcement at a regular quarterly operations meeting attended by all of Gilt's employees. We were careful to schedule the meeting for a Friday, so that anyone who was upset by the news would have the weekend to think things over and regain perspective.

We still remember this meeting as if it were yesterday. There were at least seventy people jammed into our large conference room (dozens more would join the business in the coming weeks). Despite our preparation, we had no idea how things would go. We didn't really think anyone would be angry, but surely people would have concerns about how this news would affect them. Alexis started off the meeting and spoke for a long time. As usual, she wasn't referring to prepared notes; she never writes speeches. She told our employees that they should be so personally proud of how far we'd come as a team since the spring of 2007. She reflected on all our successes to that point and reviewed all the indicators that we would continue to grow rapidly.

After several minutes of buildup, she remembers saying, "I have some important and positive news to share with you." She explained that we'd soon be welcoming a new CEO named Susan Lyne, most recently CEO of Martha Stewart, and that she was thrilled to be bringing someone of Susan's stature to our young start-up. Alexis made it as clear as she could that Susan was coming to Gilt because we were doing really well and that her arrival signaled our strength and success as a business; it was not a harbinger of doom or internal restructuring. Susan would not make major changes.

She also emphasized that Gilt was unique and special and that our culture was not going to change. Our team would continue to be built and developed, not swapped out to make room for new hires.

We were so caught up in the moment that it's hard to remember the currents of emotion that ran through those conference rooms that day. There was a lot of surprise, giddy excitement, and also some uncertainty. When Alexis opened up the floor for questions, very few people raised their hands. One person asked about Susan's leadership style; another, about changes she would make to our working environment. We remember expecting a little drama, but none was forthcoming or maybe it just didn't reach us.

A few people popped by our cubicles to express concern for us or individually inquire about what new roles we'd be taking. For the most part, our employees seemed to greet the news with a bit of trepidation but also enthusiasm; we'd handled the announcement well.

When it was over, Alexis was overcome with a powerful sense of relief. She had no idea what her new role would be at Gilt, but she would be excused from the grinding schedule of meetings that had made her feel trapped and had not made good use of her strengths as a leader. She could now shift her focus to helping Gilt's new businesses and initiatives get off the ground and lend more of her time to the company's overall strategic objectives.

———

Unfortunately we couldn't share our excitement about our new CEO with the world because Susan's first day happened to coincide with the fall of Lehman Brothers. With the entire financial and retail world soon spiraling into doom, Gilt's good news was somewhat eclipsed in the newspapers. It was strange to feel we were on the precipice of a great new era for our business with all the uncertainty around us. Our friends and acquaintances were struggling to hang on to their jobs and in many cases to their businesses. We didn't yet know how the recession would affect Gilt, but we felt confident that whatever the next few months held, we had the right person at the helm.

On Susan's first day, she stood up in the middle of our office, which resembled a trading floor (albeit considerably better dressed and with far more women), and spoke to our team for about ten minutes about why she took the job. We stood beside her as she sang our praises and everyone else's and told us how she admired what we'd done so far. It didn't feel like a show; she was genuine. When she finished, we could feel the excitement in the room. She obviously had a talent for this. Our team was behind her.

True to her word, Susan didn't hide herself away in a corner office. She set up shop in a grouping of four cubicles, opposite JCS and us. She jumped right into our culture and embraced it, even scheduling office hours each week to make it clear that she was available to anyone at any level who wanted to meet her, speak with her, and get to know her. At the beginning, she seemed to spend most of her time listening, getting up to speed on everything and to know our employee base. Everyone was relieved when she made no significant changes to what made Gilt Gilt. She seemed committed to continuing what our small founding team had started.

Susan had a great sense of curiosity and a desire to learn new things that served her well in her first months at Gilt. She now admits that she thought she knew more about technology than she did. "It was like having to learn a new language," she remembers. "Yes, I had a lot of experience in a lot of different things, but I had no experience in technology. I really had to ask a lot of questions and become a student again. I can't say that I think I made a big impact early on."

We disagree with this assessment, but it's typical Susan: she was always willing to put in the time to really dig in and understand what drove Gilt and its people; she never hogged credit from her team. She was humble and approachable and generous with her time. She didn't come in with prescriptions; she genuinely listened and tried to understand all the intricacies of the business before weighing in. This made it all the more effective when she did make decisions.

Like Meg Whitman, Susan had climbed the ladder in male-dominated environments but had developed her own leadership style, one that seemed sensitive, encouraging, even nurturing. "Often I was the only woman at the table early in my career," she says. "Women in my generation had to make a lot of it up ourselves."

For Susan, as for us, developing a distinct leadership style has been a conscious evolution throughout her career. She recalls that when she became founding editor of *Premiere* magazine, "I had always been a number two, which is a very comfortable position for a woman. So when I went to publish my first issue, I sent my editor's letter over to John Evans [then the president of the Murdoch organization, which owned *Premiere*]. He called me up and said, 'What is this?' And I said, 'It's my editor's letter.' He said, 'Why did you send it to me?' And I said, 'I just wanted to get your feedback.' Then he said, 'Susan, I don't buy a dog and bark for it.' He told me it was my magazine and that I had to own it. I couldn't come to him looking for approval. I had to have confidence in my own vision." Over the years, Susan became the kind of leader who inspired her employees to trust themselves. "It's wholly counterproductive for employees to be coming to you all the time saying, 'What should I do here?' or 'Is this OK?'" she says. "The best way to grow leaders is to make sure that as soon as they're ready, you push them to make those decisions themselves. It won't always be the right decision, but that's okay. You learn more from fixing a bad decision than by making the right call in the first place. A leader needs to be comfortable making a decision and owning an outcome."

Susan also became an intuitive thinker who knew that what

motivates one employee may not motivate another. This was why she hit it off with our engineers. "It took me awhile to realize what drove Mike and the engineering team," she recalls. "There was a moment where I said, 'Aha, you guys are very much like my writers' room at ABC.' They're people who get excited about solving something in an elegant way. And there's a pecking order that has nothing to do with who's been here longest or who makes the most money; it's really more about who can come up with the most elegant way to get from A to B."

An important part of Susan's leadership style, she says, is to create a "safe space" for engineers and for all her employees to take risks without the fear of punishment. "No one is going to argue that taking stupid risks is a good policy," she says. "But if you're trying to get people to think independently, they have to take risks, they have to make decisions, and the only way you can get them to do that is by allowing them to fail and not blaming them for it. I've never worked in any business where everything worked. You just need the ratio of successes to failures to be strong and get better over time. Anyone who doesn't have a few failures in his track record has likely played it too safe.

"The television business taught me a lot of great lessons," she continues. "One was that you had to just take a shot. Most of what you tried wasn't going to work, but when it did work, it was going to be a *big* win."

During her tenure as CEO, Susan had a huge impact on Gilt's recognition in the wider world of retail, media, and technology, far beyond purely fashion. She helped catapult us to the front pages of newspapers and expand our wings into key new business like home décor and gourmet food, pulling in critical personalities along the way. She forged partnerships with the likes of *InStyle* and Target, marking us as a serious contender in retail and e-commerce. Susan also brought in key members of our team.

No one conducts an interview—one that inevitably leaves the prospective candidate thinking, Wow, I really want to join this company!—better than Susan.

---

checklist:
SUSAN LYNE'S LEADERSHIP TIPS

A few tips that helped her reach the top.

1. DON'T EVER TALK TO SOMEONE WHEN YOU'RE ANGRY. "Take a deep breath, and make sure you have the hard conversations when you're ready to have them," Susan advises. "Say, 'Let's book time tomorrow.' Then prepare. I almost always make some notes if I know I have to have a tough conversation with someone."

2. REMEMBER THAT FAILURE IS NOT TOTAL. "I can't tell you the number of times when I've thought, I *so* screwed this up, I'm never going to recover from it," says Susan. "The truth is that if you work hard and you're pretty smart and you make more good decisions than bad, a mistake is never fatal. I wish I'd known that when I started, because it would have saved me many sleepless nights." To recover from a mistake, Susan suggests acknowledging it and quickly explaining how you'll fix it and then moving on. "Don't overapologize," she says. "Don't bring it up a month later. Let it go. Trust that you can make a good decision, even after you've made a bad one."

3. LEAVE A LITTLE ON THE TABLE. "Early in my career, another media executive who was very senior to me taught me something that I've always remembered," says Susan. "I was fighting very hard for a deal point in a negotiation, and he said, 'You're going to have a long career, and we're going to meet again. If I walk away from this negotiation feeling good about it, I'll remember it—and I will likely give a little more in the next round.' Complete victory is not always a good thing."

4. **SUSS OUT WHAT MAKES PEOPLE EXCITED.** "There are people who get excited by numbers, and there are others who prefer creative satisfaction," says Susan. "It's not always about age or even gender, but there are things that make each person want to come to work or spend extra hours finding a solution. The only way to understand somebody is to spend time trying to understand what makes him tick."

5. **FIND TIME TO LISTEN TO YOUR INNER VOICE.** "This is one of the best things I've done throughout my career," says Susan. "Even when I had babies and a husband and a job, I figured out how to carve out some time for myself, even if that meant eating alone at a restaurant by myself once a week, just to allow my mind the quiet it needed to start working again. You don't even need to bring a notebook, although that can be helpful. Just sit and see where your mind goes. These are the moments when I realize there's an issue that I need to address that isn't going to fix itself, and when I always get my best ideas."

After Alexis departed from the role of CEO in the fall of 2008, you could say she became Gilt's ultimate chameleon, taking on jobs from chief strategy officer to president to, most recently, chief marketing officer. She's never been all that concerned with title: Instead, she evaluates new opportunities based on the challenge at hand, the change she thinks she can effect, and its potential to impact the larger business.

———————

Meanwhile, two years after Susan started, we had the opportunity to welcome yet another CEO, but this time we already knew him well. As Gilt refocused on our underlying operations and infrastructure in preparation for a possible IPO (initial public offering), Kevin Ryan stepped into the role of CEO in September 2010, and Susan transitioned to the chairman spot, where she would help focus the company's strategy, firm up additional outside relationships, and lead our charge into new categories.

Kevin had become more intimately involved in our day-to-day operations in 2009. Like Alexis and Susan before him, he has an unmistakable personal leadership style, and we've learned a lot from him. He loves to foster a casual office culture. He enthusiastically plays alongside younger employees on the Gilt sports teams he fields. He is famously fond of Halloween and throws a big company party every year. In 2008 he nailed his Halloween costume with particular flourish. Alexis, Alexandra, and Susan were returning from an event—they'd just been named to the Silicon Alley 100—and after a quick change in the bathroom, we headed down to the Gilt employee Halloween party in a bar and restaurant on the Lower East Side. Susan was Sarah Palin, Alexis was Donatella Versace, and Alexandra was Princess Diana. As we mingled with other employees, we spotted him: iconic, reed-thin septuagenarian Chanel designer Karl Lagerfeld. He wore a long-haired salt-and-pepper wig tied back into a ponytail, a ruffled white blouse, and tight pants. He was even imitating the German accent. Alexis and Susan didn't immediately recognize who was behind the costume, but Alexandra could tell it was Kevin. She was speechless. The costume was A++ perfection, and it showed Kevin's joie de vivre and fun-loving attitude. That night he probably stayed out as late as any of our employees.

These days it's fun (and sometimes a tad nerve-racking) to watch

Kevin cruising the hallways of our office, interacting with younger staffers, speaking openly to people at all levels of the organization, asking them questions, grilling them. His accessibility and interest in what they have to say keep them motivated and on their toes. It also helps keep him on top of the company's pulse.

Kevin is a quick study with no patience for incompetence. He likes to play devil's advocate: if you say "black," he'll say "white"—not because he necessarily believes in white, but because he wants to hear you defend black. This managerial style can be quite difficult for some employees to get used to; newer employees often think, Is he telling me to head in another direction? Does he think I have no idea what I am talking about? But ultimately Kevin's leadership style helps his teams work out what they might have missed and identify any holes in their thinking.

The unique element his leadership has brought to Gilt is a continuous focus on new ideas and an increased emphasis on the pace of innovation. He encourages employees to constantly try new things, to experiment, and to put forward ideas worth pursuing. What should we be doing next? is always Kevin's angle, and it has helped lead the way in expanding Gilt's business beyond apparel and even housewares to travel, Japan, local deals, and even retail (or full-price) men's apparel.

CODA: A STYLE ALL HIS OWN: OUR MEETING WITH ONE OF FASHION'S MOST UNCONVENTIONAL AND EFFECTIVE LEADERS, MICKEY DREXLER OF J.CREW

One of the most memorable and colorful leaders we've been privileged to meet over the past few years is the legendary J.Crew CEO Mickey Drexler, the former CEO of Gap. Mickey is credited with building that brand's overwhelming popularity in the 1990s and is widely considered a retail genius. In the fall of 2008, Susan helped us secure a meeting with Mickey. We'd had our eyes on J.Crew for quite a while, so this was terribly exciting, even if he was just doing it as a favor to Susan.

We went down to J.Crew's offices on lower Broadway, hoping to discuss a possible collaboration with its more rarefied bridal, accessories, or cashmere divisions.

And we found that J.Crew, like Gilt, has an open, airy floor space. We—Susan, Alexis, Alexandra—were ushered into Mickey's large office area, which had a big table for meetings and was out in the open, at the end of a floor of merchandisers. He sat at a corner desk near his assistant, and we sat at a large conference table, separated from his desk by a low partition. Tracy Gardner, then J.Crew's president, joined us. Knowing Mickey didn't have a lot of time to spare, we began our carefully prepared pitch. Susan spoke first because it was her relationship with Mickey that had brought us there.

It was immediately obvious that this would be no ordinary meeting. We'd stepped into an alternate universe; Mickey Drexler follows no one's leadership rules but his own.

From the beginning, it felt as if he weren't listening to a word we said. This was just his style: he simultaneously does several other things while half nodding. As we spoke, he shuffled papers, checked his BlackBerry, and wrote e-mails, tossing out a few mmms and uh-huhs to indicate that he was following us. Alexandra had encountered other brand partners who initially seemed less than riveted by her pitch, so this wasn't a huge shock. Instead of being offended, we just picked up the pace, confidently trucking through our presentation as fast as possible.

When we started describing our membership—young, cosmopolitan, with disposable income but little free time—we finally got Mickey's undivided attention. That was when he rolled his eyes and said something along the lines of "Right. *Everyone* makes up their demographics and prototypical customer." The three of us exchanged glances. "But that *is* our customer," Alexandra remembers saying.

This was when Mickey grabbed his telephone and hit the intercom. Apparently he does this all the time to make announcements across J.Crew's many floors of office space. While Kevin enjoys picking the brains of young employees casually in the hallway, this took interoffice communication to a whole new level. Suddenly we could hear Mickey's voice not just right in front of us but booming out of loudspeakers throughout the floor. He said something like "Hey, I'm talking to this company, *Gilt* something. What is it? Oh yeah, Gilt Groupe. If anyone has ever heard of it, call me back." Then he slammed his phone back into the receiver.

His phone immediately started ringing off the hook. "Hi, oh, you know what Gilt is? Have you shopped on it? Hey, hold on a second. . . . You know what it is too? Please hold. Please hold." After ten seconds of trying to juggle countless incoming calls, he went back on the loudspeaker. "Stop calling me. If anyone shops on Gilt or has anything they want to tell me about Gilt, just come by my conference room."

Within minutes J.Crew executives and staffers started lining up all around their boss. Soon there were at least fifty people crowded into Mickey's open conference area, not counting the ones who walked by, saw how crowded the space already was, and left. We could hardly conceal our grins as handfuls of stylish, young, educated, cosmopolitan shoppers, both men and women, validated our site demographics to a tee. Our members were exactly as we'd described them: fashion-forward men and women between the ages of twenty-five and thirty-eight. Mickey seemed genuinely surprised by the zealous response from his employees. He asked the Gilt members where else they shopped online (there were other businesses like Gilt, they explained, but none was as good) and whether they shopped on Gilt every day at noon (they admitted they did; we thought that was brave).

"I should block Gilt," he said, and then added something like "Or maybe we should build a site like this ourselves!"

Then he demanded, "Why didn't I know about this?" almost as if to say, "If you liked something this much, why didn't you put it on my radar?" Mickey's reaction to all this is what makes the story one of our favorites of all time. He genuinely couldn't believe he had not already heard about Gilt.

We left J.Crew's office on an adrenaline high, laughing to one another as we hailed a cab back to the Flatiron district. Our meeting had been surreal, even cinematic. "Did that really happen?" we asked one another. "Did you see all those people?" "We couldn't have choreographed that better if we'd tried!" We knew that whether or not we ever worked with J.Crew, we had the respect of Mickey Drexler, one of the most inventive minds in the industry. We'd also learned a unique approach to communication (and we've kept in touch with him since). Each day his employees were privy to a cascade of information, questions, and informal surveys, all communicated to them directly. In the process, he undoubtedly learned from his employees and stayed in touch with their ideas and sensibilities. No one at J. Crew seemed to lack information about the business; Mickey spread news and ideas through every hallway of his headquarters daily. Watching a leader of his caliber and style operate had been thrilling. Now there was a leader who was being *different*, who was being himself and making it work brilliantly.

CHAPTER 13

HYPERGROWTH, EXHAUSTION, AND ONE HILARIOUS JAPANESE PRESS CONFERENCE

With 2009 revenue of $170 million and a current valuation
of some $400 million, Gilt Groupe appears to have more
staying power than most fashion trends.
—*THE WALL STREET JOURNAL*, OCTOBER 19, 2010

When people first meet us and hear our story, they often say things like "You make it look so easy!" While we certainly try to dress and act the part when we host a fancy party or movie screening, we also generally conceal the bags under our eyes and downplay the long, sleepless nights we've spent stressing about complex operating issues or employee concerns. Despite how composed we may appear, launching and growing a start-up has sometimes felt like trying to climb into the driver's seat of a car that's speeding down the highway at a hundred miles per hour: if we're lucky, we're barely hanging on to the tailpipes. We've taken wrong turns and been punched in the gut by the airbag more times than we'd like to recall.

Most of 2009 was like that.

It started off on a champagne-fueled high. Just a little more than a year after our launch, membership had grown to an astonishing 750,000 people. To toast our success and our brand partners, not to mention a slew of fashion industry tastemakers, we hosted a one-year anniversary bash at Shang, then a buzzworthy new restaurant in the new Thompson hotel on the Lower East Side. The hotel had a minimalist vibe, with sultry lighting, cozy round booths, and floor-to-ceiling views of downtown Manhattan. And true to form, Christian Leone had ensured an amazing turnout of boldfaced names. *Everyone* was there.

We were a little nervous as we greeted a crowd that included designers Erin Fetherston and Doo.Ri, socialites Marjorie Gubelmann and Alex Kramer, and then *Elle* fashion editor Nina Garcia. Though the economic mood was dour, everyone seemed to be caught up in a wave of excitement about Gilt. "It's cheap and discreet, so you don't actually have to show up at the sample sale," designer Peter Som told a reporter from Style.com.

We could hardly believe it when Isabel Toledo, the celebrated cult designer who had just achieved broad recognition by designing Michelle Obama's inauguration outfit, crashed the party with her talented artist husband, Ruben. The girls checking names at the door didn't even recognize the couple, and they were almost turned away. Luckily, Nina Garcia personally stepped in to usher the Toledos past the clipboards and into our party. *Phew!*

During dinner we stood up together to welcome the crowd and tell them how delighted we were that they had come to help us celebrate how far Gilt had come in just one year, in large part thanks to the brand partners, editors, and tastemakers in the room. (Nowadays Alexandra would not be nervous at all about speaking to a crowd of that caliber, but back then she sure was.) It was an unbelievable moment. Just months after the Lehman Brothers bankruptcy, we'd cemented our brand partner relationships and reputation by stepping in to help solve designers' inventory crises—and in the process, our own. It felt as if Gilt were the toast of the fashion world.

But beneath the shiny veneer, things were getting increasingly harried and stressful. The anniversary party was a brief moment of elation and reprieve during what proved to be a grueling year (or two) that was crucial to the fate of our business. We'd already spent the past year in hypergrowth, a period of explosive increase in demand that can challenge a start-up's systems and infrastructure, straining everything from Web site to warehouses to accounting.

Not to mention staff. Alexandra was darting from L.A. to Paris to London to Milan to meet with brand partners and attend trade shows, all while managing a growing team of buyers and merchandisers back in New York. Alexis meanwhile was also in the trenches, pouring blood, sweat, and tears into preparing for the launch of several new businesses, from Gilt Noir to our new Gilt Japan business. And she was getting married in February in Aspen to Jerome, her longtime boyfriend—in hindsight, not ideal timing (but really, when *would* an ideal time be in a start-up?). Unlike Alexandra, who enjoyed managing the many details of her own nuptials, Alexis was forced to farm out most of her wedding planning.

As the faces of the brand, we both also did a ton of media interviews, which was a job in itself. As membership exploded and Gilt showed signs of surviving—*thriving*—in a recession that was toppling more established enterprises, we became sought after for interviews. How did Gilt get started? What was the future of fashion? Would customers ever pay full price again? Together and separately, we appeared in television segments across the country and chatted with reporters from *Fortune*, the *Wall Street Journal, Elle,* and the *Los Angeles Times.* Neither of us slept much; for months, Alexandra suffered migraines, and we waved distracted hellos to each other as we sprinted down the hallway in opposite directions. Our schedules rarely overlapped. Often we weren't even in the same city.

The business had grown into something much larger than our dedicated founding team. But it was also starting to feel like a Mack truck barreling toward us at full speed, threatening to run us over.

Part of the stress was still inventory. While we were flush with merchandise by early 2009, we knew it wouldn't last; stores would dramatically scale back their orders in anticipation of customers' new financial realities, and designers would produce far fewer of each piece, meaning there would be less excess for us to buy. In order to surge our inventory to keep pace with our growth, we rushed to secure even more exclusive capsule collections with designers and to create new relationships with brands that could offer high volumes. We also placed more orders earlier in the production cycle, at the same time as department stores. We knew that keeping our supply of covetable merchandise strong and growing was of paramount importance.

Internally, we engaged with our board in a lively debate about how best to add nonluxury products to the mix. While the board favored adding a new tab specifically for contemporary and casual brands, Alexis felt strongly that this would confuse members and only complicate the streamlined shopping experience we'd worked so hard to create. Modern shoppers mixed clothing in their own closets; rarely did the Gilt members we knew (or we ourselves) dress in head-to-toe designer. Instead, they mixed leggings or jeans with their Gilt Groupe "splurges."

Alexis voiced her concerns, but the board felt equally strongly about creating a new lower-priced tab, Gilt Fuse, which they thought would help the site appeal to a new customer seeking more accessible price points. Alexis eventually agreed to disagree and moved on, throwing her support behind the initiative.

Debuting in summer 2009, the Fuse tab had a younger, edgier feel than Gilt; its colors were icy blue instead of stately gold; the models, younger. It sold clothing and accessories, with a larger selection of denim and Ts. But while members liked the brands, they were *not* fans of Fuse. We'd added unnecessary clicks to their fast, easy, convenient shopping experience. After receiving consistent negative feedback for pretty much the first time in our existence, we eliminated Fuse in less than a year. All our brands would now be sold together. To our relief, none of our luxury brand partners has ever complained about these lower-priced brands on our site.

While Fuse consumed a lot of our company's resources for the better part of a year, we learned many lessons from this trying time, like how to more effectively listen to and understand our customers' needs and preferences. Also, that price point (high versus low) was not a business strategy or a concern that necessarily drove a customer to one area of our site versus another. In fact, separating items by price just made it harder for customers to find the items they wanted.

As we surged our inventory, we also had to examine Gilt's infrastructure. To accommodate the tidal wave of merchandise, we'd need larger warehouses; we'd also need to accommodate our growing membership with more servers and to dramatically increase the company's staff. But how could we pause to make necessary infrastructure improvements when we were stretched so thin already?

In April 2009 we got powerful proof of what was possible if we played our cards right. While the two of us were teaching a class at Harvard Business School, Gilt's first sale with the iconic shoemaker Christian Louboutin went live, and by the time we turned our phones back on afterward (no more than a couple of hours later), *more than forty thousand pairs of shoes were wait-listed.* The sale had brought in hundreds of thousands of dollars in revenue in the first hour alone. It was proof of the amazing volume we could move if only we could ramp up our supply and build the infrastructure to support it.

It also proved the power of our medium: We could *not* have welcomed one million consumers through actual doors at noon, nor could they have purchased and wait-listed tens of thousands of dollars' worth of shoes in minutes had it not been for the Internet. Our business model could exist only online. And there seemed to be no limit to how big it could grow.

At eBay, Alexis had seen what happens when a start-up focused on the urgent at the expense of the important. Back then she'd also felt as if she were sprinting a million miles an hour to keep up with a fast-growing business, one that was growing *too* fast, leaving little time to develop proper finance, accounting, and engineering infrastructure. After a highly successful IPO in the fall of 1998, eBay's site crashed repeatedly in 1999, as the company struggled to install and then repair its Web site infrastructure and heaved at the strain of its rampant user growth. Each time the site went down, even for a period of hours, bad press and a slide in the stock price followed. After one particularly bad outage took the site down for days, the stock price plummeted 25 percent. And millions of customers were annoyed and possibly even turned off.

We wanted to avoid a situation like this at all costs. So, rather than wait too long to address issues with our infrastructure, we scrambled to prepare our systems and staff for rapid growth *before* we got into trouble. We didn't want members to feel any of our inevitable growing pains because attentive customer service was key to maintaining our luxury reputation. We needed our site to be reliable and navigable and for customers to continue receiving their purchases as fast as possible. We needed brand partners to remain confident that Gilt was the most exciting place on the Internet to sell merchandise and attract desirable new customers.

But increasing spending in the context of a start-up is always tricky. You can't take it back, so overinvesting is a big danger. We knew that it was risky to invest heavily in the middle of a deepening recession. But we ultimately determined it was an even bigger risk *not* to invest.

In the summer of 2009 we raised a new round of capital from the private equity firm General Atlantic and welcomed managing director Anton Levy to our board. We started working with a third-party warehouse that deployed Kiva robots, a system that eventually mechanized our entire distribution process and brought us to the cutting edge of e-commerce logistics. These days the majority of our inventory no longer touches human hands at all until it is taken from the virtual hands of the robot by our packer, who inspects an item and places it in a box. Before then, it's ferried by hundreds of two-foot-tall robots that zip around our massive warehouses much faster than mere mortals ever could, packing designer merchandise off to Seattle, Jacksonville, and everywhere in between on the same day it's ordered. The robots dramatically increased the efficiency of our warehouses and the speed with which we could service our customers. But they were such a huge investment that timing was key: if we'd installed them any earlier, they just might have bank-rupted us.

We also started hunting for new warehouse space. Over the next two years we moved our major distribution center from the Brooklyn Navy Yard to Andover, Massachusetts, and eventually to a massive new three-hundred-thousand-square-foot warehouse—imagine the size of ten football fields—in Louisville, Kentucky. Today over ten thousand packages per day are shipped out from that facility by our robots.

Most important, we rebuilt the entire foundation of our Web site so as to avoid outages as two hundred thousand customers rushed through our virtual doors at exactly the same time each day. Mike and Phong dropped nearly all other work to lead a project that sys-tematically rebuilt each part of our site—a daunting task, to be sure—enabling it not just to keep up with but *outpace* our onslaught of daily traffic. They started first at the registration wall, then moved to the sale pages and item descriptions before retrofitting the cart where members would collect their chosen purchases; finally, they rebuilt the checkout page. Initially, they'd worked in a fast programming lan-guage called Ruby on Rails; this had helped us build and launch the site within a few short months. But Ruby could no longer sustain the levels of consumer demand we were experiencing. So the engineers worked long hours to accomplish in months what other teams would have taken years to envision, execute, test, and roll out. While the project certainly exacted its toll, with their leadership Mike and Phong successfully averted technological crises that might have ground Gilt Groupe to a dramatic halt six months down the road.

One rule we lived by as we weathered Gilt's growing pains was that in times of rapid growth, every part of a company inevitably breaks at least once. Alexis had seen this at eBay, too. The systems, operations, and technology that get a business out the door quickly, with moderate investment, are almost never the systems, operations, and technology it needs to sustain a large-scale, world-class enterprise. As we mentioned earlier, we still believe that start-ups shouldn't invest too heavily out of the gate before gauging customers' reactions to their product. But if a company is fortunate enough to grow rapidly (i.e., hit hypergrowth), we can *guarantee* its systems will fail. It's best to anticipate what will break next and carve out time and resources to preemptively fix it. Because if you wait too long, consequences can be dire.

Almost five years after our launch, Gilt has already systematically rebuilt its technological infrastructure, warehousing, and logistics, e-mail services, shipping partnerships, inventory management systems, and pretty much every other part of the business.

———

As we rebuilt our infrastructure throughout successive years of rapid growth, we also tried to pay attention to the company culture our founding team had worked so hard to build. How would we maintain it when we were hiring so fast and Alexis, Alexandra, Mike, and Phong didn't have the time to personally interview and help train all of Gilt's new employees?

A 2010 article on hypergrowth in the *Wall Street Journal* summed up our dilemma:

Fast growth is often an entrepreneur's dream, but it can come with repercussions, including customer-service snafus and staffing chaos. If not managed well, it can also wreck a company culture, which can put a young company in "serious danger," according to Rob Wolcott, a professor of entrepreneurship and innovation at the Kellogg School of Management.

"In many ways, culture is the one thing that gives you long-term competitive advantage because it's something that is very difficult to copy," Mr. Wolcott says. "When growth becomes too hot to handle, so to speak, then everyone starts focusing on the urgent and sometimes misses the important."

We didn't want to see Gilt's culture suffer as we grew. Though we weren't as involved with every team anymore, Gilt maintained a liberal vacation policy, an open floor plan, and plenty of out-of-office events for employees (such as our annual Halloween party). Importantly, teams throughout the company kept hosting off-sites, some with Barry Carden, to examine and improve their communication.

---

checklist:
HOW TO MAINTAIN COMPANY CULTURE AS YOUR BUSINESS SCALES

1. WRITE DOWN YOUR COMPANY'S VALUES. We printed ours, which we'd agreed on in our first off-site meeting with Barry Carden, on little cards and distributed them widely throughout the office and to all new employees. At Gilt, Mike Bryzek helped codify the company ethics, or the principles by which we operate. It's important to let the values of your organization emerge organically, but also to document them so that people know what's expected of them and the values they are beholden to maintain. We've found it also helps to remind staffers of these values at quarterly meetings and to post them where all can see.

2. EMPHASIZE PERSONAL FLEXIBILITY. Alexis was herself personally flexible as CEO, and after she moved on from that position, she continued to take on a wide variety of different roles in the company. In a start-up, you need to have employees who can roll up their sleeves and get it done, taking on several roles at once. When employees are told clearly from the beginning that their roles will change and evolve, perhaps even quarterly, and that those roles may even appear to narrow over time, you'll effectively screen for personal flexibility. Employees will determine before signing on whether they can handle the pace of change; you'll have managed their expectations. Employees who understand exactly what a start-up environment entails will be less likely to resist the change that accompanies hypergrowth.

3. IDENTIFY EVANGELISTS. Mike has always been a chief evangelist of our organizational values, indoctrinating many new members of our staff beyond just his engineers and modeling the values himself. Some evangelists will emerge organically, but it also helps to appoint people at all levels to help spread the word about the cultural values by living them, bringing together informal groups and spearheading forays out of the office. Get these people involved in hiring in every department, so that they can help vet candidates for the company's values.

4. GET OUT OF THE OFFICE TOGETHER. Gilt has always been a highly social work environment. We do a lot of going out together and have always tried to invite small groups to our homes or to restaurants or bars after-hours.

LAUNCHING GILT JAPAN

In the midst of hypergrowth, Gilt was also focused on launching new businesses. We'd always known the site would sell much more than women's and men's fashion, and in each category—partly because our competition was nipping at our heels—we made it a priority to launch fast and get a foothold in the market before other companies did. By 2009 we'd launched kids' and home verticals and our men's business, and hired buyers to oversee each. We started planning an even more ambitious travel business, Jetsetter (it launched that September), not to mention the rollout of our mobile apps. It started to feel as if we were *always* sprinting to the launch.

The launch of Gilt Japan, in particular, took a tremendous amount of Alexis's attention and focus in early 2009. Discussions about Japan had been percolating in our offices and board meetings since early 2008. The appeal was simple: an untapped market, no competitors, and access to the biggest luxury spenders in the world, not to mention plentiful inventory. By April 2008, with the very strong urging of the board, we'd made the decision to launch our first international business out of Tokyo.

Since none of us had ever done extensive business in Japan, we knew we'd need to hire someone not only to head up the site but to advise us on how to alter our approach for this new market. Once again, Nick Beim provided the winning candidate: he suggested Katsu Kuwano, then the head of Match.jp and a well-known Internet impresario in Tokyo. In May 2008 we flew Katsu business class from Narita to meet our team (at the time we'd never before dreamed of spending so lavishly on airline tickets for any employee, current or prospective). It was immediately obvious that Katsu was that rare combination of e-commerce veteran and highly sophisticated fashion devotee. He was also a cultural match; our entire team and board loved him. Within weeks we'd hired Katsu to run Gilt Japan.

Katsu found temporary office space and started hiring his team. We contributed to some of these hiring decisions via videoconference, but our general strategy, then as now, was to hire well and then put faith in our people. Final decisions were left rightly to Katsu.

We wanted our Japanese team to know how committed we were (besides, we're not the types to do anything halfway), so the two of us started taking hour-long Japanese classes together once a week at our office through the Japanese Cultural Institute. We wanted to master Japanese etiquette and some basic conversational language skills. This was exciting; it felt as if we'd come full circle. Our love of cultures and languages had brought us together in a Portuguese class twelve years before, and now here we were, business partners studying Japanese so we could take our successful start-up overseas. Our first Japanese lesson was definitely one of those moments when we stared at each other and thought, Is this really happening?

In the fall of 2008, armed with our brand-new Japanese business cards and a shaky command of Japanese small talk, we made our first trip to Japan and met Katsu in Gilt Japan's new offices. During a whirlwind visit, the three of us pitched our business to ten holding companies that represented a hundred or so brands (in Japan most foreign brands enter the country through holding companies that oversee the distribution and retail of goods on their behalf). We also pitched to some luxury brands directly and spent time with the new team. Alexandra also spent time with the Japanese merchants, answering their many questions about how we did things back at Gilt U.S. (as they called it).

Alexis and Katsu also toured warehouses. In Japan speed and accuracy are highly important. There is no margin for error in shipping; incorrect items and late deliveries are absolutely forbidden. We took pains to find facilities that could ship the same day within Tokyo. Like most other spaces in the country, these warehouses were immaculate and seemed to be repainted monthly (Alexis will never forget watching two men scrub a subway platform with lavender water in Tokyo). Alexis did her best to engage in the right pleasantries and to adhere to local customs. Luckily, many words describing terms in fashion or the Internet happened to be English words with an *o* or *u* at the end (*discounto*, for example), so she could often follow the theme of a conversation even without a translator.

Katsu and his Tokyo-based team were surprised when many brands expressed an immediate interest in working with Gilt because in Japan, you often have to make a dozen visits to get to yes or, better yet, close a deal. But while we felt good about our ability to get brands on board, Alexis discovered that entering the Japanese market was going to be much more expensive than we'd imagined. The free marketing strategies we'd used in the United States, which had been essential to our meteoric growth, would not apply in Japan, where word-of-mouth marketing was proscribed by a very different set of customs. In the United States we'd been relentless with our personal invitations (between the two of us, we'd probably invited seventy thousand people to join). It would be an understatement to say that this was not replicable in Japan. While the Japanese love the concept of "invite only" and "private" sales, they don't really find it acceptable to e-mail friends outside their immediate circles with offers, or especially to profit from friends' purchases. So much for our social and monetary incentives! We knew we wouldn't be able to rely on customers to tell as many of their friends about us. The word would trickle out much more slowly. When you consider that the Japanese also have lower member activation rates compared with other countries, it was clear that each member we attracted would be more expensive.

One way—the only way, it seemed—to expedite this process was to make a huge splash in the media with our launch. At the advice of our Japanese team, we decided to organize a big press conference and several days of print and TV interviews in mid-March 2009. We'd take the stage to personally introduce our new business to the Japanese press. But while two American blondes educated at "Harvardo" would be mildly interesting if only for novelty's sake, we also needed a bigger draw, a celebrity. On the advice of our Japanese public relations firm, we settled on Mona Yamamoto, or Mona-san, as we called her, a beautiful half Norwegian, half Japanese actress who had recently captured the country's imagination by exiting a hotel with a married baseball hero. This catapulted her fame to even higher levels. If there's anything that sells well in Japan, it's European luxury goods, baseball, and a whiff of scandal.

Our Japanese team worked around the clock in the first months of 2009 to prepare for the launch, as Alexis liaised heavily with them from New York and Alexandra helped tap our U.S. brand partners to see which relationships could cross over to Japan. The site went live in beta in January with a scant fifteen hundred members (remember, we'd launched in New York, a much more innately viral place, with thirteen thousand). Gilt Japan hosted several sales in February that attracted few shoppers. This weighed heavily on Alexis's mind as she flew to Aspen in early February for her wedding.

Still, despite the stress, Alexis and Jerome managed to have a wonderful and intimate fete in Aspen, attended by Kevin, Nick, Susan, and, of course, Alexandra, not to mention the couple's nearest and dearest friends and family. Surrounded by snowy mountains, Alexis and Jerome tied the knot at the Aspen Institute under a near full moon. They had skied for a few days before that and danced late into the night. With the pressures of work and Gilt's expanding business, Alexis had had little social life for the past two years, let alone time to plan or even think about her wedding. She had even purchased her Oscar de la Renta dress on Gilt just a month in advance! But it was a magical weekend, and everything went off without a hitch.

When Alexis returned from her honeymoon in South Africa, she jumped immediately on a flight right back to Tokyo to spend a couple of weeks readying the Japanese business for its media launch.

The press conference was highly scripted and choreographed and slated to run at least two hours. We couldn't really believe any media outlets would want to listen to us (and Mona-san) for that long, but we took our Japanese team's word for it. Our script featured elaborate staging cues and even detailed instructions on how to laugh. Aim to *giggle* more than laugh, we were instructed, with one hand demurely over the mouth. Mona-san would banter with us before trying on several outfits from the Web site.

When we took the stage on a Thursday afternoon, the room was packed. We both wore Valentino—red for Alexandra, tiger-striped for Alexis. There were cameras from every major network across Japan in attendance, as well as the top newspapers, magazines, and business journals. We were delighted for Gilt's sake but braced ourselves for what felt like impending personal humiliation. A two-hour press conference/theatrical performance with several costume changes and a lot of giggling was *not* how we'd ever thought of presenting ourselves in a business press conference. It was bad enough that the Japanese equivalent of the *Wall Street Journal* was there!

To start things off, we talked for three straight minutes in Japanese, which the crowd seemed to appreciate. We had memorized our lines and knew them cold. As we spoke, there were murmurs of *Oooooooo*. Then the music commenced; it sounded suspiciously like a Japanese game show sound track. As we recall, our next line was something cheesy like "Come on down, Mona-San!" Mona-san entered from stage left in the first of three outfits. People stood and craned their necks; the onslaught of flashbulbs was like nothing we'd ever experienced. Mona-san explained why she adored Gilt and wanted to shop on the site and then, to the audience's stunned, tantalized delight, disappeared behind a screen onstage to change into outfit number two, a sexy Just Cavalli cocktail dress. She continued to chat amiably from behind the screen, before she emerged to another wall of flashbulbs. Finally she changed again, into a pink Ungaro gown and diamond tiara worth a million dollars. To our amusement, she invited a security guard onstage to guard the tiara. It was pure kitsch, but the audience seemed to love it. The diamond tiara even brought the crowd to its feet. We couldn't even speak to each other over the clamor, as every major TV channel and consumer and financial press representative in the country, about seventy total, leaned forward to ogle and capture the moment with flashing bulbs. We were momentarily blinded!

The performance ended with our presenting Mona-san with an oversize VIP invitation to join Gilt.jp as the music played in the background. Let's just say this was the closest we will ever come to an actual paparazzi pursuit. The room was so loud, and the media frenzy at such a sustained pitch, that we forgot our embarrassment and started getting excited to see what kind of impact the event would have on our next few sales.

Sure enough, within hours, news of Gilt had reached millions of Japanese and we'd signed up fifty-two thousand members. Our launch was covered by five evening and morning news programs and six papers and achieved the surprising distinction of being the top Google-searched term in the entire country that day. We'd also managed not to embarrass ourselves with our rudimentary Japanese. This was a milestone for us, as both friends and business partners. We'd created the buzz we needed to launch the site and had witnessed the power of media in Japan. Yet again, we'd joined forces and really pulled it off.

Of course the trip wasn't without its setbacks. Alexandra has blocked this whole episode out, so we'll tell it from Alexis's memories. A few days before we left for Kyoto, we'd eaten never-ending *omakase,* or chef's choice meal, at a Michelin-starred restaurant in Tokyo. Alexandra had eaten some sort of raw lotus or mushroom that was rather difficult to chew. Rather than appear rude in front of Katsu, she'd swallowed the tough root whole and felt for several moments as if she were choking before she regained her composure. That night, back at the Strings InterContinental hotel next to our Shinagawa office, she wondered if she'd scratched her esophagus (at least this was our untrained diagnosis). Alexis called her brother, Adrian, a medic, at 5:00 A.M. He wasn't deeply concerned because Alexandra could breathe fine, but he suggested she see a doctor just in case. The following morning Alexandra managed to find her way to an international clinic, where an elderly German doctor working out of a Stone Age–looking facility was unable to find anything wrong with her. Nonetheless, she still felt off, very off.

Alexandra continued to feel unwell, and it wasn't until we returned to New York that she finally got a diagnosis: *stress*. Her doctor said that there was nothing technically wrong and that her symptoms were the physical manifestation of the toll her work was taking on her body. Via a chewy Japanese delicacy, the pace and intensity of the last few years had finally caught up with her. We now refer to this as the magic mushroom incident. It was part of a series of incidents that finally convinced us to make some changes and extract ourselves, even just momentarily, from the nonstop mania of building a successful start-up.

MOVING FROM A SUSTAINED SPRINT INTO THE MARATHON

We'd experienced a lot in our lives by this point and accomplished a lot too; we thought of ourselves as strong individuals. But a start-up can wear anyone down and usually does at some point. Neither of us had paused to consider that our schedules might be unsustainable, but after Japan, the signals became harder to ignore, at least for Alexandra.

On a trip to L.A. in April just a couple of months later, Alexandra endured a twelve-hour day of meetings before having dinner with a consultant and a Gilt divisional merchandising manager named Nadine. She and Nadine then returned to their hotel, the Thompson, around 11:00 P.M. They decided to make a quick jaunt to the rooftop bar because they hadn't even managed to see the hotel yet. No sooner had they arrived on the roof deck than Alexandra looked at Nadine and said, "I don't feel well." Since she was a kid, she'd been prone to fainting. It usually happened about once a year, generally due to dehydration or exhaustion, and she could recognize the symptoms right away: light-headedness, blurry vision, muffled hearing. She quickly looked for a place to sit down on the ground so she wouldn't fall over and hurt herself. She put her head into her hands, trying not to draw attention to herself, as Nadine tried to help. That was when a manager spotted her from across the roof and walked over. He asked politely if he could escort her to her room, and though she knew standing up was a bad idea, she didn't want to make a scene. She accompanied him to the elevator, Nadine trailing closely behind.

And then, as they were waiting for the elevator to arrive to the roof level, Alexandra fainted dead away into the manager's arms like some scene in a Humphrey Bogart movie. Thank goodness this manager was there to catch her so she didn't fall and hit her head! After this, Alexandra discussed with her doctor back in New York how to slow down and get her feet back under her. Unsurprisingly, her doctor suggested yoga, meditation, deep breaths, and sleep, sleep, *sleep*.

Even cool as a cucumber Alexis was to reach her own stress apex toward the beginning of 2010. At the time she was departing on yet another long haul flight, to Hong Kong, South Korea, and Shanghai for two weeks to explore those markets for potential expansion. She had flown pretty much weekly for the past two years as we got the business up and running. Landing in Hong Kong, she picked up her typical pace, attending back-to-back meetings for two days that lasted into the night. Then she made her way to Seoul to do the same. It was the dead of winter. By the end of her second long day of meetings in Seoul, she felt her throat closing up, and that night she lost her voice. She managed to pull herself out of bed the next morning to meet with Korean conglomerates, but she could barely speak above a whisper. By the end of the day, sicker than she could remember being in her life, she'd collapsed into bed at the hotel. She was unable to leave the room all weekend and slept nearly uninterruptedly for almost forty-eight hours, as if every bit of adrenaline had been drained from her system over the past twenty months and her body was forcing itself to catch up on years of sleep of which it had been deprived. Finally, on Monday, she stumbled on to Shanghai, where she choked in the city's congestion and particulate matter while charging to *more* meetings. She regained her voice in the middle of the following week, and knew this was a sign that she needed to take a break. She'd learned at eBay, and was now relearning at Gilt, that start-ups in hypergrowth mode were like a sustained sprint; if you ran at this speed for years, you'd eventually fizzle out. Alexis decided to hit "pause" and take a couple of weeks off to regain her health.

We weren't the only ones who hit walls during stressful periods that are part of the start-up experience. At some point or another, all the members of our original team have taken at least a month off after reaching extreme burnout. Even Phong, the type to work three days straight on nothing but Red Bull and then crash for twelve hours, was forced to take a month-long sabbatical to go do yoga on a mountaintop. Mike too took extended periods of time off in 2008 and 2011. The reason is that launching a start-up is different from working for someone else. When your name is on the door, so to speak, it's personal; you can't help pouring your heart and soul into the business day in and day out. It's hard for impassioned entrepreneurs not to personalize and internalize all the starts and fits, and this takes its toll if not properly recognized and managed.

While exhilarating, launching and growing Gilt Groupe was also far more physically exhausting than any other professional experience we've had.

CHAPTER 14

GROWTH, PARTNERSHIP,
AND THE FUTURE OF FASHION
AND E-COMMERCE

Our Christian Louboutin sale was pretty spectacular. Everyone in the office still talks about it and members want to know when we'll have another. Last year we sold three Volkswagen Jettas for $5,995 each ($15,995 originally at the dealership) in minutes.
—ALEXANDRA WILKIS WILSON, QUOTED
IN *THE MIAMI HERALD*, OCTOBER 19, 2011

When we started tossing around ideas for the business that was to become Gilt Groupe in the summer of 2007, we had no idea, hunkered down together in that diner on Madison Avenue, that less than four years later, our online luxury sample sale site would sell not just women's and men's fashions but kids' and home furnishings, travel, local services (Gilt City launched in September 2010), even food (Gilt Taste went live in May 2011) or that we'd have successfully launched in Japan! These days Gilt's offerings run the gamut from Junya Watanabe blazers to luxury African safari camps to Brie cheese to the chance to jet to Paris with Lady Gaga's stylist, Nicola Formichetti, to attend the Thierry Mugler fashion show (yes, we actually sold this on Gilt City).

The company's growth into all these new categories has helped preserve the fast-paced, can-do start-up culture we've loved since the beginning. Despite the fact that the team has grown to more than nine hundred, it still seems as if we're always testing a new category, launching a new brand, and relying on our instincts as consumers to help guide us into the unknown. As of November 2011, Gilt ships to more than ninety countries, but the office still runs on Red Bull (for the engineers), cappuccino (for the buyers and stylists), and adrenaline. And in addition to our formal roles, we enjoy serving as de facto stewards and "taste barometers" while various subbusinesses decide which new brands Gilt should offer. Does this sale pass muster with Alexandra? What does Alexis think? Alexandra remembers her team being particularly shocked when she gave her enthusiastic stamp of approval to a collaboration with Target in spring 2010 that ended up offering Gilt members access to three of the megaretailer's popular designer capsule lines (Mulberry bags, John Derian home décor, and Tucker clothes) before they even hit stores. As usual, she just based her decision on her own opinion as a consumer: she *loved* Target!

As the business has grown and evolved, we've had to be (and, truth be told, we've relished being) flexible, stepping into any and all roles where we were needed, often learning by doing. As of this writing, it's possible no one has had more jobs at Gilt than Alexis has. After taking on the role of chief strategy officer when Susan Lyne came on board, she successfully launched Gilt Japan and Gilt Noir, then spent six months resuscitating Gilt Home in the first part of 2011, despite the fact that she knew almost nothing about furniture or home design (in the midst of doing all this, she also managed to have a baby). But though her path may seem anything but linear, there is a method to her decision making; she gravitates toward specific types of challenges. Before taking on a new role, she always asks herself, Does something need to be built or launched from scratch? (Gilt Noir, Gilt Japan) or, Does something need complete rethinking? (Gilt Home).

It was this second consideration that led her to accept her latest challenge. By the summer of 2011 she'd been at Gilt Home for about six months, during which time it had grown to become Gilt's most profitable business. It was time for Gilt's resident shape-shifter to move on yet again. Alexis and Kevin, by then the CEO, had several discussions over a month or so about what she'd do next, and one of Kevin's ideas in particular appealed to Alexis right away: chief marketing officer.

This was a job that would be *anything* but easy.

The reasons were complicated but urgent. Whereas we'd once worried our warehouses weren't keeping pace with our growth, we now had the same fears about Gilt's marketing. For years we, along with our team, had been launching new businesses and building out staff and infrastructure in an effort to satisfy a membership fast approaching five million. But as the company focused obsessively on growth, it was becoming increasingly obvious that marketing and branding had not evolved to anywhere near where they needed to be to support what was now a multinational e-commerce player. In other words, our word-of-mouth and grassroots marketing techniques had worked so stunningly that we'd started taking them for granted. What if their effectiveness eventually started to level off? We needed a marketing team that was empowered to invest in strategies like search engine optimization and banner advertising; to market to mobile users and work more creatively through social media; to rethink our e-mail strategy. There were plenty of tactics that our competitors used and that most other e-commerce businesses anywhere near our size used that we hadn't yet invested the resources to develop. But to do so would require money, new talent, and engineers: a company-wide mandate and focus.

Naturally, Alexis was attracted to the immensity of this challenge. She loved that she'd get to rethink an area so essential to the company, put new systems in place, and have a large and, she hoped, immediate impact. She did have a few concerns, like whether she'd be granted adequate resources to make major changes. Unlike her approach to her previous positions, she actually took a few days to think about this one before signing on, and of course she consulted Alexandra. Alexandra helped her candidly talk through considerations like work/life balance. Alexis had a new baby at home, and taking on the CMO role would surely be stressful and time intensive. Alexandra wanted to make sure her friend was being realistic about that challenge. She also wanted to hear about the resources Kevin had agreed would be available to Alexis if she signed on: money for hiring, engineering, the support of the board. "We'll make it a priority," he'd said. (Kevin had mentioned particularly that he knew Alexis could hire a great team.) Alexandra suggested that Alexis should focus as CMO on fixing a few things really well and not worry about the twenty others that might yet not be where they needed to be.

Alexis was also slightly worried that she had no specific training in marketing; if Gilt were to hire a CMO from the outside, he or she would surely have twenty years' experience. But she did have a strong intuitive sense of what needed to be fixed; of anyone at Gilt, she had the most intimate understanding of the brand she'd built. She knew the business as well as anyone possibly could. She'd also worked in e-commerce since 1997 (practically since its inception) and was intimately familiar with all the online marketing techniques Gilt might explore.

Alexandra, for her part, was impressed that Alexis, not knowing how long she'd be in the role or what would come next, was willing to jump in with both feet. "I think you should go for it," she said. She meant it.

Alexis climbed into the CMO job in summer 2011. And for the first time since launching the business, it suddenly felt as if we as individuals and as a company really had the opportunity to take a step back to look at the big picture, to think hard about what Gilt had accomplished and where it was going, and to refocus on the brand itself. It's not that things had slowed down exactly—on the contrary, more than two hundred thousand new members still sign up each month. But with our infrastructure finally sound and our team in place, we made it a priority to reexamine the things that have always made Gilt Gilt, from curation to value, to ensure they're still as important to our customers (and brand partners) as they always were. Were our business proposition and point of differentiation still clear? Were we delivering on the original promises our members found so compelling, while also giving them increasingly exciting reasons to keep coming back?

As Alexis took over as CMO, our competition was as fierce as ever. For years, new competitors and imitators seemed to pop up every other day, as online designer flash sales went from nonexistent to a crowded marketplace. The better sites looked like carbon copies of Gilt, while the other ones—well, let's just say they underwhelmed. There are now plenty of e-commerce and flash sale sites specializing in each of the categories in which Gilt operates, from home furnishings to kids' to travel. Some have come and gone; others, like Haute-Look, have sold to larger businesses like Nordstrom. Many, like Gilt, are thriving. None comes close to approximating our size and range. But we never want to get so focused on growth, or on beating individual competitors in any of our categories, that we lose sight of the bigger picture: of what we represent as a company and of our long-term goals.

Alexandra's job, like Alexis's, has changed significantly over the years. While she once spent her days darting up and down Fifth Avenue or to the garment district to meet with new brands she hoped to bring on board, all while overseeing a team that grew to thirty-five merchandisers and their bottom lines, she had since late 2009 headed up a much smaller brand relations team (the still-indispensable Christian Leone reports to her). She served as Gilt's de facto ambassador and head of relationship building. Her team was nimble; it facilitated communication throughout Gilt and between Gilt and the world of potential and existing brand partners. In a given week she might host a Gilt Noir dinner in Dallas, strategize on how to get Gilt in front of an important brand in one of our new categories, speak on a panel with a few leading tech entrepreneurs, represent Gilt on several TV segments, and/or use her long-standing relationships to help resolve an issue with a longtime brand partner. What she *never* did was spend a full day at her desk.

While we knew there were things Gilt could be improving upon, we couldn't help noticing one very encouraging thing about the brand: it's still exciting. Nearly 65 percent of purchases still occur within a sale's first hour and a half, and when the clock strikes twelve, an average of two hundred thousand unique visitors rushes through our virtual "doors," quickly generating roughly one million page views. Though Gilt offers a wider selection than ever before—we work with more than six thousand brands and have more than 22 sales per day, or 150 per week, on average—customers still feel an urgency to buy that just did not exist on the Internet in 2007. A member once clicked *one thousand times* on an item, hoping it would fall out of other members' carts (after their allotted ten minutes had expired) so she could snatch it into hers!

This new competitive urgency—we call it the gameification of retail—has had broad implications for the retail industry, injecting much-needed intensity into luxury and e-commerce during a dire economic moment. Even as the retail industry has flailed and outward displays of wealth or luxury have seemed distasteful, our members have always been proud to shop on Gilt; they still regularly approach us at events to show off what they scored on our site. Gilt offers a rush that is not about status or being rich—in contrast with an It handbag, for example—but about being savvy, an insider, someone clever enough to beat others to the best finds. The site is a truly guilt-free form of retail therapy because of the value and sense of triumph it offers.

The task at hand, we knew, was to preserve the excitement and urgency essential to Gilt's brand while also reinforcing it for the future, a world in which customers shop radically differently from the way they did in 2007 and not just because of the economy. If new financial realities have shifted customers' values, Gilt has affected dramatic shifts of its own too. The new generation of consumers is discreet, educated, tech savvy, and increasingly urban; it doesn't see consumption as a leisure activity. Instead, it demands to be able to buy its wardrobe and furnish its house or apartment on the fly, from its mobile devices (that's why 17 percent of our weekday revenue comes from mobile devices, and 30 percent on weekends). In the next decade, we don't believe the savvy shoppers brands most want to reach will spend much time browsing the mall. Consumers want to get the best stuff at the best price immediately, from wherever they happen to be, on *their* terms, without endless browsing.

As we spent the latter part of 2011 reflecting on and fortifying the Gilt brand, we couldn't help reflecting too on our relationship as friends and business partners. As cofounders of a business comprising more than nine hundred employees (rather than our initial core team of five) we still somehow feel closer than ever. Perhaps it's that sense of having experienced something very powerful together. There is no doubt our preexisting friendship has made us better executives and benefited Gilt too. After meetings with our board or with brand partners, we still ask each other, "What could I have done better? Did I make that case strongly enough?"

We each constantly remind the other what she's good at. In a start-up, you're pulled in many directions simultaneously, and it's easy to lose perspective on your primary skills and their value. Neither of us lets the other forget what she brings to the table. We are each other's advocates within the company, just as we are outside it. And we still support each other, naturally complementing each other's weaknesses. Nowhere is this more apparent than in our many press appearances. During a 2009 Telemundo TV segment, conducted in Spanish in Miami, the Venezuelan journalist was speaking rapid-fire, and Alexis, who had learned Spanish in slower-speaking Argentina, froze on camera; that had never happened before. Noticing this, Alexandra quickly stepped in to answer most of the questions. Later, in February 2010, when Alexandra was nine months pregnant with her son, we did a CBS morning show segment out of our Brooklyn Navy Yard warehouse, and Alexandra was too distracted by the journalist's hacking cough—or worried about getting it—to concentrate on the questions. So Alexis did most of the talking. In both instances, each of us was glad to have a partner we trusted as much as we trusted ourselves, someone who loved Gilt Groupe as much as we each did and represented the business better than we could have done in that moment. That's one of the best things about having a partner: chances are high that at least *one* of you will be "on" at any given time.

Even now we prefer to attend parties, dinners, and Council of Fashion Designers of America events together, mingling as a team, facilitating introductions, making sure at least one of us touches base with everyone we know. This is about efficiency, but also something more. When we're together, we exude confidence; we build each other up. Everything is instantly more fun, but we're also more effective. This is essential to our friendship, as well as, we believe, to our success at Gilt. Whether we're giving an important speech, connecting directly with celebrities to convince them to curate a sale for us (Alexandra), or taking on a major new role within the company (Alexis), we root for each other. We draw on each other's expertise; we become more than the sum of our parts. We balance each other and keep each other in check. Sometimes we even dress each other! When one of us is rushing off to an important meeting, the other will take the jacket off her back to help her friend look good in a pinch.

In the spring of 2011 Gilt received a one billion dollar valuation during its latest round of fund-raising, and we were in total disbelief. (Well, Alexandra was in disbelief, even though she'd diligently read the book *Blueprint to a Billion* by David G. Thomson. Alexis, always the big-picture thinker, found it easier to accept.) While there are many factors that we think catapulted us to the one-billion-dollar valuation, a few still strike us as most important.

We focused on relationships. Beyond just our partnership, we have learned over the last four years that starting a company is less about innovative ideas than about relationships. For us, that means, first and foremost, our indispensable relationship with each other. It also means our relationships with our other three brilliant cofounders, who prove that even people who don't go way back can develop extremely strong bonds of trust. We still regroup often with Mike and Phong to relish the early days and reminisce about the successes and missteps we've experienced together. It means the preexisting relationships we leveraged with thousands of men and women in our networks and the relationships we built with relevant tastemakers and devoted customers across the country. It also means our relationships with important mentors, from Simon Rothman to our parents, who offered key advice and encouragement, and of course our extremely positive relationships with our board and with Susan Lyne, whose leadership has helped grow Gilt and influenced us as executives.

It goes without saying that no one can build a company alone, and this has been particularly true of Gilt Groupe. No one person had the engineering, marketing, networking, fund-raising, and operational chops—not to mention guts—to launch and grow a business of this size and influence. It would be laughable to even consider that! Our company is less the product of one or two genius entrepreneurs or engineers than the result of many successful ongoing collaborations.

We took big but very calculated risks. Unlike competitors who followed in our footsteps, we weren't launching a model with proved success in the U.S. market. We set our sights on a group of designers that had never sold in the way we were proposing to sell. We knew that the Gilt idea, if it worked, would most likely permanently change the game.

We both are risk takers by nature, each in our own way. For Alexis, this means heli-skiing and venturing to Antarctica; for Alexandra, it means being unafraid to cold-call any powerful executive in the fashion industry. We both have thick skins; we're not overly sensitive. As entrepreneurs we had the confidence to launch a new e-commerce model, but enough humility to know we'd have to work *really* hard to make it successful.

Because while we are bold, no one would call us adrenaline junkies; we never wanted to take risks just for the sake of it. And we believe this is key, whether you're starting a new business or just launching a new project. We believed in our gut instincts, but we never relied exclusively on them. We did our research; we knew the fashion and e-commerce industries inside and out. We systematically accumulated proof points to confirm the validity of our idea to investors. In addition to the success of vente-privee in France, we had a formidable database of contacts in Alexandra's network. And we had experienced fund-raisers and operators in Alexis and Kevin.

When it comes to taking calculated risks, we believe partnership is key. Partners support each other and spur each other on, but they also provide built-in checks and balances on the kind of madcap ideas that strike (and *should* strike) any entrepreneur.

We applied new forms of marketing and technology to get

our idea out there faster, brand it, and make it stick. There is no doubt about it: Gilt's word-of-mouth marketing campaign was crucial to our business's ultimate success, helping ensure that we had the strongest luxury brand identity and recognition among our competitors and that we attracted the most loyal customers. It began with our initial e-mails inviting members of our networks and thousands of others whose e-mail addresses we'd dredged up, from college campus leaders to members of women's professional clubs, to join our site, and it was augmented by our grassroots marketing efforts in cities across the country. To this day, three-fourths of over five million members heard about us from friends! We believe that this not only sent our membership numbers into the stratosphere but helped us create a much more engaged, trusting membership.

Recently our drive to innovate with our marketing has led us to focus on ways to help our customers purchase on the fly, away from their computers. We started with a cool, stylish, easy-to-use iPhone app. Our app, which allows customers to make a purchase in seconds, from the sideline of a soccer game, from the grocery line, or from a lunch meeting, has been downloaded more than 1.3 million times to date. In 2010 we were invited by Apple to be one of the very first companies to debut an iPad app, which has now been downloaded more than 700,000 times.

We've also expanded our social media presence. We both actively Tweet from personal Twitter handles (@GiltAlexandra and @GiltFounder). Our customer support team interacts with members through both Facebook and Twitter. If team members see complaints or questions through social media platforms, they jump right into the conversation to solve problems or provide information. Lastly, we recently rolled out a Facebook store that is helping insert Gilt's coveted sales and products directly into the millions of conversations occurring daily on individual Facebook pages.

In today's entrepreneurial environment, things come and go at break-neck speed. While Gilt is successful now, we have no idea what the future will bring; surely we'll face challenges, and inevitably even more competition. Even as we finish this book, there are new opportunities and challenges emerging on the horizon. Alexis is eight months pregnant with her second child, this time a son. She will continue to partner with Alexandra to navigate the complexities of high-tech, high-growth businesses, but now she'll do it with two children under the age of two at home. (How will that go? She won't know until it happens.) Alexandra, meanwhile, is immersing herself further in mentoring other entrepreneurs through TechStars and other organizations, while also dedicating important quality time to her son. We both continue to look forward with great excitement and anticipation to what comes next.

We have learned that start-ups are addictive.

And we've learned that truly loving what you do makes all the difference. It is much easier to innovate and to weather the inevitable storms when you have the kind of mastery of your subject that comes from longtime, deep, genuine interest or passion. As we've said, ideas are cheap and available; it's the execution that counts. Passionate people are meticulous and visionary executors. They are relentless idea machines; they can't help thinking around the clock about their businesses. Our passion for our business as consumers and now as executives has invested us deeply in the company—its vision, mission, members, brand partners, employees, and reputation.

It is our hope that our perspective on the start-up journey inspires others, both men and women, to launch bold, risky, innovative, game-changing businesses—particularly ones that capture your imagination and reflect your passions. Start-ups today demand strong relationships, smart execution, and an appetite for risk. To meet these demands, take it from us: it's best to pool your skills and resources and innovate together, with a trusted friend, colleague, or team. This is not just much more effective; it's more rewarding. Our partnership helped us go big, and it helped us do so smartly, ethically, quickly, and intuitively.

We invite *you* to do the same.

ACKNOWLEDGMENTS

We are deeply indebted to our three brilliant cofounders, Mike Bryzek, Phong Nguyen, and Kevin Ryan. Without you, this business never would have happened. You've made the journey more meaningful at each step of the way. Thank you to Susan Lyne, a terrific role model and leader. Special thanks to Leah Park and Jennifer Carr-Smith.

We are also grateful to our coworkers, investors, brand partners, and friends who agreed to be interviewed for this book: Nick Beim, Jason Binn, Mike Bryzek, Jennifer Carr-Smith, Michael Fazio, Susan Lyne, Phong Nguyen, Leah Park, Susan Posen, and Kevin Ryan. Your insights and recollections have greatly enhanced this story.

To the ever-growing team at Gilt Groupe: you continue to inspire, galvanize, educate, and humble us, day in and day out. We are so proud to work with you and for you.

We're so appreciative that so many of our friends, family, and acquaintances generously offered their time to help guide us through the realization of this project, from giving valuable advice during the proposal stage to reading and offering insightful feedback on the drafts of the manuscript: Jen Burns, Bridie Clark, Mark Fortier, Divya Gugnani, Dan Heath, Fleur Keyes, Susan Lyne, Preston Maybank,

Alexis Oliver, Deborah Macy Osmun, Alan Wilkis, Elsa Wilkis, Judi Wilkis, Robert Wilkis, Jim Wilson, Katherine Wilson, and Kevin Wilson.

We also want to thank our members and loyal customers. We love meeting you, listening to you, and using your suggestions to improve the Gilt Groupe experience. And we thank our amazing brand partners, without whom Gilt Groupe couldn't have become the exciting destination it is today.

Thank you to our many dear friends, who have been supportive of us and of Gilt Groupe from day one. You know who you are.

And to the core team who really made the publication of this book possible:

Meredith Bryan, who, over the course of many early mornings at Le Pain Quotidien and Sant Ambroeus, helped organize our thoughts and transform them into what ultimately became *By Invitation Only.*

Our dedicated agent, Kate Lee, who encouraged us to write this book.

The team at Portfolio: our editor, Courtney Young, publisher Adrian Zackheim, and publicist Amanda Pritzker.

Georgia Lopez, for her tremendous support and organizational skills. Thank you for making our lives run so much more smoothly!

To our families: We're so lucky to have such loving and supportive parents, siblings, and families. For Alexis, Deborah Osmun, Frank Maybank, Lilly Maybank, Jane Grigorief, Preston Maybank, Fleur Keyes, and Adrian Keyes. For Alexandra, Elsa and Robert Wilkis, Alan Wilkis, and Kathy and Jim Wilson.

Most important, to our husbands, who have supported us every step of the way, and our children, who are the best thing that has ever happened to us. No success in business would mean anything without Kevin, Conrad, Jerome, Thomasina, and soon-to-be-born Baby Boy McCluskey. We love you more than you can imagine.

INDEX